PATHS AND GOALS OF
THE SPIRITUAL HUMAN BEING

PATHS AND GOALS OF
THE SPIRITUAL HUMAN BEING

LIFE QUESTIONS IN THE LIGHT OF SPIRITUAL SCIENCE

Fourteen lectures held in various locations between 23 January and 27 December 1910

TRANSLATED BY CHRISTIAN VON ARNIM

INTRODUCTION BY CHRISTIAN VON ARNIM

RUDOLF STEINER

RUDOLF STEINER PRESS

CW 125

The publishers gratefully acknowledge the generous funding of this publication by the estate of Dr Eva Frommer MD (1927–2004) and the Anthroposophical Society in Great Britain

Rudolf Steiner Press
Hillside House, The Square
Forest Row, RH18 5ES

www.rudolfsteinerpress.com

Published by Rudolf Steiner Press 2015

Originally published in German under the title *Wege und Ziele des geistigen Menschen, Lebensfragen im Lichte der Geisteswissenschaft* (volume 125 in the *Rudolf Steiner Gesamtausgabe* or Collected Works) by Rudolf Steiner Verlag, Dornach. Based on shorthand transcripts and notes, not reviewed by the speaker. This authorized translation is based on the latest available (second) edition of 1992 edited by Wolfram Groddeck and Edwin Froböse

Published by permission of the Rudolf Steiner Nachlassverwaltung, Dornach

© Rudolf Steiner Nachlassverwaltung, Dornach, Rudolf Steiner Verlag 1992

This translation © Rudolf Steiner Press 2015

A catalogue record for this book is available from the British Library

ISBN 978 1 85584 421 6

Cover by Mary Giddens
Typeset by DP Photosetting, Neath, West Glamorgan
Printed and bound by Gutenberg Press Ltd., Malta

CONTENTS

LECTURE 1

STRASBOURG, 23 JANUARY 1910 ON THE INAUGURATION OF THE
NOVALIS BRANCH

Novalis and spiritual science.
The influence of Schiller and Fichte on the young Novalis. Combination of spiritual striving and sense of reality in Novalis. Inner truthfulness—the prerequisite for spiritual experience. The appearance of Christ in the etheric and the associated task of spiritual science.

LECTURE 2

HAMBURG, 26 MAY 1910

The philosophy of Hegel and its connection with the present time.
Hegel's youthful friendship with Schelling and Hölderlin. Grasp of the absolute idea in the *Phenomenology of the Spirit* and its further presentation in the *Encyclopaedia of the Philosophical Sciences*. Hegel's monism in contrast to Leibniz's *Monadology*. Schelling's theosophy. Victory of the materialistic way of thinking in the mid-nineteenth century. New methodological approaches in Solovyov and Boutroux. Strict discipline in the thinking opens the path to the supersensory.

EDITOR'S PREFACE

At the time of these lectures, Rudolf Steiner and his anthroposophically-oriented spiritual science was still part of the Theosophical Society as it then was, and used the words 'theosophy', 'theosophical' etc. to describe his own independent spiritual research. He subsequently indicated that these terms should be replaced by 'spiritual science' or 'anthroposophy' etc. unless the reference was specifically to the theosophical stream which had its source in H.P. Blavatsky or referred in a comprehensive sense to a view for which the term 'theosophy' was commonly used in the history of thought, as is the case for example in Jakob Boehme, Swedenborg, Novalis or Schelling.

Alongside his public lectures, Rudolf Steiner in 1910 gave six great lecture cycles (GA 119–123 and 126) for the members of the Theosophical Society as it then was as well as numerous individual lectures. Those of which a transcript was made can be found within the complete works as follows: the lectures in which the same subject was presented in different places are compiled in the volumes *Das Ereignis der Christus-Erscheinung in der ätherischen Welt*, GA 118, and *Exkurse in das Gebiet des Markus-Evangeliums*, GA 124.

    The remaining lectures, on a wide range of subjects and given for a variety of reasons, are contained in chronological order in the present volume. It was no longer possible today to determine the detailed circumstances for all of the lectures and why they were given, with the exception of those listed below.

Strasbourg, 23 January 1910: Here Rudolf Steiner spoke at the inauguration of the Novalis branch which was founded on 22 October 1909. The name 'Novalis' for this branch was chosen by the seven founding members.

Hamburg, 26 May 1910: This lecture on the philosophy of Hegel was given during the Hamburg cycle on *Manifestations of Karma* (GA 120). It was not originally included in the programme and it is not known for what reason it was given.

Copenhagen, 1–4 June 1910: These lectures were given on the occasion of the inauguration of the Rudolf Steiner branch. The theosophists in Copenhagen formally belonged to the Scandinavian Section of the Theosophical Society (Adyar). It is therefore remarkable that in 1910 they named their newly founded branch after Rudolf Steiner. On 20 March 1910, the branch secretary, Evelyn Neckelmann, wrote to Marie Steiner-von Sivers on behalf of the members: 'I would like to begin by letting you know that we founded our new lodge on 11 March (1910) and since our group has set itself the task of studying theosophy as presented by your Rudolf Steiner, we have given it the name "Steiner Lodge".' The request to Rudolf Steiner to speak at the official inauguration had already been made in January on occasion of his visit to Lund/Sweden; it was undoubtedly made to the spiritual teacher and not the general secretary of the German Section. The subject matter and titles of the lectures were set by Rudolf Steiner. In a letter from Evelyn Neckelmann of 3 May 1910 it says: 'And we are particularly pleased about the prospective three lectures "Paths and goals of the spiritual human being".'

Munich, 26 August 1910: In mid-August 1910, Rudolf Steiner's first Mystery Drama, *The Portal of Initiation*, was performed in Munich which was followed by the lecture cycle on *Genesis, Secrets of the Creation*. The lecture about the current state of philosophy reproduced here was given on the last day of the event and was not originally included in the programme.

After the Munich events, Rudolf Steiner travelled to Bern to speak there about the Gospel of Matthew (GA 123). Before his return to Berlin, he spoke in Basel about *The Portal of Initiation* on 31 October 1910.

Rudolf Steiner gave more than the lecture of 13 November 1910 reproduced here in Nuremberg; he also spoke on 12 November 1910 on the subject of 'Morality and Karma'. This lecture has been printed on the basis of short notes in *Beiträge zur Rudolf Steiner Gesamtausgabe* No. 45. Michael Bauer—then branch leader in Nuremberg—wrote to Marie Steiner-von Sivers on 18 November 1910: 'These days with the Doctor could not have offered more. We experienced cognitive delights.'

INTRODUCTION

This volume of Rudolf Steiner's complete works contains the lectures he gave on a variety of occasions throughout 1910. These lectures do not fit into the other volumes given in that year, all of which are built around a theme or a major lecture cycle. In this sense, the topics which are discussed in these lectures do not pursue a common thread and build on one another as a lecture cycle would, but are unconnected except in the sense that they follow the broader themes which Rudolf Steiner discussed at that time.

Yet although they may not always be connected in their chronological sequence, there are thematic links between a number of the lectures in this volume: themes such as the relationship between philosophy and science; Steiner's mystery drama *The Portal of Initiation;* reincarnation and karma; Christmas and its symbols; Christ's presence in the etheric realm; the transformation of consciousness which had to occur once Christ had incarnated physically on earth; and the nature of clairvoyance. Ideas recur from different perspectives and in different contexts.

The lectures illustrate the diversity of Steiner's thinking and the different registers he used when speaking to different audiences on different topics. For example, in the first lecture, in the context of a reflection on Novalis on occasion of the inauguration of the Novalis Branch in Strasbourg, he urgently speaks towards the end of the lecture about the great responsibility of spiritual science to help humanity open its spiritual eyes now that the Kali Yuga, the dark age, has ended.

A few months later he uses a dispassionate, descriptive philosophical—not, in his own words, anthroposophical—lecture about Hegel to deplore the damage which is done by the fact that often in anthroposophical circles an interest in supersensory things fails to be accompanied by an equally strong interest in rigorous thinking. Such logical thinking can be particularly well trained by studying Hegel's philosophy, he tells his audience. In fact, when he touches on Hegel again in lecture 6 he is just as critical of the lack of trained philosophical thinking among some of the scientists of his day, leading them to misinterpret scientific observations.

Steiner uses the opportunity in a number of these lectures to emphasize that spiritual science, like any other science, is based on the facts and findings of scientific research; it stands on the ground of scientific facts. Where it differs from materialistic science is in the interpretation of those facts. Anthroposophy does not in any way reject conventional science, he is at pains to point out, and the findings of science should be accepted. It is in their interpretation that modern science can go wrong and cannot necessarily be accepted. Trained philosophical thinking leads to different conclusions from materialism, Steiner says. Conversely, there is nothing in the supersensory field which is the subject of spiritual science that would need to be rejected by a strictly trained thinking.

But of course, Steiner's insistence that every scientific thought needs to be rigorously tested is only one aspect of what is discussed in these various lectures. They range over a wide field, not just of human soul capacities—including negative ones—and true self-knowledge and how that can affect human karma over several incarnations; they also discuss the changes in human consciousness and spiritual insight from ancient times to the modern era, including in the context of the incarnation of Christ on earth.

In the last two lectures at the end of December about the Christmas festival, Steiner contrasts the feeling of inwardness which in the past village inhabitants felt at this time of the year, as they prepared to perform the traditional Christmas plays, with the modern cultural environment of our cities, with its trams and cars and so on. He refers to the incongruity of a tram driving through a street where a traditional Christmas market has been set up. But that does not lead him to call for a return to a time which has passed and has had its day. On the contrary, we should seek to recreate that mood of inwardness in a new way in our time—in a way which is appropriate for the modern age and modern consciousness.

Because it deals with such a disparate collection of themes, we can see in this volume that Rudolf Steiner made the knowledge and findings he obtained from spiritual science available in many different forms. At the one end of the spectrum there are the strictly philosophical lectures such as the ones about Hegel. At the other end, in the lectures in which he discusses the content and creation of one of the Mystery Dramas—*The Portal of Initiation*, or the Rosicrucian mystery as he called it in these lectures—he sets out deep insights about human beings, their development and spiritual existence.

And it is in the artistic form that we find such knowledge expressed in its essence. As Steiner puts it, if the Mystery Dramas were understood in the right way it would not be necessary for him to give any lectures for many years to come. All the things expressed in 'stammering speech' in *Knowledge of the Higher Worlds, How is it Achieved?* or *Occult Science, An Outline* could be found in a much more intensive and true-to-life form in the Rosicrucian mystery.

In this sense, art and the imagination, as in lecture 10 Rudolf Steiner describes Schiller recognizing them in Goethe, lead us to the 'archetypal foundation of things' and to our fulfilment as human beings.

Christian von Arnim, May 2015

Lecture 1

CIRCUMSTANCES have dictated that a number of our friends here in Strasbourg have founded a second branch alongside the one that is already in existence. It is to bear the significant name 'Novalis Branch'. The friends from other places who have lovingly come to Strasbourg today have shown through their visit that they understand that branches can also exist alongside one another in a town, and that the many different ways of working in various fields do not need to exclude what we have to call the harmony and concord which must rule among all those who see themselves as members of our society as it is spread across the globe. And so let us also add this branch to the great stream which we call spiritual science.

You, my dear friends from the Novalis Branch, have chosen a significant name as a signature, a symbol for your work. The name of Novalis belongs to a personality who most recently—that is in its last incarnation—worked in the eighteenth century, a personality through whose whole being there flows, whose whole being is filled with what we consider to be a sense which understands the spirit, of spirituality. And in this way you have shown from the beginning that you want spiritual science to be something which is filled with immediate life, which you seek in all the places where it can be found, not just in this period or in another period but as it lives through all periods, as it can flow into the world through one personality or another in many different ways.

In Novalis in particular we can see how the striving for knowledge of the spirit is something which can penetrate through and interweave with our ordinary everyday life. Of course, if we wanted to throw a light on the sources of the theosophical spirit in Novalis then we would have to shine it into earlier incarnations of this noble spirit. And from these earlier incarnations it would become clear to us how those things have transferred into the incarnation of Novalis which can only be theosophical spiritual life in the most profound sense. But even if we just look at the Novalis who barely reached the age of 30 and who lived at the end of the eighteenth century, if we only observe this one incarnation, even then it can become clear to us that knowledge of the spirit is not something that raises human beings up into a dreamy, fantastical world, which draws them away from direct reality, but we can see in many different ways particularly in Novalis how the spirit of reality, how real life is given its value and true content by being penetrated with spiritual science.

Novalis came from the nobility of central Germany which had a certain what I might call materialistic piety—because that exists, too—but not what one can really describe as a longing in the heart for real, living spirit. Now in order to fulfil Novalis' karma in the right way, it happened that Novalis' father, the old Hardenberg, in old age—even if he was not imbued with spiritual life, but because he joined the Herrnhuter sect, a Pietistic sect—was filled with pious feelings in certain respects. And Novalis grew out of this milieu of central German nobility which, as I said, at least had enough of the spirit so that even the old Hardenberg in his later years was able to come to a certain piety in the spirit, even if it was sectarian—this is what Novalis grew out of. He grew into—not what his family wanted, because that would have been some military or diplomatic post—he grew into a great period, into the time in which great, mighty spirits were at work with professorships at a central German university in Thuringia.

Thus at that time he would still have been able to hear Schiller lecture about history in Jena. Even if the scholarly historians of today say that Schiller was not on a scholarly level as a historian—what history should be in life, spiritual life flowing through the whole of human development, that is what Schiller provided for the souls who heard him in Jena when he taught history. A great personality spoke through Schiller. The spirit spoke through this personality, it awakened the spirit.

And another teacher was there when Novalis was young, another teacher who through the great energy of his spiritual life did things in the field of philosophy which belong to the whole of humanity but which are still little understood today. Fichte was at work at the time that Novalis was making his way into life. He worked in such a way that his whole bearing, Fichte's bearing, had something spiritual. It might be considered as something superficial. But anyone who has a feeling for these things will not consider it superficial that Fichte, when he gave his lectures in a dark lecture theatre in the evening and a candle was burning on his lectern, extinguished the candle with the words: so, my dear listeners, now the physical light has been extinguished, now it is only the spiritual light that shall burn in this space.

Demonstrating as if by magic the relationship between the spiritual and the physical not just to the soul but also in front of our eyes at the right moment, that has immense meaning for such receptive souls as that of Novalis. Such a soul can thereby become capable of receiving a belief in the spiritual life which cannot be shaken by anything. It flows through the soul with a noble sentiment which then remains throughout life when a Novalis in particular comes into such an environment. We cannot say that Novalis was someone airy-fairy. Those who believe that he was airy-fairy do not understand Novalis. No, the spirit living in Novalis said—it can be read in his writings today[1]—the sleeping and waking states of human beings are two different things. When human beings are awake then they have combined in them the inner soul—that is the name in the terminology of the time of what we would call the astral body today—with the external body. The body enjoys the soul (nice words which Novalis uses to express the relationship between the physical and the astral body). And in sleep the soul is in a looser relationship with the body—Novalis says—and the body digests the soul when human beings are asleep. That once again is a nice, brief, concise description of a relationship which we also encounter in spiritual science. It is lovely when Novalis on one occasion writes in his notes:[2] 'We are always surrounded by a spiritual world. Wherever we are there are always spiritual beings around us. It is simply up to human beings to externalize their self in such a way that they obtain an awareness of the spiritual beings who surround us wherever we are.'

And once again it is nice the way that he shows a profound understanding of the progress of esoteric human development and writes: 'In ancient times people tried to guide the soul into higher development through mortification and so on. In modern times that has to be replaced by strengthening the soul: energy of the soul. The soul has to obtain power over the body through being strengthened, it must not be weakened as a result, and then has to exercise a certain sovereignty.'

We could continue talking about Novalis like this for hours. Although we would not find a spirit who can express himself in the words and teachings as can be given by spiritual science today, we would find a spirit who in his own words expresses exactly the same thing. He was not someone airy-fairy, a fantasist. Even if his poetry followed the highest trajectory we can imagine and leads us into the highest worlds of feeling, Novalis was—and this applies to someone who did not reach the age of 30—a practical spirit who studied at a mining academy, a mathematician through and through, who experienced mathematics as a great poem in accordance with which the divine spirit wrote the world, but who showed himself to possess all the practical skills that a mining engineer needs.

Novalis was a spirit who despite such a practical outlook was able to implement for his feeling life, for his heart, directly in life what he possessed as theosophical sentiment. Truly, what we know as his relationship with Sophie von Kühn must not be seen as something connected with sensuality. He loved a girl who died at the age of 14. He really only started to love her passionately when she had already died. He felt that now he lived with her in the realm in which she had been since her death. He decided to follow her into death. His further life was a life together with a personality who was physically dead. All of this shows us what Novalis grew into through the strong feature of his spiritual nature.

We can see in Novalis how as human beings we really only need to have one characteristic to have a sense for the spirituality which brings us spiritual science. We only need one characteristic and this one characteristic is very difficult for human beings. People do not easily find access to spiritual science because it is so difficult for human beings. If we put a name to this one characteristic then it appears to people as if everyone had it. Yet it is this characteristic whose absence prevents human beings from finding access to spiritual science: truthfulness, an honest acceptance of what really is in the deepest depths of our soul. Many people apparently have it—in their own opinion. Yet Novalis in particular presents an example of how there needs to be only one moment of true honesty and how human beings would have to admit to themselves through this one moment of true honesty what the spirituality in the world can mean for human hearts.

Novalis' father had a certain trait of spirituality otherwise he would not have joined the Herrnhuter sect. But his soul was not as free and honest as is meant here. That was prevented by what lived in his soul from the outer physical world. The physical world with all its preconceptions did not permit him to get up into the spiritual world. But his son did have this truthfulness. What could be more obvious than that the father could have no idea of what lived in his son? The physical world with its division and lack of harmony—its untruthfulness which erected a partition here between what the young Novalis really was and what the old Hardenberg wanted to be but could not be because of his lack of real inner truthfulness—this physical world with all the things which it turns human beings into did not permit him to recognize the importance of his son while he was alive. His son had been dead for a few weeks and the old Hardenberg was in his Herrnhuter community. The community sang the song: 'What would I have become without you, what would I not be without you.' And as this song was being sung—the old Hardenberg had not heard it before but at that moment everything ignited which existed as spirit in his soul.

He was given over to the great impression which streamed from this song and at that moment his soul grown honest was filled with cosmic spirit, with spiritual life. And when the meeting had come to an end, the old Hardenberg asked someone who had written this song which had moved him so deeply. So he was told: 'It is by your son.' It was first necessary that everything which came from the physical plane was forgotten for a moment, and then there lived in him briefly—without knowing about the person who had introduced it—pure truthfulness, pure objectivity without the preconceptions of the physical plane. In this way spirit would find spirit if we faced each other soul to soul without the obstacles which come from the physical plane. At the moment in which human beings can find the soul of the other and the soul of the world in pure devotion to the truth, at every such moment they must be penetrated by what we might call theosophical spirituality.

What we can call theosophical spirituality is not just based on some theory, some teaching, although we must never forget that for us human beings who are born to think a teaching is indispensible. But the essence of theosophy does not lie in the teaching. Anyone who wanted to emphasize that the teaching was superfluous and the only important thing was to cultivate what we call general brotherly love would have to have impressed on them that pontificating about general brotherly love cannot bring about such general brotherly love anywhere in the world. If we only pontificate about love, then, for someone who knows about life, that is no different to telling your stove: 'Dear stove, it befits you, your stovely love to make the room warm.' But the room remains cold however much we pontificate about love. But if we give it materials to make heat, wood and fire, then wood and fire are transformed into heat and the room is warmed up. The fuel for the human soul is the great ideals, the great thoughts we can assimilate, through which we recognize the connections in the world, through which we can learn the secrets of human destiny and human life.

These are not thoughts which only fill us theoretically but which make us inwardly warm and the result of theosophical wisdom is love. And just as certainly as the stove warms the room because it heats up and not because it is being preached at, with the same certainty the teaching of the great thoughts which are at work in the world will make the soul loving. Because that is the secret of real wisdom that it is transformed in the soul into love through its own strength. Anyone who has not yet found the path from wisdom to life only shows that they have not yet advanced far enough in wisdom. But anyone who would believe that the thoughts we assimilate about the evolution of the world, the evolution of humanity, about karma and so on were of no consequence for human beings should keep making it clear to themselves in their soul that these are not just human thoughts, that these are not just thoughts which we are the first to think, but that it is these thoughts which penetrate our soul which the divine spirits have used to build the world.

It is not our thoughts which appear before our spiritual eye in spiritual science but the thoughts of the divine architects, the divine spirits of the world. What the gods of the world thought to themselves before the creation of the physical world is what we reflect in our thinking about spiritual science and in this way investigate what has flowed from the divine beings into the activity and development of the world to which we belong. And what the gods have thought is divine light. And anyone who does not want to think what the gods have thought does not, even though they do not know it, orient themselves towards the light but towards darkness. The only possible basis for a real development of the human soul is the one in which we start from what are the divine thoughts of the world. The spirits of the world have not given us these embryonic faculties for us to leave them lying fallow. They have been given to us so that we develop them. And since in this developmental cycle of humanity the thinking is our most important and outstanding ability, we have to start with the thinking. But we must not stop at the thinking. That leads us gradually to transform spiritual science into an attitude which allows us to understand the secrets of how knowledge leads to character traits, to traits of the mind. Knowledge properly understood leads to real traits of character, of mind.

We can use a single example to make that clear for ourselves, can use it to make clear for ourselves that we human beings go through a sequence of ever new incarnations. What would be the purpose of those incarnations, if they were not intended to make human beings ever more perfect? We have to look back from our present incarnation to previous incarnations and have to tell ourselves: we have become what we presently are because in the course of one incarnation after the other various characteristics have been placed in our soul; our soul has again and again assimilated forces and gathered experience. What is integrated into our soul in one incarnation then emerges in the following incarnation.

We have now become the way we were prepared in previous incarnations. But then we can pause for a moment and say: we not only look back to the past but we look forward to the future, to later, more perfect lives. What would this human life through all these incarnations be if we could not tell ourselves: the further we develop into the future, the higher the stages which will have been achieved by what today is located in us as our I.

We can only guess at what we can still become because otherwise we would already be like that. We have to ascribe to ourselves the capacity to climb ever higher. But we have to look into the future with awe and reverence; we have to tell ourselves, even if we are able to understand this or that, are able to experience this or that in the world: the greater faculties which we can obtain will allow us to experience and understand many other things.

It is impossible for someone who inscribes such a thought as has just been expressed in their soul to say: I can decide today what is true or false, I can make an ultimate judgement about what is true or false. The only thing which is befitting for such a person to say is: if I could make that decision today already then it would be impossible for even higher faculties to arise in me in the future. And if that is transformed into an attitude it will give us the modesty at every moment of our development the truly dignified humility which we need to be true human beings. In this way a knowledge of reincarnation is transformed into a sentiment, a feature of our character: into dignified humility, into true modesty.

We could put it as follows. Anyone who understands today that they pass through a sequence of incarnations and keep rising higher in their development would have to be a fool if they were to say that they were perfect; or if they were to say: it is not necessary for me to learn today because tomorrow I will experience things of a quite different order of magnitude. Knowledge turns into real features of our character. And looked at in the right way, every spiritual-scientific insight turns into a feature of our character. But it is possible for us to understand that should we not be able to use our powers at any stage of our existence then these powers would not have been given to us from the spiritual world. If we wanted to wait until the world has reached its state of perfection, thinking that we first had to be so perfect that we had ultimate knowledge and experience, then we would not have to pass through different incarnations. In other words, we have to be clear that we have to use our cognitive powers in every incarnation. We must not say: I only want to obtain knowledge in the next incarnation or at the end of my existence. For all our humility and modesty, we should use the powers we have.

Thus a justified human sense of self is set alongside the humility and modesty which flows directly out of our being penetrated with the divine-spiritual and it says to us: it is true that our knowledge will only be perfect when we have reached a high stage, but we can make it perfect precisely by being aware today already of our human dignity and using our powers today already. In this way our character will obtain something which can be compared with a set of scales. We can place on the one side of the scales humility and modesty and on the other side a justified sense of self, courage in making judgements, and can say: we have reached a certain stage in cognition, in self-consciousness. In short, we will find that whenever we simply try to introduce into our feelings what spiritual science teaches, the teachings or theories of spiritual science are transformed in our soul because they contain the thoughts of the divine spirits, are transformed in our soul, in our character, in our endeavour, our feeling.

This can show us that in spiritual science the teaching, the theory may not be the main thing but that it is the kindling, we might say, for the development of the human soul. That it is the thing which is intended to bring out higher characteristics in our soul. And anyone who demands this characteristic without knowledge lives in the worst form of deception, in self-deception, the self-deception which has entered human evolution because in the course of earth development other beings have also entered and been involved in our evolution—beings which were not just harmful but also useful. But however useful they were in that they brought us freedom and a sense of self, we nevertheless have to be clear that these gifts from the so-called luciferic beings, freedom and sense of self, must not degenerate to become extreme and radical because then they become pride and arrogance. And pride and arrogance applied to knowledge lead such knowledge into darkness. Knowledge is acceptance of the divine light, of divine thoughts. Rejection of knowledge is something which leads into darkness, and neither can it lead to higher characteristics in the soul. If we look at spiritual science in this way, then we will recognize it as one of the most important matters in humanity. We will recognize it as something which we do not just for our own sake but because we are aware of our duty towards humanity and its development.

We live today in a time which is not completely unimportant; we live in an important time. It is true that people who live in a given period often say that they live in a transitional period. Every period of human development has already been described as a transitional period, but not all of them have been such important transitional periods. But of our time today it can truly be said that it is a transitional period. In what respect is that the case? Let us look at the character of another transitional period. A transitional period in human development occurred, for example, when the predecessor of Jesus Christ, John the Baptist, appeared. When John the Baptist appeared he told people what was later repeated by Jesus Christ in the significant words: 'Repent ye, for the kingdom of heaven is at hand.'[3]

What does that mean? We will understand what that means if we recall that human beings, as they developed from incarnation to incarnation, underwent various characteristics in their soul. In ancient times of our past human beings did not yet possess the characteristics and soul faculties which they have today. It was possible for all human beings in ancient times to develop a dull, hazy, dreamlike clairvoyance, to look into the spiritual world. All human beings had the possibility not just to see the physical but look into the spiritual world. But human beings in the time when such clairvoyance was widespread did not yet have something which they have today: a clearly developed self-consciousness. Human beings at that time could not yet in a clear way say to themselves 'I am'. A firm stance at the centre of our inner being could only be obtained in that the ancient clairvoyance disappeared for a while. Human beings had to put up with separation from the spiritual world in order to develop a clear self-consciousness here on the physical plane.

Later on such clairvoyance will once again develop together with self-consciousness so that the two characteristics will occur together again and human beings will possess them again. So we can look back to a time in the distant past. At that time it was possible for human beings if they did not pay attention to the physical, if they closed their eyes and turned away from the physical and made their ears ignore the sounds, that they then looked into the spiritual world and were able to obtain direct certainty of the existence of the spiritual world. These characteristics waned and were increasingly replaced by the ability of thinking, the ability of self-consciousness, to draw conclusions, of independent judgement, those things which make up our daytime consciousness today. We can put an approximate date on the time when it gradually happened that the ancient clairvoyant faculties disappeared completely from human faculties. Before about the year 3101 [B.C.] almost all people on earth were still endowed with a hazy clairvoyance. Then, from that year onwards, it began to decrease more and more, it became increasingly weak.

But that made ego-consciousness, self-consciousness, judgement, drawing conclusions, self-aware thinking grow. So the light of spirituality grew dark and that which is the human I dawned and became brighter and brighter. The interior of human beings became brighter but spirituality grew darker. That is the year in which what oriental philosophy calls the Kali Yuga, the dark, black age, began. Something was there which—at the time that John the Baptist appeared as the predecessor, followed by Jesus Christ—reached a crisis, we might say, a decision. They had to tell humanity: you now have to learn that there is spirituality although you do not see such spirituality with any spiritual eyes. You have to learn that the realms of heaven are here. You have to understand this from out of your I. That is why Christ had to incarnate into a physical body because self-consciousness in the Kali Yuga was only able to perceive the spirit on the physical plane.

That time was a transitional period. The old faculties had disappeared. If people at the time had not heard the call of the Baptist, of Jesus Christ, they would have declined at that stage and not managed to progress any further. Those who heard these voices had to recognize the god who had descended as far as physical corporeality. They understood that the realms of heaven had come close to the I.

Christ was in the physical body of Jesus of Nazareth for three years. That was the time in which human beings were only able to see with physical eyes when a god descended to them.

We are once again living in a transitional period, in a crisis. The Kali Yuga came to an end in about 1899. And now new characteristics are developing in human beings even if they do not know it. New characteristics are developing in human souls in a natural way. It is no proof to the contrary that so many people know nothing about it. A hundred years after Christ Tacitus[4] still referred to an unknown sect of the Christians; and in Rome people still told, after Jesus Christ had fulfilled the Mystery of Golgotha 70 to 80 years beforehand, of a sect which was supposed to live in a side street and was led by a certain Jesus. The most important events had passed by innumerable people.

If people fail to perceive something, it is no proof that this most important, crucial and incomparable thing does not exist. Since about 1899 faculties have been developing unnoticed in human beings which will emerge in the mid-thirties of the twentieth century, in about 1933 to 1937. Then these soul faculties will emerge in a whole range of people because their time has arrived; faculties of etheric clairvoyance will arise. They will be there. Just as there were people with an extremely developed ego-consciousness when Christ was there, there will be people in our century who will see not just with physical eyes but who will experience as a natural development what strives to come down from spiritual levels so that soul and spiritual faculties will emerge from their soul and they will enter etheric existence. And the fortune of these people will be to understand the new world they will see.

One thing is true, and as such important for our souls, when Jesus Christ said: 'I am with you always, even unto the end of our earth cycle.'[5] He is here. Since that time he has been in our earth environment. And when the spiritual eyes open they will see him, will see him like Paul saw him in the event at Damascus. That is something which will happen in about 1933, that he will be seen as an etheric being, as a being which, although he has not descended to physical existence, can be seen in his etheric body because a certain number of people will then ascend into the etheric. But these people will lack understanding if they have not been prepared through spiritual science for what they will see.

That is why we are living in a transitional period, because we are growing into a new way of seeing.

Spiritual science has the responsible task of preparing human beings for the great moment in which—although he will not appear in the flesh, that was only possible once—he is here, and he will return in a form in which those whose eyes have been opened will see him in the world which is only visible to clairvoyant eyes. Human beings will grow upwards towards him. That is what the return of Christ will be: a growing upwards of human beings into the sphere in which Christ is. But they would stand there uncomprehendingly if they were not prepared through spiritual science for this great moment. Such preparation must be serious because it is full of responsibility. Humanity has to be prepared that more will be seen than was seen hitherto unless human beings take this faculty into darkness and make it wither—because that could also happen, that the twentieth century passes by without leading to the fulfilment of this goal. We have the responsible task of preparing human beings for this great moment through spiritual science. But we must prepare human beings spiritually, make them understand that only the spirit will encounter Christ with opened spiritual eyes. A materialistic view might believe that Christ will appear once again in a physical body. But that would not be spiritual but materialistic. If we human beings believed that, we would not have the will to work our way up to the spirit.

That is why in this time certain prophecies from the Book of Revelation will be fulfilled. Counting and building on the materialistic spirit, individuals will appear in a physical body who will say that they are the reincarnated Christ. And those will fall victim to them who have not been led to a proper understanding through spiritual science, because Maya will be great and the possibility of self-deception immense. Temptation will grow to become enormous. Only a knowledge of the spirit which is aware of its responsibility will bring human beings to an understanding of what is meant to happen.

These reflections were intended to show how spirituality through spiritual science is meant to work in individual human souls and that a knowledge of the spirit is a task of our time because we can say of our present time: important things lie ahead of us. But because the most important things might be completely overlooked by humanity in the darkness, because the great moment could pass without human beings seeing it, that is why spiritual science has to act in the right way. Penetrating with our spirit what has been communicated to us by spiritual research will provide the spirituality in each branch which we need in order to develop our own souls to an ever higher level so that we can serve humanity more and more.

Let us seek to reflect often that the saying applies to our time as much as it did at the time of Christ: repent ye, because the time is at hand. If at that time the words were 'the kingdom of heaven is at hand', today we have to look prophetically into the immediate future and say: because the human I is close to the kingdom of heaven. Let us prepare ourselves through the right kind of spiritual science so that we can enter worthily into the kingdom which calls on us. And we ourselves can only prosper if we find the way to the kingdom of heaven. If we digest what we have as experiences on earth and in turn allow what we experience in higher spiritual existence to arise again, offer it as a great sacrifice at the altar of divine existence, then we fulfil in dignity our purpose as human beings to the fullest extent. Let your activity here be imbued both by the spirit of Novalis and the spirit of spiritual science itself, which has come before our soul, and you will see that your activity will take a good course. Because if our activity is imbued with such an attitude, then what we call the light of the Masters of Wisdom and Harmony of Feelings[6] will flow into it while we are gathered in our branches. We are never without the help of these advanced individualities when we come together with the right attitude in our branches. May such a spirit unite you! May such a spirit, which at the same time is the spirit of the Masters of Wisdom, ensoul you! Act in this spirit and your activity will be part of the great work of spiritual science. Your activity will be part of the attitude which must penetrate the whole world.

LECTURE 2

We will engage today not in anthroposophical but in purely philosophical reflections. They can however be fostered in an anthroposophical group, because although the subject matter of spiritual science is the result of experiences in the supersensory world turning these experiences into a comprehensive systematic conception of the world requires sharp and, indeed, also trained thinking which deals conscientiously with every single point. And if it is the case that untrained thinking can cause a lot of damage in external science, it is the case specifically in the anthroposophical movement that—more so than through inaccurate observation—even greater damage is caused because an interest in supersensory things does not go hand in hand with an equally strong interest in logical thinking. And such purely logical thinking can be trained particularly well through a reflection on the thinking of Georg Wilhelm Friedrich Hegel.[7]

Such a reflection will also be able to throw a certain light on our present time. People talk from time to time about going back to Hegel but we cannot say that our time has the intellectual prerequisites which would advance an understanding of Hegel. The whole of Hegel's thinking grew out of a time in which there was the most intense interest in deriving the foundations of all knowledge and existence from perspectives of the highest order. And it is no coincidence but a deep necessity that Hegel lived in a time in which these foundations of the highest order were sought in the greatest variety of fields.

Hegel was born in Stuttgart on 27 August 1770. He became a

student at the Tübinger Stift (1788–93), that institution which played such an important role in the development of German intellectual life at the time. His fellow pupils included Schelling,[8] who towered over him and outshone him for such a long time, and the deep-natured Hölderlin,[9] who was soon to descend into madness—even if not because of his deep nature. They formed what might be described as a trefoil: the deep-natured Hölderlin seeking in mystical light and shade, Schelling with his energetic sharp thinking and brimming-over imagination, and the somewhat ponderous Hegel extracting his thoughts onerously from out of his soul. Schelling and Hegel subsequently worked together again at Jena University which at the time was a hothouse of intellectual life. Schelling thrilled his listeners with the mighty sweep with which he dealt with intellectual problems; he even thrilled those who did not by inclination seek to penetrate the questions of existence.

Schelling pointed to something which goes beyond all thinking in human existence, to the, as he said, intellectual intuition[10] which he thought of as a primal ability to look into the substrates of existence. Hegel was a fellow lecturer of his (1801–6). Even at this time still his thinking was ponderous because he wanted to make each thought never comprised more than it was intended to mean. And it is this slow penetrating ponderousness of his thinking which makes Hegel not at all easy to understand to begin with.

Then came the sad time of 1806.[11] During this time Hegel undertook, as he himself put it, the actual great intellectual journeys of discovery. As the cannons thundered at Jena he concluded the first of the works to emerge from a detailed, incredibly profound collection regarding the spirit, the *Phenomenology of Spirit*. This is a work which is unique in the whole of world literature. Hegel wanted particularly to clarify for himself the experiences which the soul can have when it ascends from subordinate perspectives, as it were, to the highest, to what Hegel calls the constitution of the spirit in itself. To begin with we live in the most dulled possible connection with the external world in which every this or that, every tree and every house is something with which we live together, every opinion is something in which we live. Only when we start to reflect on this and that does perception arise. From perception we then get through the thinking to an initial sense of self, an obscure inkling of the self. Only then do we get to the first flashes of a real consciousness. But here the I is still spellbound within its surroundings. It works its way out of this enchantment through the content which it is meant to have solely out of itself in that it leaves more and more of what is connected with the external world. In this way self-consciousness comes about and thus the interpenetration, the interweaving of self-consciousness with the spirit. It becomes spirit itself, grasping itself within itself, becoming spirit growing conscious within itself.

And when human beings then look back, they perceive what grasps itself as spirit within itself; they perceive the idea which they have extracted, as it were, from its enchantment in the external world. They perceive that they were previously stuck in the contradiction between subject and object, but that now—in overcoming subject and object in the idea which grasps itself, which is not just subject and not just object—they grasp what Hegel calls the absolute idea. Thus through an incredible effort of thinking Hegel had come to establish so-called absolute idealism.

Hegel's fortunes varied considerably after his Jena lectureship. He worked for a time as a political journalist in Bamberg (1807–8), then he became headmaster of and taught at a school in Nuremberg (1808–16) and thus through many different external experiences became the realistically thinking spirit which we encounter subsequently. After Nuremberg he briefly obtained a post at the University of Heidelberg where he published his *Encyclopaedia of the Philosophical Sciences* in 1817. Hegel might well have said about the reception of this work the words which legend has it he expressed shortly before his death: 'Of all my pupils there has only been one who understood me, and he misunderstood me.'

It is indeed a very peculiar feeling to have immersed something so incredibly profound into the stream of the world and at the same time to see how almost all the conditions for acceptance of such profundity are missing. We have to adopt Hegel's perspective to draw something like a skeleton of what this *Encyclopaedia* was intended to be. But I would ask you, when I speak now from the perspective of Hegel, not to start viewing me as a Hegelian. For Hegel it was a matter of continuing to develop the perspective he had developed in the *Phenomenology of Spirit*, which he had obtained through placing himself on the standpoint of the idea beyond subject and object—and now to elaborate this perspective, if I may put it like that, in order from that perspective to survey human thinking and activity in all its scope.

According to Hegel, the concepts of subject and object, of cognition and opinion and suchlike could not be contained in the absolute idea. The idea is beyond all such contrasts. Hegel wants to understand the idea as if it were being presented in all its purity, this idea which, although it is at work in subject and object, goes beyond both. This idea may well be found in human beings, in the external world, in spirit and nature, but it goes beyond both, it lies beyond spirit and nature. In Hegel's view the idea must therefore not be understood as something abstract to begin with, like an abstract point for example. On the contrary, it is something replete in itself which out of itself as the idea allows a rich content to grow out of itself, just like the plant seed implicitly contains the whole of the plant with all its individual parts. Thus according to Hegel the idea allows a content to grow out of itself which is independent of spirit and nature, which, when it is applied, must be applied to both.

Before, then, considering the meaning of spirit and nature we obtain a perspective higher than both and then see in nature a manifestation of the idea and equally see the idea coming to expression in the spirit. We thus have to obtain a perspective from which the idea is developed in such a way as if the human being were not present at all. Human beings then surrender to the very own process of the world of ideas developing in itself and out of itself. This perspective produces what in the meaning of Hegel can be called the science of logic. Here we are not dealing with a subject and object, as in Aristotelian logic, but with the independent movement of the idea located above subject and object.

Any thinking which only wishes to devote itself to the things of the external world finds it difficult to gain entry to the strictly closed ranks of the Hegelian concepts. We feel as if violence is being done to us, as if we are being shoehorned into a system of ideas which has nothing whatsoever in common with the normal, everyday rationale of reason. The idea is meant to think, not I: that is the feeling we have. That is why people mostly also do not engage with Hegel's world of ideas. But if we do so nevertheless, well, we might correct Hegel here or there— that is very easy particularly with Hegel. But that is not really the point. The point is that people undergo enormous self-discipline in their thinking through the study of Hegel; because there is nothing like Hegelian logic to learn where a system of human concepts, indeed, a concept as such can occur.

A concept can only be recognized with all its implications if it can be thought of only in a certain location within a whole web of concepts. In order to clarify that for himself, Hegel starts with the emptiest concept, the concept of being, which is normally just placed without people generally being aware where they have placed it. Now this concept is meant to be completely empty in Hegel. So as we enter Hegel's logic we have right at the start to ignore all later content which this concept has obtained, that is, we have to be very disciplined in our thinking. Thus the concept of being is not established by human beings but it is what faces human beings when all other concepts have been excluded from it.

Now Hegel wants to find the method for developing concepts; in other words, one concept has to develop from another. Thus the concept of being, if we look at it in the right way, must immediately elevate itself above itself. As soon as we apply the abstract concept of existence to a thing, that abstract concept is no longer pure. It is then already related to a this or that. In this way we learn to understand that being is nothingness, but, please note, only within the concept. Through such a self-referential dialectic we have thus derived the concept of nothingness from the concept of being.

Once we have created discipline in our thinking in this way, we have educated ourselves at this point of Hegelian logic already in a way of thinking which in Hegel's further discussion of being and nothingness is only ever applied in the way as has just been explained. Being and nothingness now produce a third thing: becoming. But in order to grasp becoming it has to be brought to rest. Thus in fourth place the concept of existence emerges from the concept of becoming. This is the only way that existence can be used in Hegelian logic, as being which has inverted itself into nothingness, which together with that has produced becoming which, brought to rest, produces existence. And Hegel continues, using this method. He obtains the concepts of one and many, quantity and quality, measure and so on.

Thus we have an organism of the idea in the first part of Hegel's *Encyclopaedia*. Only once we have grasped all the preceding things can we reach the concept of purpose which stands at the end of Hegelian logic. Such absolute logic does indeed achieve an immense self-discipline which should be held up to our time at least as an ideal. It teaches us to express a concept only if we have its content completely in our consciousness. We must not, then, have anything in our concepts other than what at some point in our lives we have clarified for ourselves as the development of the concept. Subsequent concepts which appear in Hegelian logic are subject and object, knowledge, essence, causality which are now however clear in our consciousness.

Once Hegel had established the complete system of concepts in this way, he was able to show how concepts reveal themselves in what we might call their enchantment. The concept cannot only be in the subject because then any talk about nature would be meaningless. On the contrary, our concepts underlie natural phenomena, have made them. Thus it is irrelevant with regard to the concept whether it appears internally or externally. Externally it is hidden from us. Nature is the concept or idea in its otherness, as Hegel says.[12] Anyone who says anything different about nature goes beyond what they know for certain. The result is a kind of natural philosophy, a natural science which seeks the development of the idea externally after it has first been sought in itself, in its purer existence, in logic.

To begin with, the idea comes to expression in subordinate phenomena where the concept is most hidden so that we might be tempted to refer to natural phenomena devoid of the idea. That is what happens in mechanics. But even within mechanical phenomena Hegel's disciplined thinking distinguishes between two things. He distinguishes ordinary mechanics such as underlies phenomena like thrust, force and matter—relative mechanics, as he calls it—from absolute mechanics. In other words, he considers it inadmissible to apply the ordinary concepts of relative mechanics to the heavenly bodies. Only when we develop the concept of absolute mechanics do we find the idea which lies in celestial mechanics. There is, however, no trace of that distinction in today's science. Hence Hegel's polemic against Newton[13] who particularly was most intent on applying the concepts of relative mechanics without further thought to the concepts of absolute mechanics.

Starting from the concept of absolute mechanics, Hegel proceeds to the concept of the real organism. He identifies the three elements of the organism as:

> First, the geological organism. In Hegel's sense, the complete structure of the earth must not be understood as the laws of a small area being extended to the whole earth, as is done by geology today. Hegel sees what we might call a rigidified organism in every mountain range, in every geological form.
>
> Second, the plant organism in which the concept reveals itself in equal value with the idea, in uniformity with the idea.
>
> Third, the animal organism which in a certain sense already presents the existence of the idea in the external world.

What the idea appears to be in earth existence, the enchanted idea as it were, has thereby exhausted itself. Human beings now emerge from these enchanted ideas. Initially they have to be understood through their natural characteristics. That is the subject matter of anthropology. In their perception, human beings find themselves in a dulled state in external existence, but when they rise to consciousness and from there to self-consciousness, they detach themselves in a sense from external existence. This is where anthropology is followed by the 'phenomenology of spirit'. Within this phenomenology human beings finally grasp themselves as spirit. They recognize themselves as subjective spirit in that initially they struggle free from the enchantment of nature. Gradually the idea itself appears to them once again. What it was in the first, very first, concept of existence now comes to the fore. Once human beings have in this way recognized the idea in itself in logic and outside itself in nature they now understand it where it is in and of itself.

Now this initially subjective spirit turns itself into objective spirit. The idea highlights what it is as such in what are the spiritual institutions: marriage, family, law, morals. All of that is combined in the state. What emerges in the state as objective spirit, as realization of the idea, what can be found in the interaction between states, that is world history. Thus world history is the existence of the idea after its passage through the subjective spirit.

And the question arises: can we close the circle at the end like a snake biting its tail, that is, can we get back to the absolute idea, to a realization of the idea which overcomes the subjective and objective again? The absolute idea can in its absolute reality initially appear as something preparatory so that it is not enchanted, hidden as in nature but such that it shines through appearances. That is the case in art. Beyond world history, Hegel thus creates the first realization of the absolute idea in art. But here it still has something of an objective, of an external nuance. But it can also act in such a way that it no longer has a nuance of the external but a nuance of the internal. That is the case in religion. So it is the realization of the absolute idea on the second level.

But the idea can also overcome the nuance of externality, which it still has in art, and the nuance of internality, which it still has in religion. It does so in understanding itself at the point where it catches hold of itself, in philosophy in a Hegelian sense.

And thus the circle is closed. In the whole field of history there is nothing which is as self-contained as the Hegelian system.

Later on he elaborates individual parts, such as the philosophy of right (1821), a field in which a strictly disciplined thinking is particularly beneficial. Now Hegel says something remarkable in the preface to the *Elements of the Philosophy of Right*:[14] when reason takes hold of the idea, everything must be understood because we see the idea, that is the action of reason, in things. Everything real is therefore rational in a Hegelian sense.[15] These words can, of course, be immediately refuted with the arbitrariness of ordinary reasoning if we fail to take account of the context of Hegel's thinking.

If we therefore place Hegel's philosophy in outline before our souls in this way, we have recognized immensely disciplined thinking as the basic tenor of his philosophy.

Hegel then taught this philosophy from 1818 to 1831 in Berlin where he died on 14 November 1831, the same date that Leibniz[16] died who had set out exactly the opposite philosophy. Hegel's philosophy is centred on the idea which remains wholly with itself. In Leibniz the idea is scattered in the immense number of monads. But just a single monad which contains the pre-established harmony would, if it developed, need to take the path of the Hegelian absolute idea. Thus Hegel's system lies in the development of a single monad. Hegel set up the strictest monistic, Leibniz the strictest monadological system. For as long as we remain in Hegel's columns of thought we remain in a strictly closed loop of the spirit. How do we get beyond that if we measure Hegel's system against *Monadology*? That is indeed what happened to one thinker, that for him Leibniz's *Monadology* broke open Hegel's monism. That is what happened to Schelling.

Having been silent since 1814, he was appointed to Berlin in 1841, ten years after Hegel's death. He tried to go beyond Hegel with whom he had worked in the past and from 1802 to 1803 had published the *Kritische Journal der Philosophie*. They were unusual lectures which he now gave in Berlin.

There is only one way to get beyond Hegel. It is only possible by drilling a hole from outside at the point where in Hegel the I grasps itself in the *Phenomenology of Spirit*. We also remain stuck in Leibniz's monads if we do not drill a hole there in the same place. If we start at that point we get beyond the I which only grasps itself, then we get to supersensory experiences which really go beyond what Hegel comprehends in his system. And that is indeed what Schelling does. He started to teach theosophy, real theosophy, even if in an abstract form, and he met with the same success which a person would have today who wanted to teach theosophy at a university.

Schelling teaches a triplicity of the foundation of the world, a threefold potency: first, the capacity to be; second, pure being; third, the combination. Thus he set out then what today we seek in the threefold Logos.[17] Then Schelling sought to understand the secrets of the ancient mysteries in his *Philosophy of Mythology*. He sought to teach what we investigate today—helped by supersensory experiences which have become possible since then—for example in what my book *Christianity as Mystical Fact* says about the mysteries of antiquity. Then Schelling strove for an appreciation of the Christian mysteries in his *Philosophy of Revelation* which attempts to throw a light on Christianity from a theosophical perspective. Schelling was only able to give these lectures because he had previously stood at the lectern with different views. Now the rage against him was all the greater. All the textbooks and other histories of philosophy today present this last 'theosophical period' with great horror, a period in which he went totally mad having previously established the insanity of his 'intellectual views'—as they put it.

But with this transition from Hegel to Schelling an age simultaneously arose which lived completely under the spell of natural science. And since then we are experiencing a strange spectacle through the observation of which we will be able to see why theosophy, spiritual science, has to be received today in particular in the way it is received.

There is no one who admires the results arising from facts more than I do, and yet the following has to be said. The discovery of plant and animal cells by Schwann[18] and Schleiden[19] in the 1830s was a great attainment but petty opinions followed on from it. The theory of energy and matter arrived which considered anything spiritual to be merely the froth on physical processes. The worst product of such a way of thinking was the strict framework within which Büchner[20] framed theoretical materialism in his book *Kraft und Stoff*. Büchner's audacious courage is something to be admired of course. The other researchers were simply not brave enough to think their thoughts through to the end.

But more subtle minds also went different ways from Hegel and Schelling under the constraints of natural science, such as Hermann Helmholtz[21] who did great things in the fields of psychophysics, the physiology of the senses, physiological optics and the theory of sound. His discoveries led him to reject Hegel through the way that experiments were conducted and through the suggestive power of the experiments, not through his thinking, so that he said: when I open Hegel and read a few pages of his *Natural Philosophy* that is pure nonsense.[22]

And there was another subtle and cognitively trained spirit whose thinking was misunderstood: Julius Robert Mayer[23] who discovered the law of the conservation of energy. His law did indeed have great physical importance and this was acknowledged. But Mayer's thinking about the mechanical equivalent of heat in his work *Die organische Bewegung in ihrem Zusammenhange mit dem Stoffwechsel* (1845) was never understood. People much preferred to read Helmholtz—he was much easier to understand. Thus people preferred to read his work *Wechsel-wirkungen der Naturkräfte* (1854) in which he proved the correctness of Mayer's law on the basis of the impossibility of perpetual motion.

Then the achievements of Darwinism came along and such a bold spirit as Haeckel[24] who, however, was averse to any intellectual culture and could therefore not see anything in Hegelian philosophy other than a tangle of concepts. This courageous spirit was now called upon to develop the scientific facts in the sense of external, material historical development. Thus he was the founder of the materialistic Darwinism of the 1860s and 1870s. No philosophical direction of thought rose up against that. The world was no longer capable of being gripped by philosophy; there was nothing of a reciprocal relationship between philosophy and science.

Thus a thinker as important as Eduard von Hartmann,[25] who in his *Philosophie des Unbewussten* (1869) called materialistic Darwinism before the court, we might say, of a spiritual philosophy, was abused as a dilettante who has no idea about science. There were many publications against him, including a brilliant anonymous one: *Das Unbewusste vom Standpunkt der Philosophie und Deszendenztheorie* (1872). Haeckel said about this publication that it was so excellent and showed up the errors of the philosophy of Eduard von Hartmann so thoroughly that he himself (Haeckel) could have written it. And Oscar Schmidt,[26] Darwin's[27] biographer, very much regretted that the esteemed colleague wished to remain anonymous. Then a new edition of this work appeared and Eduard von Hartmann revealed himself as the author.

Thus philosophy in the most unsubtle way provided the evidence that it is very well able to understand science even if trained thinking leads it to quite different conclusions from those of materialism. It is indeed the case that this struggle is not just word against word but cultural forces are opposing one another.

Subtle minds always retained their understanding of both things, philosophy and science. But they could only ever be heard in the smallest circles because of the dominant suggestive power of science. Thus the extraordinarily subtle history of philosophy by Vincenz Knauer,[28] *Die Hauptprobleme der Philosophie,* which set out great perspectives, could only be understood in the smallest of groups. Indeed, not even what the narrow Herbartian[29] philosophy was able to produce against outer materialism had any effect. So it happened that a strictly logical mind, even if trained in scholasticism, which wanted to build the bridge to scientific method within itself could not even do that within itself. This is what happened to Franz Brentano[30] who wanted to combine scientific method with strictly logical thinking in his *Psychologie vom empirischen Standpunkt*, the first volume of which appeared in 1874. But his disciplined thinking was not able to make any headway; he himself was still too much subject to the constraints of scientific materialism. He could not deal with himself and so the second volume, which had been announced for the autumn, failed to appear.[31] And today Brentano lives as an old gentleman in Florence and the second volume has still not appeared.

I myself witnessed the terrible struggles which this division could cause in the individual soul. I saw how the methodological aspect in training the thinking directly lost its power through the suggestive power of science. It happened during a formal meeting of the Vienna Academy in the 1880s at which I was present when Ernst Mach[32] gave a lecture about economy in looking at natural phenomena. He indeed failed to find a way to grasp natural phenomena within his method. With each sentence it was painfully clear how all methodology of thought disappeared, how everything shrunk to the principle of the least use of energy in understanding nature. In this way thinking was reduced from the ruling position it held in Hegel to the least conceivable economic importance.

Thus Hegel remained what we might call under an enchantment and even a Kuno Fischer[33] was not able to release him from his spell. It turned out to be true what Rosenkranz[34] said in the introduction to his Hegel biography: we philosophers in the second half of the nineteenth century are, at best, the grave diggers of the philosophers of the first half of the nineteenth century. And with that he meant—biographers.

A new revival in the methodology of thinking then appeared to be provided by the works, going back to Kant,[35] of Otto Liebmann,[36] Zeller[37] and so on. Liebmann wrote one of the most sharp-witted treatises which have ever been written in the field of epistemology. He used every means to attempt to establish a transcendental epistemology but finally nevertheless ended up with a kind of epistemology which we might crudely describe as comparable to a dog chasing his tail. He did not get beyond the starting point of his epistemology.

And that is how we reached our present state. Clausius[38] importantly developed the theory of heat which influenced the physiology of the senses, which in turn influenced epistemology. Once again, then, a spell was cast on philosophy by science.

Thus those who spoke on the basis of the former trained thinking were silenced. It is true that in the 1880s a researcher, starting from Kant, really sought to develop epistemology further but he was not heard. Thus circumstances forced him to abandon that area completely and move over to aesthetics. It was not until 1906 that he—it was Johannes Volkelt[39]—published a small epistemological work *Die Quellen der Gewissheit unserer Erkenntnis* (The Sources of the Certainty of our Knowledge). The conditions for a true epistemology existed as little as for a true understanding of Hegel.

Our time is much more satisfied by something like Spencer's[40] encyclopaedia which goes a tiny bit and very superficially beyond science. And when indeed the concept of the smallest economic measure, as set out by Mach, returned from the New World in the Pragmatism of a William James,[41] it was enthusiastically received as something new. Certainly, the strict columns of Hegel's absolute logic and the totally unphilosophical reasoning of Pragmatism make rather curious bedfellows.

But what is good cannot be suppressed completely, only for a time. Healthy thinking stirred, on the basis of the power arising from a people we might say, where a misunderstood Kantianism was not able to coat the thinking like mildew. Thus the Russian philosopher Solovyov[42] did indeed bring new important methodological approaches in that he was based in the strength of a young people which, if you want to put it like that, had not even produced a proper culture, but not in an old one like Franz Brentano. The Frenchman Boutroux[43] introduced a new usable concept into historical development. Such endeavours continue to be ignored. But the truth continues to smoulder under the ashes. It can become overgrown with preconceptions and impotence but it nevertheless continues working as self-discipline in the thinking.

And those in particular who believe that they have to represent spiritual science must hope that such self-discipline of the thinking will smooth the path for spiritual science. They must find the way to the strictest Hegelian logic because that is the only way to provide a firm foundation in the thinking for what they have to bring down in often loose forms from higher spiritual worlds. Thus, if we may put it like this, there is nothing in the supersensory field which would have to be rejected by a strictly trained thinking. Sharper, self-disciplined thinking will find the transition, the bridge which leads from the last highest product of the physical plane, the thinking, to the supersensory.

LECTURE 3

WE will deal with a specific subject in these three days. We will talk about the paths which the soul of the human being can take in the context of a spiritual-scientific view of the world, about the goals of theosophical life. To this end today's lecture will provide a kind of introduction. Tomorrow and the day after we will then advance to the actual inner part of our reflections. Today our standpoint will be more of an outer one, I might say, and start with the question: is what we feel to be the spiritual-scientific view of the world something which has been brought about through the convenience of individual personalities or do its foundations lie in the soul of our time itself? Do we have something before us which is connected with the deepest needs of our age?

We can best approach an answer to these questions if we are clear that all those who come to spiritual science from all kinds of different professions, be they rich or poor, strong or weak, are seeking souls. All of them are seeking souls who do not always know precisely what they are seeking, but feel that they are seeking something. They are often souls who have gone all kinds of different ways and have let those things act on them which the present can provide: souls who have sought to satisfy their longing in this or the other field of art; souls who have looked around in what science can offer; souls who more or less darkly, more or less brightly have felt after laborious searches that they cannot find in the present what coincides with the searches of the soul. Such souls are frequently touched by what the spiritual-scientific movement can give and say: yes, here an impulse

lives which is different from elsewhere, different from what has its
origins in the life around me.

What do such souls feel, or what can they feel if they come into
contact with what we may call theosophy today? We must not think
that these seeking souls who find their way to spiritual science are the
only ones who are seeking. They have been chosen or they choose
themselves from a great number of seeking souls. Anyone who listens to
what is spoken out of the deepest needs of our time will see that there
are many souls who say: we thirst for the means to have the great riddles
of the world answered for us and we do not find that all the things
provided by tradition, all the things which modern science has to say can
answer these riddles.

Let us listen for a moment to what these souls, the best among them
have to say. They say approximately the following, and with these
words, which flow out of hundreds and thousands of such seeking souls,
we encounter something like the longing heart of our time: we look
back into the distant past and see how from centuries to centuries, from
millennia to millennia the various ideas about God and nature have
followed one another, replaced one another and led to conflict between
their representatives. Many things have been passed down to us, millions of people confess to such ideas and follow them out of an honest
sense of truth. But just as many can no longer confess to what has been
passed down out of such a feeling of truth; they feel out of a sense of love
of truth that they have to let the old views go.

What was it like in the far distant past? At that time people might
for example look at the river flowing from the heights down into the
planes, look at the beneficial effect of that river and ask themselves:
what speaks to us out of the rush of this river? What is it that is at work
in this river? And they found something in it which they also found in
themselves. They found that it was based on a spiritual something, a
divine being, they found in the flowing river a divine spiritual power
which rewarded them, which gave people what they needed for their
well-being. They found something spiritual at work in the blowing
wind, the rolling thunder, the flashing lightning which was the same as
in the flow of the river, the sound of the surf. They saw something in it
of which they said: what lives in my soul is related to the murmur of the

brook, the rage of the storm. They may speak a different language but there is something similar there nevertheless and I feel I can understand it.

Something similar was felt by those to whom Moses brought down the tablets of the law. They felt that a being spoke out of them which was infinitely greater than the father of a family, but what spoke out of the thunder and the venerable head of the family was nevertheless related. They felt the spirit throughout. They experienced a living bond between what lived in them as pain and joy and the external world—a bond which these people in times immemorial were able to understand.

That is what the best say. And if you go where serious science speaks, not trivial superficiality, you can hear the following. Our ancestors looked up to spiritual powers. They did not just see rippling water, blowing wind, the fire of lightning. They saw spiritual beings in these natural forces, gnomes, undines, sylphs, salamanders. Whatever we might think about these people, they were understood by their contemporaries, those people who wrote their belief as poetry into the external world, belief which gave them strength and stability.

And now the best of these seeking souls add: we can no longer believe in gnomes, undines, sylphs and salamanders, in spiritual beings of nature, because we have been taught that iron laws work down as far as the smallest atom; and we have to think of the external world as a construction of these. We can no longer fill it with life as our ancestors did, can no longer hold sacrificial ceremonies and rites which send up our voices, can no longer say when we are racked with pain: do not despair because life in the spiritual world will give you all the greater comfort. And a large number of people say: our whole world has become different. We no longer build on what was built on previously. If in earlier times someone had been pierced by a rusty piece of metal, they would have sought comfort with spiritual beings. Today we do better to go to the doctor and use the resources of external medicine. That is what we use today to treat what previously would have been treated with what lives in the soul.

Some argue against this that we cannot be without the belief in a spirit, we cannot do without that. A spirit is at work in all laws, is at work in thunder the same as in the atom. And a person only needs to have gone beyond the most terrible trivialities of materialism not to be able to deny such an insight. When seeking souls use the word spirit in this way, what do they mean? What is spirit? Where do its roots lie? How do people obtain an idea of the spirit?

A strange view is being spread today. In America people are talking about a new religion.[45] The latter only wants to recognize a god who works in the laws of nature down as far as the atom. No one today can imagine a god in human form, the representative of this teaching says, but we cannot do without a divine spirit. And so this personality says this peculiar thing: the laws of chemistry are not enough. But from where should we take the content of an idea of God? And so we hear the following: we have to think of the spirit which is at work in nature in such a way that it possesses the characteristics of the human soul. People are not therefore prepared to imagine a god who possesses human characteristics but they do want to have something which gives substance to such an idea of God.

And here we have the result: we cannot do otherwise, we cannot take the content of our idea of God from anywhere other than the human being. And the representative of this world-view further points out that in earlier times divine beings were venerated who inspired and filled people with their power and urged them towards a task. We cannot now of course believe any longer that there are supersensory beings who act as inspiration. But the future will venerate advanced helpers, wealthier spirits who have something to give to the poorer ones.

So you see, in place of what happened in earlier times feelings nevertheless occur which cling to those who can give comfort. After each earthquake, for example, there will be those who can give comfort to the many who have lost their dear ones. There will be human love when the supersensory helpers no longer exist.

Can you not see the strange contradiction which occurs here? We are to look to those who give comfort. But where do they obtain the things in their soul which they need so that they can give comfort and love? Thus we find among the best ones that although they seek, the soul must feel that it faces emptiness.

And what happens in science? Is comfort found in what science has brought us? Let us fully acknowledge the beneficial effect of science but we must not forget one thing. How much of the purely physical pain which human beings have had to suffer since prehistoric times has been relieved? People have certainly not become stronger and healthier since then. Of course there are many medicines which provide relief. But we have to draw attention to a contradiction here. External science believes that nothing can be lost. When we rub something, for example, the energy occurs as heat. Something that disappears reappears as a different kind of energy. Analgesics reduce pain and people talk as if the pain had disappeared. Here there is a contradiction with that simple law. When the pain disappears, it reappears somewhere else. We can alleviate as much external pain as we want; it is transformed into soul pain. And people are not aware that these things are connected with the relief of outer pain. This should not prevent us from doing what we think necessary to relieve outer pain, but we have to learn to understand the connections and not indulge in illusions in the spiritual field.

They have no idea, these seeking souls, that people situated in outer life today can, for example, be drawn into the powerfully developing field of industry and technology by what is presented to their eyes. But those who look more deeply can see: this intoxication, this enthusiasm has to be paid for with something. You know that souls are becoming increasingly desolate, that they feel the answers to the riddles of existence less and less. Of course we should make available in all areas what can relieve pain but we should not forget that, even when we satisfy the outer body, we can allow the soul to starve, can inflict more and more pain on the soul through unrelieved longing. That is the mood which overcomes people who not only observe human activity in a loving way but who have an overview of the course which the future will take.

There is much talk of the goals which people can set themselves. But in the intoxication which overcomes their soul when they are gripped by the swirl of external life today they fail to notice that the soul has to remain a seeking one. And why? Let us place before our soul only at the deepest level the discrepancy in what we feel today. When we cut our finger and make it heal again with the best medicines known to us, we know that the same laws of nature are at work as in our environment. We have been formed out of the whole of nature, out of the laws which govern around us. But at the same time we feel the necessity to see something other within ourselves. We see that spirit flashes out of people's eyes, spirit speaks out of their hands, spirit sounds out of their voice. And in recognizing this we also feel ourselves as the bearer of the spirit. We feel that we have been created out of our environment but not alone from it. What rules this environment? The laws of physics, laws of chemistry, what we know today as the iron laws of nature. That is not sufficient to explain the spirit. The things provided by physics, chemistry and biology are not enough for that.

Where are the roots of what we can address as spirit? The spirit is within, inside ourselves, but homeless and rootless. We can understand the chemical composition of the blood, can precisely grasp the combustion process which takes place in us and everything which is subject to the laws of physics and chemistry in the external world. But as soon as we see external nature with the spirit removed everything becomes rootless. We cannot say that in the same way that the blood is subject to the laws of the blood circulation so something spiritual follows the laws of the environment. Spirit cannot be found in the latter, the seeking, lost soul of the present says. I will not find the answers there which torment me. From where will they come?

Now we can see where the problem lies. We see that our ideas about the external world are becoming ever clearer. But then human beings want to be rooted in something with their spirit, with their soul. The soul cannot but want to do that. It cannot escape from itself into a desolate, chemo-physical existence. That is where the split occurs. The soul has the need to imagine a spiritual being but nowhere in the external world can it find what corresponds to its present-day ideas about a spiritual being. That gives rise to a deep untruth. People today cannot believe in sylphs, salamanders, undines and gnomes. But the thing which could give them satisfaction does not exist. The soul stands there without substance.

The deeper this is experienced, the less truthful it becomes when we talk only about the spirit. Either we find the spirit or we have to insert it artificially. It might appear to many that what has just been said is too far removed from daily feelings. But we will find souls everywhere whose pain has its origin in these foundations. What spiritual science brings seeks to respond to this great search. It endeavours to build a bridge between the soul itself and that which is outside, be it that the soul is listening to the raging storm or watching the gentle play of the waves.

People are no longer capable of idealizing gods acting in the air and water from out of the characteristics of the human being. We have to prohibit ourselves from seeing an anthropomorphic image of ourselves in what we describe as divine beings. That is what the present time has learnt. But the converse is the impotence of the seeking soul. On the one hand it is told: if you find a god you must not give him human characteristics. On the other hand we have the consequence that we are not able to create a replacement for ourselves. Because these seeking souls are missing anything that would justify this almost self-evidently arising fact; they are at a loss. Where can they find the firm foundation that would give them security?

That is only possible if human beings once again acquire the right to conduct research into the spirit, if they look more deeply into their interior. People in earlier times made do with less. People today are no longer satisfied with the former. Spiritual science tells people today: you have taken the wrong path. Are the characteristics which human beings have found to date all the characteristics? Are there not deeper foundations? Do we not find something hidden of which we can say, 'Yes, this could be related to what I feel to be the divine'?

There has to be something which has deeper foundations than all the things which people have understood about themselves until now, which gives them the right to transfer human soul characteristics to the divine. But how do we find the path to the foundations hidden in our own interior?

Here spiritual science points us to the paths which previously only few people went. Today many people need to be told about these paths. For there are two paths: firstly the path of mysticism and secondly the path of occultism in the true sense of the word.

Let us look at these two paths. What is the path of mysticism? In order to understand this, we only need to place a particular moment before our soul. You all know that we say in spiritual science that the person in sleep is not the same being as when awake. On going to sleep, the inner part of the human being leaves and on waking descends back into the physical body and the etheric body. Generally people do not take account of the fact that something else still happens in this process. Do we ever see from the inside that which descends? Then there is a mighty transformation in human beings. In the moment in which they descend, they do not see their etheric body and physical body from the inside. Otherwise they would see that their corporeality is illusion, Maya. As ordinary people we see the environment and that part of us which we can see from the outside. Human beings do not see what works and lives within them. They only see the external part which they also see in stones and minerals because their gaze is diverted to the external world as soon as they descend into their lower bodies.

Those who strove for a conscious awakening were the mystics. They experienced a conscious descent into the external human being. All the images of the inner life which are familiar to the mystics are what human beings can see when they turn their gaze away from the external world, from what normally captures their gaze. The mystics experience what human beings are when they look at themselves from the inside. There they do not, for example, see how the blood circulates but they see that the blood is the bearer of divine activity; they see that the blood is a shadow of divine reality. That is what the mystics experience: the spiritual motor of their own being instead of external Maya.

What the mystics tell us is true. Let us listen to what they report: this descent is connected with what we call trials, temptations, the awakening of selfish drives. Read the descriptions of what the soul is capable of unfolding in terms of base instincts. We have to go through whole layers of passions, desires, selfish inclinations of which we barely think ourselves capable. All of these things have to be overcome when we want to penetrate to the deep layers of our own being. It is a wise provision that our gaze is directed away from our own interior to begin with because human beings are not mature enough to descend consciously into their own interior. They have to fight everything that rears up in them when they have trodden the path of overcoming their own egoism. Only then do they find the true human being who is concentrated in the smallest space, the point of the I. Only there are we fully within ourselves, know ourselves in good and evil, see what human beings really are when they find themselves beyond the layer which is formed by the instincts and desires, and when they have outgrown everything which they have become through education and convention. We have to pass through this layer if we want to penetrate into our interior.

There is another way to obtain an understanding of the spirit within ourselves. It is not easy to follow and is protected against those not ready for it because it also contains its own dangers. Alongside the important moment of waking up there is also the moment of going to sleep which is equally important for looking at the human being. Let us look at it in greater detail. At the moment when they go to sleep, human beings pass over into the spiritual world, into the world apart from physical reality. Their consciousness stops; it is extinguished. Normal human beings do not in a conscious way have the spiritual world around them. If they were to penetrate the spiritual world before they were ready, then they would be afflicted spiritually to the most extreme degree with what in the physical world is being blinded. They would be blinded by a direct view of the spirit infusing the external world.

Once again it is necessary to strengthen human beings to such an extent that they are not blinded by the spirit infusing the external world. That is done by means of the occult path. Through this they find their I not closely compressed in their own interior but poured out over the whole external world, at one with the external world. That is the occult path.

In learning to tread both these paths, the path of mysticism and the occult path, an important fact appears before the eye of human beings. Let them find the point where they are most compressed in their own interior, and let them be poured out over the whole of the external world; then they will ultimately experience one great, mighty thing. What you experience when you descend into the depths of your own self and when you pour yourself out into infinity is the same thing: mysticism and occultism, they go in opposite directions, and they lead to the same goal. Human beings discover something that has been asleep in them, that is enchanted in the external world, that can be found in the deepest part of their own soul and outside in the world of appearances. They find what lives as spirit behind appearances and they find the spiritual in themselves when they have united with the mystical path of knowledge and with the occult path of knowledge. That, then, is the bridge with which the chasm can be bridged before which the seeking soul of today stands when it recognizes that it itself is something other than the world appearances outside yet cannot combine itself in its characteristics with what surrounds it outside.

Today there is the possibility of finding a path which shows how that which lives in us is nevertheless the same as that which lives in the external world. The seeking souls which stand outside our endeavours do not yet know it. That path is shown by spiritual science. The theosophical movement wants to be a signpost towards this goal. It will provide answers to the questions which are posed by the bleeding, struggling souls of today. These questions will sound into the present and spiritual science will give the answer. That gives it its inner justification and shows that it is not the arbitrary result of some people's mind but a need of our time. Spiritual science will once again indicate ways and means to find the harmony between what lives in the environment and in the human soul. It will lead us to recognize the laws at work in nature not as empty abstractions but as thoughts of divine spiritual beings. In this way it will rediscover the spirit in the external world. Souls today are empty and desolate because they cannot do that. They can only obtain comfort, help and strength in seeking the paths and goals of the spiritual human being. That shows the profound justification of such spiritual-scientific striving.

When we understand spiritual science in its deepest sources, we will give the soul the nourishment which it craves, will open up sources of spiritual action for it and, because all things external are an expression of the spiritual, over time also health. The longing and searching of the present time give spiritual science its goals.

Lecture 4

W HEN we speak about the paths and goals of the spiritual human being, we will repeatedly be faced with the question: why should we think about following such special paths? Why are we pointed by spiritual science towards setting ourselves such goals? The answer to that has to turn into sentiment and feeling for us. It has repeatedly been pointed out that forces are slumbering in human nature and in nature which are striving to develop and which can be developed. Apart from the human being who can see and hear in the physical world, each person has a higher human being within themselves. The latter exists in embryo as a kind of seed. Spiritual science makes us aware of that with ever greater urgency. This is a human being of whom ordinary consciousness does not know a great deal.

We have to have a clear sense of the following. The thing of which we have an overview right now is our ordinary, everyday human being. But the one who is slumbering in us, who is predisposed within us as a seed, is a spiritual human being. Whether the latter develops or not is dependent on our ordinary human being. We can prepare the ground with the forces of our ordinary human being, but we can also leave it unprepared and not bother with it. Then we neglect our duty towards our spiritual human being. We can prepare the ground for this higher human being through spiritual science itself, through what it can give us as teaching and information. If we transform such insight into sentiment and feeling, that will give us the answer to the question: is it not a higher kind of egoism to concern ourselves with ourselves in this way?

For as long as we have not learnt about spiritual science, it is our karma to wait. But once we have heard about the higher human being slumbering in us it is our duty to do those things which can bring those forces to development so that we can better fulfil our tasks in the world. We cannot therefore speak of egoism in this context but only of the obligation towards our spiritual human being.

That is the correct attitude of the theosophist with regard to external life. Theosophy tells us a number of things which have been obtained through spiritual research. But that does not mean that everyone who wishes to live theosophy needs to be a researcher into the spirit. The more we can tread the path of our inner development, the better it is. But before we ourselves achieve results in the field of spiritual research we have to allow others to tell us its content. If we have considered the question for a sufficient length of time, external life will confirm the reports of the spiritual researchers. Once we have understood this information with healthy logic, we have obtained the possibility of ascending to higher worlds. Reason and logic are safe guides in this respect.

The question can arise: how should we use this information? How should we approach it? Take the truth which we describe as the law of karma. It says that we find events in later lives on earth which refer to earlier incarnations. The more we make use of such laws of spiritual research in life the more we will see how true they are. Just as we will never find a triangle in the sensory world whose angles do not produce the total sum of 180 degrees, so the circumstances of life must always confirm what has been found as a law in spiritual research. And if the karmic effects do not appear to us to agree, then this will most likely correspond to the minor deviations which may arise when measuring a circle with a planimeter. The result might perhaps be 361 degrees the first time and 359 the second time but that does not invalidate the law itself. Equally the law of gravity is not upset if a push makes the plumb bob of an Atwood machine[46] swing to the side. It only proves that a different result is achieved if a new force is applied.

Spiritual research further shows how we are faced with repetitions of previous periods within the life between birth and death. What we acquired for example in early childhood between the ages of 3 and 7 returns in its karmic effects in very old age. If we study how someone spent their early childhood, we will discover a remarkable connection in old age with these childhood years. If they developed healthy needs instead of having been subject to the outer constraint of specific rules, their old age will take a different form. But it frequently happens that people graft on to or cram into the child's soul what they consider to be the right thing. But that is beside the point because each child must develop the want to do this or that from his or her own volition. It then turns out that a person can retain their health in old age, that they can retain a freshness and inner strength into the final period of their life.

There are meanwhile even more significant connections. You can learn much from the handwriting of people about the way their past has developed.

In the age from 7 to 14 it is necessary that human beings are educated not to make use of their reason prematurely. Authority must have the effect that truth appears to us as such. If we can admire the people who surround us in that section of our lives this can stand us in good stead in the last but one section of our lives. To look reverently up to the wonders of nature and a prayerful mood are beneficial factors for later. Happy acceptance of authority returns in transformation in such a way that it becomes apparent that such a person has authority. Reverence which children in this period are able to develop has the consequence that they become people who without needing to do anything only need to be in the company of others in order to appear to have a benedictive effect. The hands which were never able to fold in reverence will never be able to give a blessing. Those who have never learnt to bend their knee will never be able to give a blessing. Once you have fully understood such a law you will find it confirmed. In this way we can already trace the effects of the law of karma in the period of a human life. Thus life everywhere gives us proof of laws which are at work in all fields.

Circumstances can of course occur which conceal the law. In physics we have the law of falling bodies for example. Imagine an object which at a given moment moves through space without any support wholly without external influence. As a result of the law we have just mentioned, this object will approach the earth with increasing acceleration until it hits the earth. The object will move towards the centre of the earth in accordance with very specific laws; it will fall. Imagine further that suddenly the falling object is hit by a horizontal impact. In this case the naive observer waiting for the arrival at the relevant spot on the earth of the object falling vertically as the result of the law of gravity will wait in vain. The object remains absent. Does that mean that the law of falling bodies has been negated? Of course not. It is just that another force has been added through the horizontal strike and the object now moves towards the earth under its influence in a curve which corresponds completely with the law of gravity and the subsequent additional force. At the place where under these circumstances the object hits the ground its fall will be seen by an observer as something completely random, unpredictable. But that is not so. The laws are complete and incorruptible.

The same applies in full to the law of karma, although we can only rarely follow it in all its compounded and entangled effects. That is why people are constantly inclined to doubt their karma. But however much external Maya confuses us, we should only let ourselves be instructed by what has become law in our soul. Many who want to develop the forces of the spirit within themselves will not find it easy because life, the physical always squeezes in. All it needs is an obstacle in our life and we easily allow ourselves through a wrong judgement to be carried away into hurling an insult for example without thinking of the consequences of our action. We hit a person and are unaware that we have raised our hand against ourselves because this blow will come back to hit us at the given time. The law of karma is everywhere at work. Everything that happens to us in life happens under the law of karma. But just because we consider this law simply as a teaching, a theory, that does not yet make us theosophists.

There are two feelings we have to make our own if we want to work on our spiritual human being. On the one hand we have to tell ourselves: everything about us could still achieve greater perfection, there is no limit to our ascent. At every moment the feeling of imperfection must be an incentive to want to climber higher and higher on the ladder of perfection which has no highest rung. We have to keep placing that before our soul because otherwise we will not advance a single step in our work on our spiritual human being. On the other hand we should say to ourselves: a second step is necessary. At every moment we should feel that an infinite possibility of perfection lies in us. We should make our hidden human being as large as possible. That appears to be a contradiction and human beings must feel it as such. Our development is packaged between these two points, the feeling of our own imperfection and the striving to make the hidden human being as large as possible.

Those who strive as mystics to enter into their own interior, who wish to make progress through inner contemplation, must pass through the first point. They have to make humility their own. The best rule which mystics can make for themselves is this: to think of everything they encounter in their own interior as being as imperfect as possible and to disregard their own personality completely. Because anyone who descends into their own interior must be prepared to experience terrible things. Stories of tragic events take place in the inner world of human beings who dare to enter the depths of their own being. A Tauler,[47] an Eckhart,[48] a Paul[49] have something to say about that. And what was the help they sought against the dangers? Paul said: Not I, but Christ in me wishes to act.

Take with you the master, the ideal, but alongside have the feeling that egoism has to be driven out. It is not their own I which should feel, want and conceive everything. Their unworthy I had to be driven out. This feeling is very similar to the feeling of shame in ordinary people. Wanting to be someone else, wanting to organize something else into one's own soul, that is the path of mysticism.

And what belongs to the path of occultism? The path of occultism leads into the external world. If human beings want to follow the occult path they have to live in such a way that they gradually have to learn to become used to enduring the higher world when they leave their body during sleep. They must acquire the feeling of perfecting themselves to infinity. But here too a danger lies, like for the mystics when they descend into their own interior. We described the dangers which affected the mystics, they themselves spoke about them. Nothing is said about the path of the occultist. Each person must familiarize themselves with this danger on their own.

When we look into our own interior, it would be bad if we had not learnt to feel ourselves as a unity which is infused throughout our whole being. Such being able to hold fast to a unity is torn apart by each passion which overcomes us. Anger, jealousy, hate destroy our power of being able to direct our gaze at the unity. And the worst thing is if we have not learnt to concentrate, if we are driven all over the place. We have to learn to feel ourselves as a unity firmly and unaffectedly.

If as occultists we seek the path into the external world, we have to discard our personality as it has just been characterized. Here we must not seek a unity which underlies the whole of the external world. Because when we turn outwards towards the spiritual world we encounter an endless variety of beings and circumstances. If an occultist were to attempt to penetrate the all-embracing unity which underlies the whole manifest world they would perish. Imagine a drop of red liquid and this drop is poured into a large basin of water. Liquid as the drop is, it would immediately dissolve into the mass of water, it would dissipate. That is what would happen to the insecure I if it wanted to enter the world of the all-embracing unity. We must not dare to penetrate there alone because we would lose ourselves like the red drop is lost in the mass of water.

If we want to enter the astral sphere we are directed towards a multiplicity. We have to start with the multiplicity, with the beings who are higher than us, with those who have themselves in stages passed through a higher development, with the hierarchies of that world. We must not want to skip anything because it would be a presumption to want to penetrate straight to the highest. We have to learn in stages to study with the help of the higher beings if we want to understand the all-embracing unity. The arrogance to want to penetrate to the highest will most certainly lead us to stumble. We must not allow ourselves to be misled through our monotheistic ideas to believe that when the veil which separates us from the spiritual world slides aside, we will only see a single divine all-embracing unity. We see a multiplicity and we have to turn our gaze to the multiplicity.

But how are we meant to find our way? Pythagoras[50] said: do not seek multiplicity with your eyes, ears and senses, seek it through the number! We should approach multiplicity armed with the number. Just as the mystics have to decant the ideal of higher perfection into their interior, so the occultist has to appeal to the number. And here there is a characteristic which is absolutely necessary, namely security. We have to feel secure. Because if human beings waver, what are they? They are a will-o'-the-wisp, a flickering light and the world is a labyrinth. We need Ariadne's thread to find the way back. The number gives us firmness, that is what we have to keep our eye on.

If you wish to enter the spiritual world you have to step out of yourself, have initially to go into the chaos of multiplicity. How do we find the factor? Where do we find an ordering principle? We find it through the number, through the laws of numbers. We have to penetrate the nature of the number and learn to know its true value. The number alone can become our guide in the labyrinth. The number can teach us many things and profound secrets underlie certain numbers.

Take the number two. Everything that appears in life is revealed in the number two. Right not without left, light not without dark. Everything that manifests externally is subject to the number two. The number two is the number of revelation, the number of manifestation.

The number three is the number of the laws of the soul: thinking, feeling and volition. To the extent that something organizes and structures itself in the soul entity, it is subject to the number three. Where the number three is revealed as one of the laws, there is an underlying soul element. We can find the number three in innumerable relationships. In the three logoi we have the three basic forces which refer back to something divine and of the soul.

The number seven applies with regard to all things temporal: Saturn, Sun, Moon, Earth, Jupiter, Venus and Vulcan, which designate the seven consecutive evolutionary states.

Where we see something simultaneously working together we obtain the number twelve: the twelve gods, the twelve apostles and so on. The reduction of the fixed stars to the twelve signs of the zodiac is also connected with this. The number twelve teaches us another law as well. Think of materialism. Is materialism wrong? It does not need to be so as long as people do not carry it into the soul element. If we want to be materialists we have to pay homage to vitalism,[51] then we learn to understand material life. But we have to choose a different perspective for the soul and spiritual entity. If we wish to understand the world in its abundance, we have to be able to adopt a variety of standpoints. We have to follow the practical path of the spirit.

Now we might hear someone express the principle: you have to create a certain system for yourself if you want to penetrate into the higher worlds. But that is the worst way we could go. We should, in contrast, first step out of our own personality: from the centre which this personality occupies in its existence to the horizon of our physical existence; and only here at the horizon should we adopt a specific standpoint, first the materialistic one, and look at it from the inside, from the one perspective, by which means, as already mentioned, we learn to know material life. Only then can we walk around the horizon and choose twelve different perspectives.[52] That is the only way which can lead to real knowledge. Practical occultists have to become very selfless before they can walk the horizon in a circle. They receive unity in external and internal things in that they have to forget their personal I twelve times.

LECTURE 5

I F we asked a person in everyday consciousness, 'What is it that we call the I?' we would get the answer that such self-consciousness had to be sought within the boundaries enclosed by the skin. Our view can be proven through the fact that the seat of the soul must be sought in the head and the heart. But spiritual science sees that differently, only it is not easy to understand.

We come closer to the spiritual reality if we try to clarify the supersensory facts for ourselves. People cannot come close to the truth with the concepts and words which they use without this research. We will get a good understanding of that if we make use of a single picture.

Think of a seafarer sailing the seas. Here the external factors are the important, the determining thing. How he sails the ship depends on the state of the ocean, whether islands appear in the ocean, what the sky is doing and other things. The captain and sailors make their decisions on the basis of all these external facts, the external facts are what matter to them. Now some might think that when the ship reaches port she is at rest, all work stops for a period. But that is not the case. A different kind of work starts. There the ship no longer does the work but work is done on the ship. Damage from the voyage is repaired. The hold is filled with new cargo and so on. In this way the voyage and the time that the ship lies in port can be compared with human life, with life during the day and life during the night. Only there is one difference and this is that human beings are not involved in the work during the night. During the work in port the ship must be made serviceable by the workers and sailors for her next voyage. But everything which in the daytime work of human beings provokes action through the senses stops working at night. Our senses, which have done the work in our body during the day, are at rest during the night. The work of the day rests like the ship in port. And yet work does take place in the human being which makes him or her capable of starting a new day's work.

In this way we can come closer to the concept of what the actual spiritual part in the human being is. It is not enclosed by a person's skin but extends beyond the physical human being. The actual spiritual entity extends its feelers into the human being, it sends the essential part, the spiritual part into the human being.

Where is the actual I located in the human being? We find the spiritual human being, the supersensory ego-human being surrounding the physical human being. And when we look at the human aura, which is formed like an egg, then the ego-consciousness will work most effectively in the shell, in the auric egg. It is this fact which leads to a proper solution of the problem.

I referred to twelve points on the horizon. The occultist has to know them. They exist there even if they are not recognized by everyone. These twelve points constantly send their forces into human beings; they are attacked from these twelve points in the various points of their aura. It is only because their I surrounds them that they are capable of making the cosmic forces one with themselves. Human beings must feel that they are part of the cosmos. That makes them capable of perception and in that way it becomes possible for them to acquire capabilities of apprehension which correspond to the points we have just talked about. They are embedded in these twelve points. The divine spiritual forces act into the human being through these points. If you are able to contemplate and observe this you will understand the paths and goals of the spiritual human being.

Human beings have to be able to integrate this feeling into their lives. Spiritual science enables them to become familiar with the sum of forces through which they can fulfil this transformation in themselves. Let us consider our simple everyday lives. Someone might hasten through the world and encounter many things on which they could reflect, which they could work on in their spirit, but they do not make the least effort to transform what they have experienced into work or, indeed, even just think about it more deeply. The only thing they want to do is have 'experiences' and rush from one sensation to the next.

Then there is another type of person who goes through life without paying the least attention to the external world. They brood on and speculate about their own thoughts. They do not notice what is going on around them; they are constantly brooding. Neither extreme is of benefit for human beings. But there is a middle position and that is this: to interweave everything we experience with our own thoughts. This middle state is the most beneficial one for human beings in the external world.

Let us assume a young man is preparing for his exams. He has worked hard, the time of the exam approaches and with it the anxiety about the exam. The young man keeps thinking that on the day of the exam he might be asked the one question about which he feels least secure, about which he knows least. That is at work in his thoughts. The exam goes well, it determines the rest of his life. It is the gateway to his further life. Now it can happen that in the further course of his existence he is pursued by a dream and in this dream the anxiety about the exam of his youth appears, all the things he thought he did not know at the time. The soul is intimately connected with this and the occult observer sees the web that is spun in the dream. What is woven there has not contributed at all to the life that has passed. But the occultist knows that it will turn into useful forces in the next life.

It can also happen differently. The dream stops at the age of 45. Observing himself, the person discovers that quite new characteristics appear. It might be experienced, for example, that in his advanced years he has a lot more courage than he possessed in his youth. The states of anxiety of his youth and the associated will to overcome them have been quietly at work in the inner human being. Forty-five years later these forces have turned into their opposite. There is always something weaving and working inside the human being and the thing which is at work there is the astral body. It works for so long in the etheric body until what has been experienced has been interwoven with the etheric body and has become a true characteristic. In normal life it only appears as a characteristic in the next life but quite unusual cases like the one just mentioned can also occur.

In this way human beings process their external experiences and the same thing happens with the extrasensory situations of life which require us to process them with our I. How does the spiritual human being work with regard to external circumstances? The external circumstances come to us but the web that transforms our abilities is spun from inside. We weave into the human being the things which originate in the eternal spirit. We have to approach the external but the spiritual approaches us.

Let us assume that a person for one or another reason becomes interested in something, for example looking more closely at a tree. They have to approach the tree, must give themselves up to the tree in order to achieve a result. But it is different with spiritual results. They come to us, we have to wait for them to arrive.

The key thing about external experiences is that they are transitory in nature. But those which come to us by way of theosophy are based on spiritual ground. We weave them into our interior as something everlasting. We have to go towards external things, but the spiritual has to come to us and the more we make ourselves capable of receiving the spiritual the more it ripples towards us from the spiritual worlds and turns into our property. The human beings who live as poets among us and have created and produced something are always those who in times past allowed the supersensory to flow into them. We have to learn to think more. We have to be able to think logically and in a reasoned way and then make our soul very still. Then we will not have waited in vain. The spirit will correspondingly flow into our soul to which we ourselves have opened the way. We have to learn to preserve the mood of anticipation. The best thing is not the thing we brood on. We are meant to obtain everything through the work we do on our thinking, not through ourselves. We can only fertilize our spirit through sharp thinking and then waiting. It has to stream into us when we have learnt to observe the proper processes and these processes have to work together with the thinking, feeling and volition.

There are three parts of our soul life: thinking, feeling and volition. A person sees a rose. They recognize it as such through their thinking life.

They admire the form and colour; that awakens certain feelings in them. They stretch out their hand to grasp the rose and thereby express an act of will. But important results depends on the way in which the person now treats these characteristics which can be crucial for the rest of their life.

For example, a person might meet another one towards whom they feel a pronounced antipathy. They see that they cannot free themselves from the person they dislike and the feeling that is aroused by that constraint makes them angry. Thinking, feeling and the will are involved in this process.

The different courses which these processes take can often be observed in daily life. The anger of one person quickly ebbs away; they do not want to carry such feelings around with them for long and the better feelings gain the upper hand. Another, in contrast, carries their anger with them for the whole day; they do not find the flexibility to shake it off. The first person who quickly shakes off their agitation will remain a mentally healthy person; they might reach a great age. But the other who becomes angry at every little thing and carries their anger around with them for a long time will age early. Such constant agitation will eat away at their body.

There is a saying, never go to sleep angry. That is when the affects start to weave in the soul and we weave the passions into the human being. What we experience out of the spirit acts on our soul and it is quite a different matter whether our experiences only remain theoretical or whether they are transmitted to the feelings.

Let us assume a person incorporates much of a spiritual nature in themselves and what they incorporate penetrates the human being. What is incorporated really only becomes productive for the spiritual human being when they embrace what is incorporated with enthusiasm and love. Only at that point does that work also become work of the inner human being; they draw out the spiritual and make it a part of their spiritual I. It is the feelings which help us to make our spiritual acquisition our own.

Human beings live in an aura and when the theosophical truths are incorporated by the spiritual human being the aura is strongly set in motion. The I is the motor of that movement. How is that process revealed to the clairvoyant eye? When love and enthusiasm for the great spiritual thoughts take hold of the human being, everything comes to life in the aura and the result of this higher thought life is such that it has a cleansing effect on the aura. All material wishes and musings gather into balls and these balls become denser and denser as our spiritual work increases; they become smaller and smaller, until the purifying light of spiritual thinking has dissolved and dispelled them.

When the clairvoyant eye sees a person watching a sunrise, similar phenomena can be observed. Something similar happens in the aura of the observer in the reverent joy which the person can feel in this natural spectacle. For as long as such a person lets something beautiful act on their interior the effect of this process is a dissolving one in the aura and many bad things are turned to good. Being able to take pleasure and the ability of contemplation have a purifying effect on the soul and in such moments the soul is capable of assimilating new spiritual things because the stream of higher forces has found an entry.

But the opposite can also happen. When a person does not allow a great natural spectacle which has acted on them to linger in their thoughts, if nothing remains in them of all that beauty and they turn to other things after fleeting enjoyment, the following can happen: everything conglomerates in the aura of such a person. A soul and spiritual task which they came across was carelessly ignored and now lives itself out in the dark. Then it can happen that lies find entry into their interior. Working on the ability to let an event leave an impression on and be preserved in the feelings, that is the work of the spiritual human being.

If all of us learnt this, then spiritual science would lead to paths and goals which would be widely beneficial. If the only work which was done was brainwork, if there was strife and discord among theosophists, little of what is bad would be transformed into good. The law of karma will show human beings how to work in the right way.

For those who can have enthusiastic feelings about theosophy and know how to find consolation in it, the higher spiritual sciences are a blessing because they bring consolation and strength under all circumstances. No one leaves these sciences without consolation. The greater our goals, the more our striving will be penetrated by ideals and human beings will carry them out into the world. We pursue spiritual science and interweave it with our inner human being. It penetrates us and we can carry it out among other people.

We have to work on these goals as much as we are able. We do not have the right to leave the paths and goals of the spiritual human being unobserved. It is our duty to interweave the soul element with the physical world. Human beings are the entrance gate, the only spiritual gate in the physical and material world through which the heavens can flow in. We can dissolve the lead of materialism by allowing the spiritual truths to penetrate. Only when human beings work on human development do they contribute to life and not to death. Walking the paths and goals of the spiritual human being means pursuing the task of turning the supersensory into the soul element.

LECTURE 6

If I make the attempt today to sketch out the current state of philosophy and science, then the reason for that is that in the widest circles of spiritual-scientific views there is not always the clarity as to the way we as anthroposophists can establish a proper relationship with what otherwise exists at present in spiritual and scientific endeavours. I have occasionally included philosophical matters in the courses of spiritual-scientific lectures, taking specialist areas as a starting point. I have spoken specifically about the philosophy of Hegel[53] and its connection with the present time.

Today I want to take a somewhat broader view of the subject and talk in general about the current situation of philosophy and science. Since I announced what the subject would be and the participants in my courses already know about the form which such philosophical interludes take, you will not be surprised when I say from the beginning that I am not particularly concerned about popularity. I rather want to call forth a feeling as to how we, as strictly scientific people, can find the relationship between spiritual science and other intellectual endeavours of the present. It is hardly surprising that there is not a great deal of awareness in this regard—as to what has to be said in a lecture like the one today—in the theosophical literature. The theosophical writers are not, as a rule, philosophers and are not aware of the difficulties which accrue to philosophers if they try with their basic scientific characteristics to approach the field of spiritual science.

I can, of course, only highlight individual examples but I want to choose them in such a way that, when I have finished, you can obtain a feeling of how we should think about the matters I refer to. Here I will begin by saying that it can from the start make a certain impression on a receptive soul if we talk in the field of spiritual science about supersensory knowledge, the ascent of clairvoyant research to supersensory knowledge. It must occur to those who believe that they need to approach these things from the premises of the philosophy of today, if they are talked about at all, that the objections which philosophy raises against various things it calls direct experience, direct perception must apply in the same way to everything we produce in the spiritual-scientific field.

As long as we dress our supersensory experiences in words for example which, when we speak them—you may not even be aware of it—make use of spatial or chronological ideas; as long as it can be shown to us that we do that, as long as we are unable to structure our terminology in such a way that we do not insert spatial and chronological ideas in our observations in the relevant place; for as long as a Kantian or some other epistemologist of the present time can come along and object (either in the old form or in the various forms which these theories have assumed in more recent times) that it was an epistemological certainty that time and space were themselves mere categories or forms of our thinking, and if we also dressed our clairvoyant results in such forms which are taken from time and space, we would by doing that— providing something that is tied to our conceptual ability, so as a result we would basically express something with our clairvoyant results which—I know the term is open to challenge here—is merely subjective. That is a possible objection which can always be made. I mention it as an example of many other objections which can rightly be formulated on epistemological premises.

Only if we can raise such objections adequately for ourselves as scientists of the spirit have we obtained the full inner right to postulate certain things. That does not provide a reason for not lending ourselves to certain information out of an inner sense of truth. We should do that because the inner sense of truth can lead us in the right direction. But we are only armed to respond to the intellectual movements of the present time if we raise such objections ourselves and—at least within our own elaborations—can respond to these objections.

We have to distinguish between two kinds of objection. The objections against spiritual science will, of course, rain down on us from all sides. If we are in the position to know ourselves what is raining down on us, to identify it for our ourselves, and then are simply not heard with what we have to say about it, then the fault lies with the others. Then we can wait—as we must do—until people have become mature enough to understand our explanations. But if our explanations give an amateurish impression with regard to the intellectual movements of our time, then the fault lies with us if we cannot secure the construct of our teaching in the appropriate way.

We have to be capable of doing that: of distinguishing between those things where the fault lies with us—and in very many areas it lies with us, it lies in the theosophical literature, it lies in the ease with which some people think they can find their way into the field of spiritual science. We have to distinguish between the things which are our fault and the things where we can calmly wait because we are able to put for ourselves precisely the arguments which the intellectual movements of the present time would use for their objections. But if we want such a thing, we have to be clear for ourselves above all where the failings of the intellectual movements of the present time lie. We have to be able to ask ourselves a little how these intellectual movements of the present time have developed.

You know from my lectures that I do not like to shoot my mouth off about my opinions. The opinions of an individual person are basically not of any great value. I have always tried to allow the facts to speak for themselves, also in the field of spiritual science. That is why I do not want to lecture today either about theories which are rooted in opinions but allow the facts to speak. I want to present a fact which can illustrate how inadequacies in the thinking have developed in the course of the nineteenth century which have prevented the penetration in a certain deeper way into what the thinking can still supply if it only draws the consequences from its premises in a sufficiently penetrating, truly sharp way. Theosophy often turns out to be so faint-hearted with regard to the objections against it because its intellectual weapons have grown blunt.

If we speak only about the thinking—I know all the objections which can be raised against what I am about to say, but the matter will nevertheless present itself in this way for anyone who penetrates into the intellectual development of the nineteenth century—if we begin by starting from pure thinking, then we have to say that a certain climax was reached with Hegel in philosophical development as regards the sharpness of thinking, as regards the crystallization of the thinking in the soul. It is to misunderstand Hegel to talk about him as frivolously as his opponents in the second half of the nineteenth century did. They imagined that Hegel was intent on removing all content from the pure thought as to what it had to say about the world. The only thing is that they failed to take into account that Hegel nowhere pretends that the human subject wanted to take anything of real world content out of the pure thought. We have to take into account that Hegel does indeed take the viewpoint that it is the thought itself, the inwardly alive thought, the active and productive thought which fetches the content of the world out of itself, and that we with our subject of cognition are only the stage on which the thought works.

If we take the matter in the way that it actually presents itself in the course of the intellectual life, we have to say: Hegel's monumental greatness lies in this tendency. But also, it contains the whole of the weakness of Hegelian philosophy. The greatness, in that for anyone who truly wants to come to grips with him Hegel can become the teacher of a disciplined thinking which we can acquire in no other way. Theosophists in particular should acquire such disciplined thinking. After all, a great number of errors, of incorrect convictions simply arise because our thinking does not extend as far as the crystalline clarity of an intellectual discipline as can be learnt through the Hegelian system. In each lecture in which we feel a responsibility towards knowledge and truth we should, as it were, be filled with the results of such intellectual discipline. We should get into the habit of nowhere using a word that has not first been felt and experienced by us in its full scope and content. If—penetrating what appears to some to be so abstract, so dry and sober, penetrating Hegelian logic—we inoculate ourselves with this discipline in our thinking, then we reach the point where we never use the words being, becoming, existence other than in those places where in the whole structure of the lecture those words can be inserted; because we have first pursued the whole development of the content of such concepts from the simplest, emptiest concepts to those with the greatest content.

The philosophical lecturer of today and all of today's literature is fundamentally immensely far removed from such inner discipline of thought. I could easily show you that in world-famous philosophical books of the present the authors are not even able to sustain the content of a concept in a concise and precise way for more than three lines and after three lines use the concept they used earlier in quite a different way. It is quite obvious that this must lead to the inner muddle of the whole edifice which is represented by our thoughts. It would be easy, as I said, to demonstrate this in world-famous philosophical books of the present time.

Now Hegel's opponents believed that they could easily put him to flight because they did not understand the nature of the thought and the way it interlaces on the stage of the subject of cognition, but they believed—something that was never in Hegel's mind—that he wanted to remove, as it were, the world content from the direct subject of cognition. That this cannot be, that we can never remove any substantial cognitive content from the respective subject of cognition if it remains only in the concept, that is something we have to be clear about. That is why Hegelian philosophy had to remain unproductive with regard to the productive progress of the intellectual life—that is its weakness—because its underlying idea that it is the thought itself which works out of itself may be correct, but it does not follow from this that it is the subject of cognition itself which has to produce the objective content of the world. What is the only way for the subject of cognition to obtain cognitive content out of itself? It is only possible if the subject of cognition fertilizes itself, makes itself capable of producing cognitive content. But such a capability can never happen on the plane of pure thinking. Through the pure thinking we obtain a kind of overview, a kind of bigger review of what the human spirit has produced in the course of world history. From a certain midpoint we can survey the thoughts which have been produced. But we cannot obtain new cognitive content.

That was felt by Hegel's opponents. The only thing is that they based their opposition on false premises. But that is why Hegelianism on its own produced two things: a sheer immeasurably great discipline of the thinking, and the inability to obtain productive cognitive content. In other words, Hegelian philosophy cannot have an ongoing productive effect through itself. This is the point where the productive cognitive forces have to be applied, where also Hegel's subject of cognition which has been elevated to the level of the thought has to resolve to allow to flow in what you can find, for example, as a means of fertilization of the subject of cognition in my book *Knowledge of the Higher Worlds. How is it Achieved?*.

So let me say, if we start with direct sensory existence and the way human reason works on it, we reach that level which we can describe as the life and activity of the subject of cognition on the thought plane. But then further progress is only possible if we have the fertilization from the opposite side of sensory existence by those means which are set out in my book *Knowledge of the Higher Worlds. How is it Achieved?*. Now you will find in the literature in which I have attempted gradually to draw attention to these things—to begin with in a preparatory way through my earlier writings, summarized most recently in my *Philosophy of Freedom*—the path we can take from outer sensory experience, from the outer work on the material of existence, to the place where the thinking resides. You will find characterized there also the specific characteristics both of the setting of the thinking and the scope of pure thinking with regard to the subject of cognition. In my subsequent writings, which deal with the actual field of spiritual science, you will find characterized the other side of the world with its cognition-fertilizing forces. You will find an epistemological characterization of clairvoyant research, the scope of clairvoyant research which flows from the other side, as it were.

If we wanted to sketch this subject out, we could say: if we characterize for ourselves the thinking plane with the subject of cognition on this thinking plane, then there flow from the side of sensory perception all those things which can be obtained through the senses by way of the external sensory material of existence. We feel the Hegelian self-weaving within the thinking plane, what is called the dialectic of pure thinking. But then we come to a standstill if we take only this path. We have to wait until we are able to let flow into us from the other side that which we can receive by way of what is described in my book *Knowledge of the Higher Worlds. How is it Achieved?* So we can see that these things come together and that the Hegelian system was a wonderful summary of the human spirit at a specific time, but, once this had occurred, those things had quite properly to happen to which the Hegelian system could not rise. The plane where the subject of cognition has to be located is fixed. It cannot be raised; it can only be described from the other side with that which can equally be epistemologically assured—so that we do not remain one-sided but acquire the possibility to gain an insight into the strictly epistemological method also in those areas where we leave the sphere of just the senses.

When we look at all of this, we can ask: how can it be that philosophy itself shows itself to be so reluctant to engage with those logical forms which can equally be used to determine what comes from the other side, through which we can determine epistemologically what comes from the other side? The reason for this is that the philosophy of the nineteenth and into the twentieth century has so far neglected to take the step which should have been taken out of a Hegelianism understood in the right way. And so it happened that the philosophy of the nineteenth and twentieth century could not find the connection to what lies beyond the thinking plane. However, the deeper reason also has to be sought in the fact that Hegelian philosophy was little understood in the further development of philosophy. Because if we rise to the plane of pure thinking, then it is quite inevitable—because we stand at the boundary to the spiritual world—that we can also feel those logical reasons which allow us to recognize that it is quite justified for the supersensory world to flow in.

You can thoroughly feel this when you encounter such an ascent of human cognitive knowledge to the pure thought and then the way that the higher worlds are allowed to shed their illumination in the lectures of our dear Dr Unger,[54] lectures which cannot be praised highly enough. Hence we have to emphasize that it is the greatest blessing that we are in a position to have such a person among us as Dr Unger, who is able in this spiritual and philosophical field to elaborate and execute the epistemology of the pure thinking with regard to the subject of cognition which is located as the I on the thinking plane. And thus these lectures in particular can give you something of an indication for obtaining assurance in the relationship between spiritual science and the other intellectual endeavours.

If you pursue this philosophy, some of which has already been set out in Dr Unger's remarks, some of which still remains to be set out, then you will see that this philosophy will have a quite different character as philosophy to what exists today as contemporary philosophy. A truly not insignificant thinker[55] recently said something about the latter which basically cannot be challenged. If we look without bias at what has been produced in Germany and other countries then we can see that what this thinker said really is coming true: that today we have metaphysics without a transcendental conviction, epistemology without objective meaning, logic without content, psychology without soul, ethics without commitment and religion not grounded in reason.

That is a characteristic of our time as experienced by a not inconsiderable philosopher of the present. As I said, I want to let the facts speak for themselves, let what is happening speak. Whether it has to be said that he had no inclination to engage with the spiritual-scientific path or whether in the suggestion of his thinking he could not do so is neither here nor there. But we have to say that this is how someone can think who is fully engaged in contemporary activities but cannot find the way out to supersensory content through the thinking. Certain prerequisites have to be fulfilled in the thinking which today cannot really be found in any other philosophy than in what I have tried to establish in my book about *Truth and Knowledge*, in what is set out in *The Philosophy of Freedom* and in the carefully executed operation of Dr Unger's thinking. All of this provides the approach to an energetic philosophy from out of the field of spiritual science which avoids mixing anything of a theosophical nature into its reflections, which aims to be strictly philosophical and precisely through such academic rigour will fulfil its task into the future.

Now we might ask, how can it happen that, although it was thought that Hegelianism had been overcome, nineteenth-century thinking in all civilized countries could not rise to come to terms with the thinking aspect in the subject of cognition in such a philosophical way—how could that happen? It cannot be my task to go into the profound cultural historical reasons—I have done that elsewhere—but today I want to remain in the field of pure philosophical characterization. The reason is that facts occurred, that it cannot escape anyone who attentively follows the course of intellectual life in the 1850s, 1860s, 1870s and 1880s as to how basically the thinking itself remained strong only in a single field of nineteenth-century intellectual development, as to how elsewhere it became too dull to draw the consequences to be found in itself. There is only one field in which nineteenth-century and early twentieth-century science demands the highest respect even from the strict thinking of the spiritual researcher, and that is none other than mathematics. Everything that has been done within the scope of the field of mathematics bears the traces of sharp, penetrating thinking. Hence also someone who for example undertook their theoretical studies in the natural sciences such as theoretical physics and chemistry towards the end of the nineteenth century could very much have the feeling: the things that are handed down in such complicated formulas which had to be learnt in for example thermodynamics, undulation theory,[56] Clausius' theory[57] and so on are not the fault of mathematics. Anyone who went through that and had the philosophical wherewithal had the feeling: it is not the fault of mathematicians, mathematics has become a wonderful instrument to work everything out in finely chased systems; what was blunt were the intellectual weapons.

Thus it was easy to have the feeling when working with the mathematical formulas in the various fields of physics and chemistry: as long as one remained within mathematics everything felt secure, but as soon as one had to deal with the philosophical characteristics of what one was actually calculating the ground started to sway in all respects. That is what emerged from the minds of those who spoke in philosophical terms at the time. Nothing could be experienced other than the purest philosophical dilettantism which particularly revealed itself when natural scientists started to philosophize, such as Du Bois-Reymond[58] in his paper 'Seven World Riddles' or his lecture on 'The Limits of our Knowledge of Nature'. But nothing has improved. So we may say: we have experienced the extraordinary phenomenon that the thinking in the form that is of necessity required of it by spiritual science has only remained strong and exact in mathematics. The strict requirements of the thinking are today not satisfied in any field of research—the strict requirements we demand from the perspective of spiritual science— other than in the field of mathematics.

Now I do not here wish to deal with certain contributions—with their characteristics—which can be applied to the cognitive field particularly from a mathematical perspective. I merely wish to draw attention to the symptomatic aspect of these things, draw attention to the fact that specifically in the field which has retained its wonderful inner strength, in the field of mathematics, there has come to expression most clearly how the thinking of the nineteenth century is ready in itself to break through the barrier which separates the human subject of cognition from the supersensory world. And be they only hypotheses, sometimes boldly proposed and undertaken purely computationally, we do nevertheless have to take what has happened in the mathematical field in such a way that it is an expression of the longing of human knowledge to go beyond the sensory world. And here we have seen specifically in the mathematical field how this longing has been realized. After all, has not mathematics in its forms in general, where we refer to them as geometry, considered certain things to be immutable since the time of ancient Euclid![59]

Who would have believed, for example, that there is anything more immutable than the theorem that the three angles of a triangle are equal to 180 degrees, or another theorem: if you have a straight line here and next to it a point, then in the sense of Euclidean geometry you can draw only a single parallel line through this point next to the straight line. In other words, in the sense of Euclidean geometry the sum of the angles of a triangle is equal to 180 degrees and we can only draw a single parallel line next to the straight line. That follows from the premises of Euclidean geometry. Why should anyone believe that this could be different? And yet, and this is the important thing—as I said, I could say a number of things for and against the content but I will only deal with the symptomatic aspect, with the longing to leave the sensory field; I only wish to give a characterization—we have the peculiar thing that we have seen geometries other than the Euclidean arise in the nineteenth century. So the inner precision of the thinking attempted with the means which underlie the chiselling out of geometrical truths through the thinking—this thinking attempted to crystallize out of itself a geometry, or geometries, which apply to something other than our ordinary sensory space. Because for the latter it is true that the three angles of a triangle together form 180 degrees and that one can only draw a single parallel line through a point next to a straight line. And geometries arose in the nineteenth century which do not only aim to apply to our sensory space. No. Riemannian[60] geometry and Lobachevskian[61] geometry are two real geometries born out of human thinking in accordance with strict mathematical laws.

In the sense of Lobachevskian theory the three angles of a triangle together are always less than 180 degrees and in the sense of Riemannian geometry always greater than 180 degrees. In the sense of the latter you cannot even draw one parallel line through a point next to a straight line and in the sense of the former you can even draw two. These things are not so easy to take. Because when mathematicians set a certain constant as equal to zero in certain formulas which can be used to express every special relationship given in Lobachevsky's theory, they get Euclidian geometry as a special case of Lobachevskian geometry. You can extract Euclidian geometry from Lobachevskian geometry.

I do not want to discuss here that the results of clairvoyant research tell us that the determinations of neither the one nor the other geometry are correct. They are only evidence that these thought operations can take us beyond the sphere which in the first instance encloses our space. But this has to be said: if we are aware of the import of these geometries, then we can obtain an idea that circumstances exist which are quite different from those in the sensory world. Because the latter is ultimately expressed in the formulas of geometry. If now different formulas from those of Euclidean geometry apply to a world, then that world is a different one from ours. And we can say: with Riemannian and Lobachevskian geometry we can see the longing of geometricians to get beyond the sensory world, to grasp something in their thinking which does not lie in the sphere of the sensory world. That is why these non-Euclidean geometries are of symptomatic importance for our century.

And it is of no less importance that the Frenchman Poincaré[62] worked on these theories in a very clever epistemological way. But unless we are willing to take the step into the field of spiritual science, we will, if we stay with the pure utilization of these extra-Euclidean determinations, only get to the point which Poincaré reached: that all our geometrical determinations show nothing other than the formulas which our cognitive capacity possesses to encompass the facts in the easiest possible way. Poincaré works that out very clearly. And Germans too have the possibility to learn of the importance of what actually underlies the whole subject through the meritorious translation of his book by the Munich mathematician Lindemann.[63]

So we have to say, even if we can only give a brief indication, that in one field such precision of thinking has still truly come to expression in our time and that this precision in the thinking is well characterized in such endeavours—however dry and hypothetical they may rightly appear in individual cases: there is a longing for knowledge to take us out of the world which directly surrounds us.

It is generally useful if we are aware of the precision which people can acquire through mathematical training. Because everything which is justifiably produced in the spiritual-scientific field must, in so far as there is a thinking element, be infused with this strictly disciplined thinking. It may vanish behind the facts; but anyone who produces something of a spiritual-scientific nature must be aware that such thinking should stand in the background. Otherwise spiritual science becomes something which can easily be trampled to death by anyone who has no connection with the spiritual. And we cannot say in all instances that there is bad will if we are not understood. Because that is something which increasingly has to move centre stage in the spiritual-scientific field, that we make the same demands of our own thinking as the strictest mathematician makes of his. Since we have clairvoyant research at our disposal, we will be protected from constructing mathematical edifices against the wind, as it were. I say that because there are arguments against the edifices of Riemannian and Lobachevskian geometry. I merely wished to characterize the cognitive longing.

But that it would be useful to be familiar with mathematical structures is something which I tried to show in my *Philosophy of Freedom*. It contains a chapter[64] I would like to call 'The pleasure value of life'.

Up to the time that I wrote this chapter about the pleasure value of life there was a lot of talk in philosophical circles about the pleasure balance of life, and the factual world was used in an apparently mathematical formula which was meant to give the pleasure balance so that all pleasure in life was summated in a and all absence of pleasure in the same life in b. The difference between the two, the surplus of pleasure over the absence of pleasure, was called the pleasure balance. In bringing pleasure and absence of pleasure into a formula like this, a method of differentiation was chosen which we can call the mathematical formula of subtraction. The essential thing in my chapter is that I showed how it is impossible to combine pleasure and absence of pleasure in such a way that they are brought into a relationship of minuend and subtrahend. Whatever is produced in that way will never correspond with real experience. I showed that we only obtain the pleasure value if we do it like this: if we divide a by b then c gives the quotient of the pleasure value

$$c = \frac{a}{b}.$$

If you conscientiously investigate the facts of life you will find that this is true everywhere. In order to be able to do what is expressed about a fact of life in this formula, we have to have at least some overview of what can follow from mathematical structures.

Take the question for instance: how can the pleasure value in this formula become zero? How, in other words, can life become completely tedious? Through no other fact than if the denominator of the fraction—the b—is infinity. Because in forming a quotient you can only obtain a zero if the denominator contains infinity and if the numerator is 1. That is to say this premise fits with the facts of life in quite a different way. The latter will show you—even if people give themselves over to illusions—that there is always a certain pleasure in life. It exists where there is any life at all.

So we can see how it can be useful to use arithmetical formulas in the right way. If you use the wrong differentiating formula, then you can easily obtain a surplus of lack of pleasure and can say: weariness of life is justified as a magnitude. You can also see how useful it is to be able to make strict mathematical logic into your ideal, as it were.

If we disregard mathematics and look at the individual fields of philosophy, then we have to say: we find the impossibility everywhere— look in the field of logic, even if it has been refertilized to a certain extent from the mathematical side through the theory of probability—that a self-contained thinking can draw its own consequences. And here I want to draw your attention to the most important fact in development— using an example in the development of our intellectual life throughout the nineteenth century—to a spiritual-scientific fact which occurred with a certain buoyancy in the spiritual life around the middle of the nineteenth century.

At the time Julius Robert Mayer,[65] and then independently from him Helmholtz, found what has since then been called the theory of the mechanical equivalent of heat, of the so-called conservation of *vis viva*. Now soon after this had happened, Helmholtz constructed another theory on the theory of the conservation of *vis viva* which was then widely accepted and which many today still consider to be unassailable: namely that in the interplay of *vis viva* in the cosmos there is a constant conversion from other, let us say from the actions of the vital leading forces in the world, be they the forces of magnetism or electricity, be they other purely mechanical forces—the conversion of such forces into heat. Now it is never possible in the sense of Carnot's law[66] as it is called fully to complete the conversion process from energy into heat while maintaining the same quantum of energy. We have to say that it is never possible to convert all heat back into *vis viva*. Incidentally, if I wanted to describe the so-called second law of thermodynamics I would have to give several lectures about it. But today I only want to give a characterization. In this context it is not important that we set out here every detail of what you can learn about it.

It is therefore the case in the sense of the second law of the mechanical theory of heat, and in the sense of what Hermann Helmholtz made of that in the fifties of the previous century,[67] that in all processes of our existence a quantum of heat must ultimately exist in the conversion of heat into energy which can no longer be converted back into another force. As a consequence all our physical and mechanical processes ultimately have to take the course that their energy is converted into heat. And as there will always be a residue of heat, all these processes finally have to lead to all other energy being transformed into heat, to all living forces ultimately being converted into heat. That would give us what we can describe as the heat death of our earth. No further process could follow, of course, if everything were transformed into heat.

Thus the thinking about physical matter in the middle of the nineteenth century ends up with this law, ends up with the statement which, if we consult what could be thought about physical matter at the time, is actually quite correct: it ends in a confirmation of the heat death of our earth. And the only consolation which Helmholtz could find was:[68] it is still a long way off and no one needs to be afraid that they will be affected by the heat death. And all we can discover shows us that this process is so minute that we can hope life will continue as vigorously as before for millennia without the earth suffering heat death. But for anyone who proceeds more thoroughly in the acquisition of knowledge this remains simply a philistine consolation.

I only want to characterize with that something which I could have characterized with many other examples: how the progress of scientific thinking to that point—the lecture which Helmholtz gave about this matter was given in about 1852—meant that the configuration of the thinking had to come to certain results.

This lecture was criticized at the time (1856) by a Hegelian, Karl Rosenkranz.[69] He now brought out all the heavy weaponry which was available in the arsenal of Hegelian philosophy. And anyone who knows Karl Rosenkranz, the earnest, we can say the sincerely earnest Hegelian, knows that Karl Rosenkranz should not be taken as lightly as people often want to take him. He brought out everything he could bring out from the Hegelian school. So here we have the other stream, namely the one following this line of thinking. This went in the direction I have tried to show. The result of physical thinking can be shown in Helmholtz, the result of philosophical thinking in Rosenkranz. Here we see that important objections are raised about the mechanical theory of heat. Rosenkranz chides Helmholtz for really only thinking in analogies. His laws had to be abstracted from the processes which took place in the clock, the Girandoni air rifle and other things. It is true of steam engines that something of the living forces we call forth is lost to the environment which cannot be brought back. As long as we proceed

from such processes, which have what I might describe as finite surroundings, for as long we cannot avoid in what we have gained there the
kind of results which Helmholtz obtained in his treatise on the
mechanical theory of heat. In this context Karl Rosenkranz rightly
points out[70] how it does not follow at all, as soon as we move beyond
the immediate situation on earth, that there is no possibility, that the
heat radiating into space must be lost in the same way as happens with
the steam engine. The situation could be completely different.

I cannot deal today with what spiritual science has to say[71] when it
comes to speaking about the theory of heat. That is where the secure
ground lies which I was able to characterize for you in the lectures which
I have just held about the biblical creation story.[72] The Hegelian
remained unproductive because he could not find the transition to this
ground. Thus heat remained nothing for him other than an inner
trembler. Yet with the concepts which are simply given if with regard to
strictly disciplined thinking about finite mechanics, which only applies
to the immediate surroundings with all its formulas, including the
formula

$$\frac{m\,v^2}{2}$$

—all these formulas apply to our immediate circumstances—with these
concepts he turns to absolute mechanics. In the ascent of his scientific
system, Hegel went from so-called finite mechanics to absolute
mechanics which he applied to the movement of the heavenly bodies.
Here the formulas are transformed so that the formulas we obtain from
the steam engine as they apply ordinarily to heat in the sense of
Helmholtz simply cannot be applied to the processes which encompass
larger entities in space. But to appreciate the possibility that one can
ascend from finite mechanics to absolute mechanics requires an inwardly
self-directing logic which was simply missing in the philosophy of the
nineteenth century, including Karl Rosenkranz. Because there is a
strong suggestion throughout all of his objections, to which he is also
subject, which takes its starting point from the dominant scientific ideas
of the nineteenth century. They got the better of many thinkers. It truly
requires self-directing thinking if one wants to break through these
scientific views.

I could easily show that even as far as the law of the conservation of matter, which plays such a big role, the correct thing can only become known if we are aware of the inner structure of the thinking. I could show that this law as it exists in physics today is nothing other than an outward projection into space of independent laws of thinking in which, furthermore, the thinking has to work with blunt weapons. We can see here what we know today in the field of spiritual science: that what is within ourselves appears objectively to us in higher regions—I do not even want to refer to the conservation of energy—that what I have now said about the conservation of matter applies in a wider sense. So we can see how through the suggestion of scientific findings, with regard to which we should always remain on purely factual ground, the thinking element of the human being has turned out to be blunt in this field because philosophy was not able to penetrate the skin which is formed not by scientific facts but by the interpretation of the facts found through research.

Spiritual science stands fully on the ground of scientific facts. I would consider it to be one of the greatest deficits of spiritual science if it did not go hand in hand with a real scientific investigation of the facts. But the interpretation of the facts which have been researched is another matter. When researchers tell us about the facts they discover in their laboratories, then we should gratefully accept their findings; then we accept the statements of nature itself, and to deny them would be nonsense. If we do not accept them then we show that we do not have any sense of truth. But if we were also to take the so-called monistic considerations and allow them to be impressed on us as if they were facts, then we would take the opinions of people as fact. This happens in that the opinions of people have crept insidiously I might say—but no one is accused of being a fanatic—into popular literature. For a few pence we can purchase not just scientific facts but also the opinions which are presented in such a way as if they were facts, which are highlighted as it were to say that if people do not believe them they do not believe the scientific results. But we can adhere to the latter and nevertheless say that their explanation is nothing other than inter-pretation undertaken by blunt weapons of thinking.

Just as this thinking is blunt with regard to the simplest physical and chemical things, so it of course shows itself to be all the more blunt when higher areas are considered, such as physiology. The times have long past in which a gifted anatomist such as old Hyrtl[73] could bring the anatomical structure of the human being to life for his pupils in the first years of their medical studies. We are dealing today with a way of doing things which is not at all aware of one thing in particular. In order to characterize this matter, I would like to dress it up in a different way.

It would be my most urgent wish in the spirit of what I myself consider to be a spiritual-scientific movement that those who have a professional physiological and medical training would familiarize themselves with the facts of spiritual science so that they could work through the results of physiology with regard to its factual nature. I myself will be able at most to provide an outline next spring of such a spiritual-scientific physiology.[74] A lot of work is required in this respect. The most wonderful material is available in our physiological literature which we simply have to be familiar with, but we also have to familiarize ourselves with the border areas and in turn how physiology is influenced by a true psychology which today very much lies buried under rubble.

Here it would be a longing of spiritual science for those with physiological training among us to undertake a strictly precise survey of certain physiological and anatomical results of recent times. It is true, however, that anyone who knows the factual material is aware that in certain areas which we would need nothing has yet been done. But anyone who familiarizes themselves with what has already been achieved in this field could easily do that, could familiarize themselves with it in such a way that they do it productively. Then, if they are infused at the same time with knowledge of the spirit, they will not get into a situation to create a foundation for physiology in which each organ is considered of equal value in the dissection of the organism.

What is the key thing which prevents physiology from getting anywhere today? We have the heart, lung, liver and so on; they are all studied as if they were laid out next to one another as organs of equal value. That is not the case. All these individual organs have various antecedents in terms of their value. And when we hold a piece of liver in our hand we do not hold the same matter as when we hold a piece from the heart muscle and so on. Here it is a matter of adding a certain factor to the purely outer sensory situation which I cannot describe in any other way than as a certain objective evaluation of the organ concerned. This will become clear to physiologists if they undertake a precise comparison of an organ in the fully developed human organism with a real embryology. Then they will realize that embryology works in such a one-sided way today because in a certain sense it only pursues an ascending process and not the descending one which runs in parallel. We do not proceed in the correct way until we bring out something at each stage of embryological development which contains a factor of decadence and another factor of productivity as does a mathematical function. And when we get into a position in which we can apply what we have determined in terms of value to the full form of the organ in the organism, when we do not simply place the heart and the liver next to one another as organs of equal value—they are of different qualitative value—then we will have arrived at the moment when the greatest light will be thrown specifically on the magnificent results of our world of physiological facts.

The things I have characterized with regard to physiology in this way could equally apply to biology, history and cultural history. This is an area of work which lies ahead of us and which has to be built on. Here you can see in a vivid way the situation of philosophy and science in contrast to what we have in terms of positive results through what I might call favourable circumstances, through our human karma. We have the most excellent results all around us through factual research. Anyone who familiarizes themselves with these facts will see a wonderful development. What is missing is the sharp penetration, the energy in philosophical thinking which when it is applied—courageously applied—to the facts can present these facts in their proper light. That was contained in epistemological terms in my basic epistemological work *Truth and Knowledge*. There you will find reference made to the kind of epistemology which counts on our epistemology not to remain without objective meaning but to appear in such a way that the epistemological results fertilize our subject of cognition so that the latter can be immersed in what is given us through the situation of science in general. If from the beginnings which should develop out of our spiritual-scientific movement in this field, in all fields of science, we work in the proper way with seriousness and dignity, if we do not remain at the level of a certain theosophical amateurism but strictly immerse ourselves in what is available scientifically, then we will come to have a metaphysics—instead of a metaphysics without transcendental conviction as is truly the case today—which with the weapons which are forged for it by a productive epistemology penetrates through the outer field of the senses into the supersensory.

Then it will have conviction because it will rest on metaphysics, because it will be able to fertilize the human subject of cognition. Logic will obtain its content because the laws of thinking will turn out to be the laws of the world. Ethics will also be able to possess what we can call commitment because productive cognition will flow into our impulses. We will have ethics with commitment. Then we will also have a psychology not without the soul but a psychology with the soul because the human longing for knowledge is directed towards the question of the soul and its destiny in the world.

This was intended as a slight attempt to show you where we actually stand when we allow our gaze to wander from what we can spiritually feel in us to what has been investigated around us, to what exists scientifically around us. If I were to characterize for you every single thing that exists scientifically, I would have to give many lectures. But more will happen over time. I only wanted to show the tendency which can lie in our spiritual science when the possibilities it contains are sought not just for egoistical reasons—to satisfy our immediate personal goals—but when they are sought in order to contribute to the work on the spirit, on the cultural process of humanity.

LECTURE 7

Most of the people present will know that, apart from repeating the performance of the drama *The Children of Lucifer*[75] from the previous year, we endeavoured in Munich to perform a Rosicrucian mystery which tried to set out in a variety of ways the things connected with our movement. This Rosicrucian mystery is on the one hand meant to be a kind of sample of how all the things which drive anthroposophical life can flow into art. But on the other hand we should not forget either that this Rosicrucian mystery contains many of our spiritual-scientific teachings in such a way as might only be discovered in the course of several years. And specifically it should not be misunderstood that if people made a reasonable effort to read the things which it contains (not between the lines, they are there in the words, even if in a spiritual way), if people made the effort to understand the Rosicrucian mystery in such a way that these things were sought in the coming years, then it would not be necessary for me to give any lectures for many years ahead. Many things would be found in it which I otherwise set out in lectures on any given subject. But it is more practical for us to seek these things together than if we do it individually. It is good in a certain sense that what lives in spiritual science is also available in such a form.

So following on from the Rosicrucian mystery, I want to speak today about certain particular features of human self-knowledge. But for that it is necessary that we remind ourselves—in a characterizing way—how the individuality works in the body of Johannes Thomasius in the

Rosicrucian mystery. Hence I would like this lecture, which will deal with self-knowledge, to start with a recitation[76] of those sections from the Rosicrucian mystery which refer to the self-knowledge of Johannes.

Scene 2

Landscape: rocks and springs. The entire scene is to be thought of as taking place in the soul of Johannes Thomasius. What follows is the content of his meditation; later Maria.

> (There sounds from the springs and rocks: *Know thou thyself, O man!*)

Johannes: 'Tis thus I hear them, now these many years,
These words of weighty import all around.
I hear them in the wind and in the wave:
Out from earth's depths do they resound to me:
And as a tiny acorn's mystery,
Confines the structure of a mighty oak,
So in the kernel of these words there lies,
All elemental nature; all I grasp
Of soul, of spirit, time, eternity.
It seems mine own peculiarities
And all the world besides live in these words:
'Know thou thyself, O man. Know thou thyself.'

> (From the springs and rocks resounds: *Know thou thyself, O man!*)

And now—I feel
Mine inmost being terrified to life:
Without the gloom of night doth weave me round,
And deep within my soul thick darkness yawns:
And sounding from this universal gloom
And up from out the darkness of my soul
These words ring forth: 'Know thou thyself, O man.'

> (From the springs and rocks resounds: *Know thou thyself, O man!*)

It robs me of my very self: I change
Each hour of day, and am transformed by night.
The earth I follow on its cosmic course:
I seem to rumble in the thunder's peal,
And flash adown the lightning's fierce-forked tongue—
I Am.— Alas, already do I feel
Mine own existence snatched away from me.
I see what was my former carnal shape,
As some strange being, quite outside myself,
And infinitely far away from me.
But now another body hovers near;
And through its mouth I am compelled to speak:—
'Ah, bitter sorrow hath he brought to me;
So utterly I trusted him of old.
He left me lonely with my sorrow's pain,
He robbed me of the very warmth of life,
And thrust me deep beneath the chill, cold ground.'
Poor soul, 'tis she I left, and leaving her
It was in truth mine own self that I left;
And I must suffer all her pain and woe.
For knowledge hath endowed me with the power
Myself into another's self to fuse.
Ah me! Ye quench again by your own power
The light of inner knowledge ye have brought,
Ye cruel words, 'Know thou thyself, O man.'

(From the springs and rocks resounds: *Know thou thyself, O man!*)

Ye lead me back again within the sphere
Of mine own being's former fantasies.
Yet in what shape know I myself again!
My human form is lost and gone from me;
Like some fierce dragon do I see myself;
Begotten out of primal lust and greed.
And clearly do I see how up till now
Some dim deluding veil of phantom forms

Hath hid from me mine own monstrosity.
Mine own self's fierceness must devour my Self.
And through my veins run like consuming fire
Those words, that once with elemental force
Revealed the core of suns and earths to me.
They throb within my pulse, beat in mine heart;
And even in mine inmost thoughts I feel
Strange worlds e'en now blaze forth like passions fierce.
They are the fruitage of these very words:
'Know thou thyself, O man. Know thou thyself.'

(From the springs and rocks resounds: *Know thou thyself, O man!*)

There,—from that dark abyss, what creature glares?
I feel the chains that hold me chained to thee.
So fast was not Prometheus rivetted
Upon the naked rocks of Caucasus,
I am rivetted and forged to thee
Who art thou, fearful, execrable shape?

(From the springs and rocks resounds: *Know thou thyself, O man!*)

Oh yea, I know thee; for thou art myself:
Knowledge doth chain to thee, pernicious beast,

(Enter Maria unnoticed by Johannes.)

Chain mine own self—pernicious beast—to thee.
I willed to flee from thee; but I was blind,
Blinded by glamour of the worlds, whereto
My folly fled to free me from myself;
And now once more within my sightless soul
Blind through these words: 'Know thou thyself, O man.'

(From the springs and rocks resounds: *Know thou thyself, O man!*)

Johannes: (As though coming to himself, sees Maria. The meditation
passes to the plane of inner reality.)

Thou here, my friend?

Maria: I sought thee, friend, although I know full well
How comforting to thee is solitude,
When many varying thoughts of many men
Have flooded o'er thy soul. I also know
I cannot by my presence help my friend
In this dark hour of strife—yet yearnings vague
Drive me in this same moment unto thee;
When Benedictus' words, instead of light,
Such grievous sorrow drew from thy soul's depths.

Johannes: How comforting to me is solitude!

* * *

Yea, I have sought to find myself therein,
So often when to labyrinths of thought
The joys and griefs of men had driven me.
But now, O friend, that, too, is past and gone.
What Benedictus' words at first aroused
Within my soul, and all that I lived through
When listening to the speeches of those men,
Seems but indeed a little thing, when I
Compare therewith the storm that solitude
With sullen brooding hath brought forth in me.
Ah me! when I recall this solitude!
It hounded me into the voids of space,
And tore me from my very self in twain,
Within that soul to whom I brought such grief
I rose, as though I were that other self.
And there I had to suffer all the pain
Of which I was myself the primal cause.
Ah cruel, sombre, fearful solitude
Thou giv'st me back unto myself indeed,
Yet but to terrify me with the sight

Of mine own nature's fathomless abyss.
Man's final refuge hath been lost to me:
I have been robbed of solitude.

Maria: I must repeat what I have said before.
Alone can Benedictus succour thee;
Only from him may we obtain support
And that firm basis which we both do lack.
For know thou this I also can no more
Endure the riddle of my life, unless
His gentle guidance solveth it for me.
Full often have I kept before mine eyes
This truth sublime, that o'er all life doth float
Appearance and deception if we grasp
Life's surface only in our moods of thought.
And o'er and o'er again it spake to me:
Thou must take knowledge how illusion's veil
Weaves all around thee; and however oft
It may appear to thee as truth, beware;
For evil fruitage may in truth arise
If thou shouldst try within another's soul
To wake the light that lives within thyself.
Yet in the best part of my soul I know
That even this oppressive weight of care
Which hath o'erwhelmed thy soul, dear friend of mine,
As thou didst tread with me the path of life,
Is part and parcel of the thorny way,
That leads unto the light of Truth itself.
Thou must live through each horror and alarm
That can spring forth from vain imagining
Before the Truth in essence stands revealed.
Thus speaks thy star; and by that same star's speech
It doth appear to me that we shall walk
One day united, on the spirit-paths.
And yet whene'er I seek to tread these paths
Black night doth spread a curtain round my sight.

And many things I am compelled to see,
Springing as fruitage from my character,
Intensify the darkness of that night.
We two must seek clear vision in that light,
Which, though it vanish for a while from sight,
Can never be extinguished in the soul.

Johannes: But then, Maria, dost thou realize
Through what my soul hath fought its way but now?
A grievous destiny is thine, dear friend,
Full well I know. And yet how far remote
From thy pure nature is the avenging force,
That hath so wholly shattered mine own soul.
Thou canst ascend the clearest heights of truth,
And scan with steadfast gaze life's tangled path;
And whether in the darkness or the light
Thou wilt retain thine own identity.
But me each moment may deprive of Self.
Deep down I had to dive within the hearts
Of those who late revealed themselves in speech.
I followed one to cloistered solitude—
And in another's soul I listened to
Felicia's fairy lore. I was each one;
Only unto myself I seemed as dead;
For I must fain believe that primal life
Did spring from very Nothingness itself,
If it were right to entertain the hope,
That out of that dread nothingness in me
A human being ever could arise.
For I am driven from fear into the dark
And from the darkness back again to fear
By wisdom stored within these living words:
'Know thou thyself, O man. Know thou thyself.'

(From the springs and rocks the words resound: *Know thou thyself, O man!*)

(Curtain)

Scene 9

Same region as in Scene 2. Johannes, later Maria.

> (From rocks and springs resounds: *O man, feel thou thyself!*)

Johannes: O man, feel thou thyself! For three long years
I have sought strength of soul, with courage winged,
Which doth give truth unto these words, whereby
A man may free himself to conquer first;
Then conquering himself may freedom find
Through these same words: 'O man, feel thou thyself.'

> (From rocks and springs resounds: *O man, feel thou thyself!*)

I note their presence in mine inmost soul,
Their whispered breathing thrills my spirit-ear;
And hid within themselves they bear the hope,
That they will grow and lead man's spirit up,
Out of his narrow self to world-wide space,
E'en as a giant oak mysteriously
Builds his proud body from an acorn small.
Spirit can cause to live in its own self
All weaving forms of water and of air,
And all that doth make hard the solid earth.
Man too can grasp whate'er hath ta'en firm hold
Of being, in the elements, in souls,
In time, in spirits and eternity.
The whole world's essence lies in one soul's core,
When such power in the spirit roots itself,
Which can give truth unto these self
same words: O man, experience and feel thyself—

> (From rocks and springs resounds: *O man, feel thou thyself!*)

I feel them sounding in my very soul,
Rousing themselves to grant me strength and power.
The light doth live in me; the brightness speaks
Around me; soul light germinates in me;

The brightness of all worlds creates in me:
O man, experience and feel thyself;

(From rocks and springs resounds: *O man, feel thou thyself!*)

I find myself secure on every side,
Where'er these words of power do follow me.
They will give light in sense-life's darkened ways:
They will sustain me on the spirit-heights:
Soul-substance will they pour into my heart
Through all the eons of eternity.
I feel the essence of the worlds in me,
And I must find myself in all the worlds.
I gaze upon the nature of my soul,
Which mine own power hath vivified;
I rest within myself; I look on rocks and springs;
They speak the native language of my soul.
I find myself again within that soul,
Into whose life I brought such bitter grief;
And out of her I call unto myself:
'Thou must find me again and ease my pain.'
The spirit-light will give to me the strength
To live this other self in mine own self.
Oh hopeful words, ye stream forth strength to me
From all the worlds: O man, feel thou thyself.

(From rocks and springs resounds: *O man, feel thou thyself!*)

Ye make me feel my feebleness, and yet
Ye place me near the highest aims of gods;
And blissfully I feel creative power
From these high aims in my weak, earthly form.
And out of mine own Self shall stand revealed
Those powers, whereof the germ lies hid in me.
And I will give myself unto the world
By living out mine own essential life;
Yea, all the might of these words will I feel,
Which sound within me softly at the first.

They shall become for me a quickening fire
In my soul-powers and on my spirit-paths.
I feel how now my very thought doth pierce
To deep-concealed foundations of the world;
And how it streams through them with radiant light.
E'en thus doth work the fructifying power
Of these same words: O man, feel thou thyself.

(From rocks and springs resounds: *O man, feel thou thyself!*)

From heights of light a being shines on me,
And I feel wings to lift myself to him:
I too will free myself, like all those souls,
Who conquered self.

(From springs and rocks resounds: *O man, feel thou thyself!*)

That being do I see
Whom I would fain be like in future times.
The spirit in me shall grow free, through thee
Sublime example, I will follow thee.

(Enter Maria.)

The spirit-beings, who did take me up,
Have woken now the vision of my soul.
And as I gaze into the spirit worlds,
I feel in mine own self the quickening power
Of these same words: O man, feel thou thyself.

(From springs and rocks resounds: *O man, feel thou thyself!*)

Thou here, my friend?

Maria: My soul did urge me here.
           I saw thy star shining in fullest strength.

Johannes: This strength can I experience in myself.

Maria: So closely are we one, that thy soul's life
           Allows its light to shine forth in my soul.

Johannes: Maria, then thou also art aware
             Of what has just revealed itself to me.
             Man's first conviction has just come to me,
             And I have gained the certainty of self.
             I feel that power to guide me everywhere
             Lies in these words: O man, feel thou thyself.

(From rocks and springs resounds: *O man, feel thou thyself!*)

(Curtain)

In the two scenes 'Know thou thyself, O man' and 'O man, feel thou thyself' we have before our soul two development stages in the unfolding of our soul.

Now I would ask you not to find it peculiar in any way when I say that actually I have no objection to this Rosicrucian mystery being interpreted in the way that I have on occasion also interpreted other poetic works in our circles. Because in a certain sense we may say that what I have often said in connection with other poetic works which I was permitted to interpret can come before our soul in a living and direct way through this Rosicrucian mystery. I have never refrained from saying that as little as the plant, the flower knows what the person looking at the flower finds in it, the flower nevertheless contains what that person finds in it. When I was having to interpret the work *Faust*,[77] I explained that the poet in writing it down did not necessarily know all the things directly himself, did not experience them directly in the words which were then later found in it. I can assure you that at the time that I wrote the individual scenes I was not aware of what I will now subsequently say in connection with this mystery, of which I do know what it contains. The scenes grew out of themselves like the leaves of a plant. It is simply not possible to produce such a form by first having the idea and then implementing it in its outer form. It was always quite interesting for me when one scene after the other was created like this, and friends who got to know the individual scenes said it was strange that it always turned out differently from what one imagined.

Thus this mystery stands like an image of human evolution in the development of the individual human being. Let me emphasize: as far as the concrete feelings are concerned, it is impossible to wrap oneself in abstractions to represent anthroposophy because every human soul is different and basically, since it experiences its development itself, has to be different. In everything which is given as a general teaching, we can only receive guidelines. As a result we can only provide the complete truth if we build on the individual soul, on a soul which represents its human individuality in all its uniqueness. So if someone were to look at Johannes Thomasius and try to convert what is said about him specifically into theories of human development, they would do something that is completely wrong. If they thought that they would experience precisely the same thing as Johannes Thomasius they would be in error. Because the broad sweep of what Johannes Thomasius has to experience applies to every human being, but in order to experience it in its unique character one has to be Johannes Thomasius. And each person is Johannes Thomasius in his or her own way.

Thus everything is represented in a very individual way. But as a result, in building on the specific figure, everything that is the development of the human being in his or her soul is given in as truthful a way as possible. That is also why such a broad basis has to be created, why Thomasius is first shown on the physical plane, why reference is made to individual soul experiences, to those things which are of importance when in a time which is not too distant he left a being who was devoted to him in faithful love. That happens often enough but this individual event has a different effect on the person who endeavours to undergo a development. It is a profound truth that the person who undergoes a development achieves self-knowledge not through introverted brooding but through submersion in individual beings. Through self-knowledge we have to experience that we come from the cosmos. We can only submerse ourselves when we transform ourselves into another self. The first thing we are transformed into is what was once close to us in life.

It is an example of the experience of our own self in another when Johannes first, as he penetrates deeper into his self, submerses himself with this self-knowledge in another being, in the being whom he caused bitter pain. So we see how Thomasius submerses himself in such self-knowledge. Theoretically we say: if you want to understand the flower you have to submerse yourself in the flower. But self-knowledge can best be achieved when we submerse ourselves in the events in which we ourselves were involved in a different way. We undergo external events for as long as we are in our own self. The thoughts we think from other beings becomes an abstraction with regard to true self-knowledge.

For Thomasius, what other people have experienced initially becomes his own experience. There was one person, Capesius, who described his experiences. These experiences are such that we can recognize how they relate to life. But Thomasius takes something else from that. He listens. But his listening—this is characterized subsequently in Scene 8—is of a different sort. It is as if for him the human being were not present at all with the ordinary self. Another, deeper force reveals itself as if it were he himself who crawls into Capesius' soul and experiences what happens there. That is why it becomes of such infinite importance that he is alienated from himself there. That we tear ourselves away from ourselves and are realized in the other cannot be separated from self-knowledge. That is why it is so important with regard to Thomasius that he is forced to say after having listened to the speeches [in the first scene]:

> A mirrored picture 'twas of fullest life
> That showed me to myself in clearest lines:
> This spirit-revelation makes me feel
> That most of us protect and train one trait
> And one alone in all our character,
> Which thus persuades itself it is the whole.
> I sought to unify these many traits
> In mine own self and boldly trod the path
> Which here is shown, to lead unto that goal;
> And it hath made of me a nothingness.

Why has it made a nothingness out of him? Because through self-knowledge he has submersed himself in other beings. Introspective brooding makes people proud, arrogant. Because we submerse ourselves in a foreign self, true self-knowledge initially leads to suffering. Johannes follows [in the first scene] the other people in such a way that he listens to Capesius and experiences the words of Felicia in this other soul. He follows Strader into the solitude of his monastery. Here we initially have abstraction. He has not yet reached the point to which he is now led [in the second scene] through pain. Self-knowledge deepens through meditation in the inner self. And what has been shown in the first scene shows the deepened self-knowledge [in the second scene] which presents the concrete arising from abstraction. The usual words we hear ringing out over centuries as the mark of the Delphic oracle obtain a new life for human beings, but initially a life of alienation from ourselves.

As someone who has obtained knowledge of himself, Johannes is submersed in every outer being. He lives in the air and water, in rocks and springs, but not in himself. All the words which we can only make resound from outside are actually words of meditation. And as soon as the curtain rises we have to imagine the words which resound much more loudly in any self-knowledge than can be presented on the stage. Then the person obtaining knowledge of himself is submersed in the various other beings; that is how he learns about the things into which he is submersed. And then the same experience which he has already had previously appears before his eyes in a terrible way.

That is indeed a deep truth that such self-knowledge, when it takes the course as has just been characterized, leads us to look at ourselves in quite a different way from the way we did previously. It leads us to experience our I as a foreign being, as it were.

The outer envelope is really the closest thing for human beings. People in our time will feel much more closely connected with it when they cut their finger than if they are hurt by a false judgement about a fellow human being. It is a great deal more painful for people today when they cut themselves in the finger than when they hear a false judgement! And yet the cut is only to their physical envelope. But that we feel this, that we experience our body as a tool, is only the result of self-knowledge.

People can get close to experiencing their hand as a tool when they take hold of an object. But we learn to experience the same with this or the other part of the brain. Such an inner experience of the brain as an instrument occurs at a certain level of self-knowledge. At that stage the individual things are localized. When we knock in a nail we know that we do so with a tool. But we also know that we use this or the other part of the brain for that. Because these things become objectively alien to us, we learn to know our brain as something separated from us. Self-knowledge supports such objectivity with regard to our envelope and then our envelope ultimately becomes as alien to us as an outer tool. We truly begin to live in the external world when we start to feel our bodily nature as something objective.

Because human beings only experience their physical envelope, they have no clear understanding that there is a limit between the air outside and the air in their lungs. They nevertheless say that the air inside is the same as outside. If we take the substance of the air, then they are inside and outside. That is the same with everything, with the blood, with everything that is physical. But physically they cannot be inside or outside, that is simply Maya. Precisely because the physical interior becomes an exterior they continue truthfully into the rest of the world and the cosmos.

The first scene recited today was meant to present the pain of the feeling of alienation from oneself. The pain of becoming alienated from ourselves because we find ourselves in everything that is external. The physical envelope of Johannes Thomasius is like a being that is external to him. But in return for experiencing his own body as being external, he sees coming towards him the other body, the body of the being he has left. That approaches him and he has learnt to speak with that being's own words. He says to it—his self has expanded to it:

> Ah, bitter sorrow hath he brought to me;
> So utterly I trusted him of old.
> He left me lonely with my sorrow's pain,
> He robbed me of the very warmth of life,
> And thrust me deep beneath the chill, cold ground.

But the reproach only enters the soul in a living way when the foreign pain with which we have linked our own self has to be expressed because our own self has submersed itself in another self. That is a deepening. Johannes is truly in that suffering because he has caused it. He feels as if he has flowed out into it and reawoken. What does he actually experience there?

If we take everything together, we find that the ordinary, normal human being only experiences something similar in the state which we call Kamaloka. Human beings to be initiated have to experience in this world already what the normal person experiences in the spiritual world. They have to experience within the physical body what are Kamaloka experiences which are otherwise experienced outside the physical body. That is why all characteristics which we can incorporate as Kamaloka characteristics exist as experiences of initiation. Just as Johannes is submersed in the soul to which he caused pain, so ordinary human beings must submerse themselves in the souls to whom they have brought pain. They have to feel pain in the same way that they would if someone slapped them back. The only difference in these things is that the initiate experiences them in the physical body, the other person after death. The person who experiences them here lives in quite a different way from Kamaloka. But what people experience in Kamaloka can be experienced in such a way that they have not yet truly obtained freedom. And that is a difficult task, to become truly free. Human beings feel as if they are shackled to physical circumstances.

It is one of the most important developmental experiences in our time—it was not yet like this in the Graeco-Roman period, it has only become of particular importance now—that human beings can experience how incredibly difficult it is to get away from oneself. That is why an important initiation experience is expressed in the words in which Johannes feels himself shackled to his own lower body where his own being appears to him as a being to which he is shackled:

> I feel the chains that hold me chained to thee.
> So fast was not Prometheus rivetted
> Upon the naked rocks of Caucasus,
> I am rivetted and forged to thee

That is something which is connected with self-knowledge, the mystery of self-knowledge. We only have to understand it in the right way.

The question as to this mystery could also be described in this way: has the fact that we have become human beings on earth, that we have submersed ourselves in our earthly envelope, made us better human beings or would we have become better human beings if we could be in our interior alone, if we could simply throw off our envelope? Superficial people when faced with spiritual life could easily ask: why submerse ourselves in the earthly body at all? The simplest thing would be to stay up there and then we would not have this whole miserable situation of having to submerse ourselves.

Why have the wise powers of destiny submersed us? In terms of our feeling little can be explained if we say that divine-spiritual forces have worked on this earthly body for millennia and millennia. Precisely because it is like that, we should make more of ourselves than we have the forces to do. Our inner forces are not enough. We cannot now already be as much as the gods have made if we only want to be what we are in our interior, if we are not corrected through our envelopes. Life presents itself as follows.[78] Here on earth human beings are put in their bodily envelopes; these are prepared by beings through three worlds. Human beings are first meant to develop their interior. Between birth and death they are something bad; in Devachan they are better beings again, taken in by divine-spiritual beings which infuse them with their own forces. Later, in the Vulcan period, they will then be complete beings. Here on earth they are beings who indulge in their pleasures. The heart, for example, is constructed so wisely that it can resist the onslaught which human beings direct towards it with their excesses, with coffee for example, for decades. Then human beings trek through Kamaloka in the way they are today through their own forces. There they should learn to know what they are through their own forces. And that is truly nothing good. Human beings, if they were to describe themselves, could not give themselves the attribute of beauty. On the contrary they would have to describe themselves as Johannes does [in the second scene]:

> Yet in what shape know I myself again!
> My human form is lost and gone from me;
> Like some fierce dragon do I see myself;
> Begotten out of primal lust and greed.
> And clearly do I see how up till now
> Some dim deluding veil of phantom forms
> Hath hid from me mine own monstrosity.

And inward things are expanded like elastic into our bodily envelopes and hide from us. We do indeed get to know ourselves as a kind of fierce dragon when we get to know initiation. And that is why these words are drawn from deepest feeling, these words of self-knowledge not of introspection:

> Oh yea, I know thee; for thou art myself:
> Knowledge doth chain to thee, pernicious beast.

Basically both are the same, once as object, the other time as subject.

> I willed to flee from thee.

But such flight only leads human beings to themselves.

And then we get into the company which appears, which we get into when we truly look into ourselves. Such company which we find within ourselves are our desires and passions, those things which we did not notice earlier on because each time when we looked inside ourselves our eyes were diverted to our surroundings. Because in comparison to the things into which we wanted to look, the world is a wonderful place. There, in illusion, in the Maya of life we stop looking into ourselves. But when the people around us say all kinds of stupid things and when we have had enough then we escape into solitude. And that is very important for certain stages of development. At that point we can and should collect ourselves. That is a good means of self-knowledge. But there are nevertheless experiences in which we get into company, in which we can no longer be in solitude, when those beings in particular appear—within us or outside us, it doesn't matter—who do not leave us alone. Then that experience occurs which we should have. It is simply the case that such solitude brings the worst company:

> Man's final refuge hath been lost to me:
> I have been robbed of solitude.

Those are real experiences. But do not let the intensity, the strength of these experiences in themselves be a challenge. Do not think, when such experiences are presented with great intensity, that we should suffer fear and anxiety. Do not think that this should help to prevent someone from submersing themselves in these waters themselves. We do not experience them immediately as strongly as Johannes does because he was meant to experience it like that for a certain purpose, in a certain sense even prematurely. Regular self-development takes a different course. That is why what happens with Johannes in a tumultuous way must be understood as something individual. Because he is an individuality which has suffered shipwreck, everything can take place in a much more tumultuous way under these laws. He learns to know them in such a way that they profoundly throw him off balance. But one thing was meant to be awoken by describing it for Johannes in this way, namely the feeling that true self-knowledge has nothing to do with any kind of trivial words, that true self-knowledge has no other option than first to lead through pain and suffering.

Things which previously served to refresh human beings acquire another face when they appear in the field of self-knowledge. We can beg for solitude, certainly, when we have also found self-knowledge. But at certain moments of self-knowledge solitude can be the thing which we lose if we seek it in the way we knew previously, in moments when we flow out into the objective world where the solitary person suffers the greatest pain.

We have to learn to experience such outpouring of ourselves into other beings in the correct way if we want to feel what has been put into a drama. A certain aesthetic feeling has been executed, everything in it is spiritually realistic. Anyone who thinks realistically—a realist with true aesthetic feelings—feels a certain pain in an unrealistic depiction. Even things which at a certain level can give great satisfaction can be a source of pain at another level. That is dependent on the path of self-knowledge. A Shakespeare drama, for example, something which is a great achievement in the external world, can be a source of aesthetic satisfaction. But a certain moment can occur in development where we can no longer be satisfied by that because we feel ourselves torn apart inside when we go from one scene to the next because we can no longer see the necessity of one scene following on from the previous one. We can experience it as something artificial that one scene is placed next to another one. Why artificial? Because there is nothing that ties the two scenes together other than the writer Shakespeare and the audience. The sequence of scenes contains an abstract principle of causality, not something intrinsic. That is the characteristic feature of Shakespeare's dramas, that nothing is indicated which interweaves and holds them together karmically.

The Rosicrucian drama has become realistic, spiritually realistic. It makes great demands of Johannes Thomasius. He is on the scene without being actively involved in any important way. It is in his soul that everything takes place and what is described there is the development of the soul, the real experience of what is experienced in the development of the soul.

The soul of Johannes realistically spins the one scene out of the other. Here we can see that realistic and spiritual are not contradictory. Materialistic and spiritual things do not need to but can contradict one another. And realistic and spiritual things do not need to contradict one another either and something spiritually realistic can be wholly admired by a materialist. Shakespeare's dramas can indeed be thought of as being realistic with regard to their aesthetic principle. But you can also understand that an art which goes hand-in-hand with spiritual science ultimately means that for someone who experiences their self in the cosmos the whole cosmos becomes the being of their I. Then we also cannot bear it when something confronts them in the cosmos which bears no relationship to the being of the I. Art will learn something in this respect which allows it to get to the I principle because Christ first of all brought us the I. This I will come to expression in a great variety of fields.

But this concrete human element in the soul and in turn being distributed externally also reveals itself in another way. If at the time someone had asked which person is Atma, which is Buddhi, which Manas, it would be horrible art, terrible art if the depiction had to be interpreted in this way: this character is the personification of Manas. There are theosophical bad habits which attempt to interpret everything in this sense. We would have to say about an artwork which can be interpreted in this way: poor work of art! Certainly, with regard to Shakespeare's dramas this would be fundamentally wrong and ridiculous.

These things are the childhood diseases of theosophical development. It will overcome them eventually. But it is nevertheless necessary to draw attention to these things occasionally. It is not inconceivable that someone might attempt to discover the nine components of human nature in Beethoven's Ninth Symphony.

And yet it is correct in a certain way that what is unified human nature is in turn distributed among various people. One person has a particular hue in their soul, another person a different one. In this way we can see people before us who represent different sides of human nature as a whole. But that has to be thought of realistically; it has to come out of the nature of the person. The way that people confront us in the world, that is how they represent the different sides of human nature. And we become a totality in developing from incarnation to incarnation. If the underlying relevant fact is to be represented, the whole life has to be spread out.

Thus what in a certain sense is meant to represent Maria in the Rosicrucian mystery is spread out among the other figures which sur-round her as her companions who together with her represent a single egohood. We can particularly see characteristics of the sentient soul in Philia, characteristics of the intellectual or mind soul in Astrid, char-acteristics of the consciousness soul in Luna. The names were given with this in mind. All names are such that they have been specifically given for the individual beings. Not just in the words, but in the way that the words are set—specifically where the spiritual is to act in Devachan, in the seventh scene—the thing which is meant to characterize the three figures of Philia, Astrid and Luna has been precisely gradated. The way in which the seventh scene starts is a better characterization of the sentient soul, intellectual soul and consciousness soul than could otherwise be given in words. Here we can show people what the sentient soul, the intellectual soul and the consciousness soul are. In art we can show the levels in the way that these three figures are depicted. In the human being they flow into one another. If they are separated, then they present themselves in the way that Philia places herself in the cosmos, Astrid places herself in the elements, Luna flows into the activity of the self and self-knowledge. And because they present themselves in this way, the Devachan scene contains everything which is alchemy in the true sense. It contains all of alchemy. We just gradually have to discover it.

But it is not only given in the abstract content but in the interweaving and nature of the words. That is why you should not just listen to what is said, and specifically not just to what the individual is saying, but to how the soul forces speak in relation to one another. The sentient soul inserts itself into the astral body; we are dealing with flowing astrality. The intellectual soul inserts itself into the etheric body; we are dealing with flowing etheric beings. We see how with inner firmness the consciousness soul pours itself into the physical body. Thus what works in a soul-like way as light in the soul is given in the words of Philia. What works in an etherically objective way so that we are faced with true things, that is given in Astrid. What gives inner firmness so that it is combined with the physical body, that is given in Luna. That is what we have to fulfil. Let us listen to the soul forces in Scene 7:

Philia: (Sentient soul)	I will myself imbue With clearest rays of light From cosmic spaces wide. I will breathe deep within Sound-substance that gives life From distant ether-bounds, Dear sister, that thou may'st Succeed in this thy work.
Astrid: (Intellectual soul)	Through all the streaming light I will weave darkness in To cloud its radiant beam. I will make dense and thick The living life of sound; That glowing it may sound And sounding it may glow, Dear sister, that thou may'st Direct the soul-life's rays.
Luna: (Consciousness soul)	Soul substance will I warm, Life's ether harden too. That they may thus condense And may thus feel themselves As living in themselves

> And powerful to create,
> Dear sister, that thou may'st
> Prove wisdom's certainty
> To mankind's seeking soul.

See how in Philia we have:[79] 'Dass dir, geliebte Schwester ...', that in Astrid we have the darker, more solidified: 'Dass du, geliebte Schwester...'; 'Dass dir ...', 'Dass du ...'. And now we have it interwoven in Luna with something that weighs even more heavily: 'Der suchenden Menschenseele.' Here the U is so interwoven with the neighbouring consonants that it becomes even more densely solidified.

These are the things which can indeed be characterized. What matters is the 'how'; that is something we have to understand. If we compare the words which Philia speaks further on:

> Ich will erbitten von Weltengeistern,
> Dass ihres Wesens Licht
> Entzücke Seelensinn,
> Und ihrer Worte Klang
> Beglücke Geistgehör

with the quite different nature of the words that Astrid speaks:

> Ich will die Liebesströme,
> Die Welt erwarmend,
> Zu Herzen leiten
> Dem Geweihten

then the inner weaving and nature of the Devachanic cosmic element occurs precisely where these words are executed.

We have to use these things, and that is why I mention them, to make clear for ourselves that when self-knowledge begins to immerse itself in the external weaving and nature of the world, the key thing is to give up all one-sidedness and to learn to feel how otherwise we can only experience in a philistine way what exists at each point of existence. That is what makes us human beings into such rigid beings, that we are tied to the point in space and believe that we can express truths in words. But words are things which are less well able to express the truth because they are tied to the physical sound. *We* also have to feel the expression, if I can put it like that. That is why it is important that a significant process like Johannes Thomasius' process of self-knowledge can only be experienced properly once he starts courageously to gain and grasp self-knowledge.

That is the next act after self-knowledge has devastated us, that we start to take into ourselves what we have learnt in that we have understood the cosmos to be related to ourselves, having recognized the nature of the beings, that we embolden ourselves to live what we have recognized. Because it is only half the matter that we submerse ourselves like Johannes into a being whom we have caused pain, whom we have thrust down into the cold earth. Because now we feel things differently. We take courage to compensate for the pain and submerse ourselves into this life and speak differently in our own being. That becomes what we initially see in the ninth scene. Whereas in the second scene the being called out to Johannes—

> Ah, bitter sorrow hath he brought to me;
> So utterly I trusted him of old.
> He left me lonely with my sorrow's pain,
> He robbed me of the very warmth of life,
> And thrust me deep beneath the chill, cold ground

the same being called out to him in the ninth scene, after Johannes had experienced himself in the place where all self-knowledge drives us:

> Thou must find me again and ease my pain.

That is the other side: first the devastation, then the compensation of experience. The other being calls to him:

> Thou must find me again.

Such elevation of the experience of the world, such filling oneself with the experience of the world could not be represented in any other way. True self-knowledge as we surface in the cosmos could not be described if not in the words with which Johannes awakens. It naturally has to start in the second scene:

Tis thus I hear them, now these many years,
These words of weighty import all around.

Because after he has submersed himself in the ground of the earth, after
he has united with the ground of the earth, the strength is created in the
soul to let the words arise in this way. That is the key thing in the ninth
scene:

For three long years
I have sought strength of soul, with courage winged,
Which does give truth unto these words, whereby
A man may free himself to conquer first:
Then conquering himself may freedom find.

Those are the words 'O man, feel thou thyself!' in contrast to the words
in the second scene 'Know thou thyself, O man!' In this way we always
encounter the same scene again. Whereas on the one occasion the scene
leads downwards—

It seems my own peculiarities
And all the world besides live in these words:
'Know thou thyself, O man. Know thou thyself.'

it is then reversed. It changes. The scene reflects the process in the soul.
  So you also heard the devastating words:

But then, Maria, dost thou realize
Through what my soul hath fought its way but now?

*   *   *

Man's final refuge has been lost to me:
I have been robbed of solitude.

Then the ninth scene shows how the being first acquires assurance and
then security. That is the congruence. They have to be self-evident
experiences and not constructs. In this way we are meant to feel how in a
soul such as that of Johannes Thomasius self-knowledge is refined into
self-experience. We are also meant to feel how this experience of
Johannes Thomasius is distributed across individual human beings and
thus his own knowledge across all of the human beings in whom a part

of his being comes to expression in the individual incarnations. At the end a whole company stands in the sun temple like a tableau and all of them together are a single human being. The characteristics of a single human being are distributed across all of them; it is basically a single human being. A pedantic person might say: there are too many parts, it should be nine instead of twelve. But that is not how reality works, that it is in harmony with the theories. It is more in harmony with the truth than if we had the individual components of the human being muster in the regular way.

Let us now place ourselves in this sun temple. There are the individual human beings who have been placed in the way that they really belong together karmically, how karma has placed them together in life. But if we now think of Johannes as being here

Johannes Thomasius

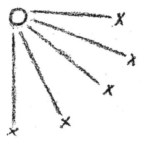

and think of each individual character being mirrored in the soul of Johannes, and each human being as being the soul community of Johannes—what, then, has happened, if we accept it as reality. Here karma has truly brought these human beings together as if in a node. Nothing is unintentional, purposeless, aimless, but what individual human beings have done not only reflects an individual event; each one reflects a soul experience of Johannes Thomasius. Everything takes place twice: in the macrocosm and in the microcosm of Johannes's soul. That is his initiation. In the same way that Maria for example stands in relationship to him, so an important component of his soul stands in relationship to another component of his soul. These are absolute congruences, strictly executed. What is an external action is an internal developmental process when it takes place in Johannes. What endeavours to happen here is what the hierophant expresses in Scene 3:

> Within our circle there is formed a knot
> Of threads that karma spins world-fashioning.

It has been knotted. And this properly tied knot shows where everything leads: on the one hand absolute reality, the way that karma spins, but not purposeless spinning. We have the knot as the initiation process in the soul of Johannes and we have the whole thing in such a way that a human individuality still stands above all these human beings: the hierophant who intervenes, who guides the threads. We only need to think of the hierophant and his relationship with Maria.

But this in particular can show us that this process is something which can illuminate self-knowledge here in Scene 3. Leaving the self in this way is no fun. It is a very real process, an abandonment of the human envelopes by inner strength. Then these human envelopes are left behind and become a battlefield for subordinate powers. Where Maria sends the beam of love down to the hierophant, that cannot be represented in any other way than: down there the body which is taken hold of by the power of the adversary and says the opposite of what takes place above; up there a beam of love radiates downwards while down below a curse arises. Those are the contrasting scenes: in Devachan where Maria describes what she has really done, and in the third scene where below the cursing of the demonic powers against the hierophant takes place as the body is abandoned. There we have two scenes which complement one another. It would really be quite terrible if they first had to be constructed.

Thus I have based today's lecture on one side of this mystery drama and I hope that we can link some specific characteristics with that which underlie initiation.

The circumstance that some things had to be sharply emphasized when real processes of initiation were represented should not make you despondent or fainthearted with regard to striving for the spiritual world. The only purpose of the description of the dangers is to steel human beings against the powers. The dangers are there, the pain and suffering lie ahead of us. It would truly be a bad endeavour if we merely wanted to move up into the higher worlds in a comfortable way. In reaching the spiritual worlds we cannot enjoy the same comfort as we have when we roll along in modern trains or in the way modern material culture treats external life. What I have described here should not deprive us of our courage but our courage should be strengthened precisely through acquainting ourselves in a certain way with the dangers of initiation.

Just as in Johannes Thomasius, whose inclination made him unable to wield his brush, this is transformed into pain, but then pain into knowledge, so everything which causes suffering and pain will be transformed into knowledge. But we have to be serious in our search for this path. We can only do this if we attempt to make clear to ourselves that the spiritual-scientific truths are not that simple. They are such deep truths about life that we can never finish trying to understand them in detail. The example in life, in particular, allows us to grasp the world and we can talk even more precisely about the developmental conditions if we present the development of Johannes as if we were presenting the development of a human being in general. The book *Knowledge of the Higher Worlds. How is it Achieved?* sets out that development as it can take place in every human being; that is simply the possibility how it can be in reality. When we represent Johannes Thomasius, we describe a single human being. But that robs us of the possibility to describe the development in general.

I hope you will take the opportunity as far as possible to say that I have basically still not properly told the truth. We have two extremes and have to find the gradation between both. I can only ever stimulate some thoughts. These then have to continue living in the hearts and souls.

In the thoughts I put forward[80] about the Gospel of Matthew I said: do not try to remember the wording but when you have stepped out into the world try to look into your heart and soul what the words have turned into there. Try to read not just the cycles but also to read seriously in your soul.

But for that something first has to be given from outside, something has to have entered first. Anything else would be self-deception of the soul. Understand how to read that in the soul, and you will see that what has sounded from outside will sound inwardly in many different ways. That would then be the correct anthroposophical endeavour if every time what had been spoken was understood in as many different ways as there were listeners.

Never can the person who wishes to speak about spiritual science attempt to be understood in just a single way. He wishes to be understood in so many ways as there are souls present. Anthroposophy can cope with that. But one thing is necessary. I do not say this to say something negligible. One thing is necessary, namely that every single way of understanding is correct and true. It can be individual but it must be true. Sometimes the individual part of apprehension consists of the opposite being understood of what has been said.

So when we speak about self-knowledge, we also have to be clear that it is more useful to speak in such a way that we seek the errors in us and the truth outside us.

We do not say: seek the truth within yourself! The truth is indeed found outside. We find that it is poured out into the world. We have to become free of ourselves through self-knowledge, have to pass through such stages of the soul. Solitude can be a very bad companion. But we can also feel the whole extent of our weakness if we reflect the feeling in our soul of the magnitude of the cosmos out of which we have been born. But then we take courage, become bold enough to experience what we have learnt to know.

Then we will find that out of the loss of the final assurance in our life there does indeed grow the first and last assurance of our life, the assurance which, in rediscovering ourselves in the cosmos, allows us to overcome and find ourselves anew:

> O human being, experience the world in yourself!
> Then, striding beyond yourself,
> You will more than ever have found yourself
> In your true self.

If we feel these words as experiences, then they become stages of development for us.

LECTURE 8

BERLIN, 31 OCTOBER 1910

The light of the sun is flooding
The breadths of space;
The song of the birds is filling
The heights of air;
The tender plants are shooting
From the kind earth;
And human souls in reverent gratitude,
Rise to the spirits of the world.

As those of you who attended the performance of the Rosicrucian mystery in Munich will know, this children's song introduced the content of this mystery. During this hour a number of spiritual-scientific things will develop before us following on from what lies in this mystery, we might say has been given life.

It is, if I may say so, a long spiritual process which led to this mystery. When I think or look back on it,[81] its seeds go back to the year 1889. It is not just approximately, but with a precision which can be observed in these things, that I am taken back to the source of this Rosicrucian mystery. And I can trace very precisely which paths these seeds followed in these three times seven years; and they did so, I may say, without any particular input by myself in that they led a life of their own in these three times seven years. It is very peculiar to follow such seeds on their path until they reach what we might call composition. They follow a path which we might call going into the underworld. There they need seven years to descend. Then they return and for this ascent they again required seven years. Then they have arrived at the point where they were basically with regard to the human being when they started their descent, and then they continue on the other side for seven years in the other direction, we might say ascend to the heights. That gives us two times seven years plus seven years, that is 21 years. At that point one can start with composition with some prospect that what is intended with these seeds really can take shape. And if I were not aware that an independent organism which has truly led a life of three times seven years within itself lives in this Rosicrucian mystery I would not dare to continue talking about it in any way. But thus I feel not only justified, which is not the issue, but in a certain way obliged also to speak about those things which not only live between the lines, not just in the characters, not just in the what and the how, but what also, I don't even want to say lives, but has to live in many things specifically of this Rosicrucian mystery.

I have mentioned on several occasions[82] since the Munich performance of this Rosicrucian mystery, something which after all is true, that I would not have to say anything more about many, many things in the esoteric, the occult field, that I would not be required to give any more lectures if all those things which it contains acted on the souls of our dear friends and many another person directly from out of the Rosicrucian mystery. And in words such as they are commonly used in lectures, I would have to say many, many things, not just for days, weeks or months but for years if I wanted to outline what the Rosicrucian mystery intends and is able to say. All the things which you find—and with regard to occult things it is certainly justified to speak like this—in a kind of stammering speech in the book *Knowledge of the Higher Worlds. How is it Achieved?*, the things it contains as a description of the path up into the higher worlds, all those things combined with what it was permissible to say in another form in *Occult Science. An Outline* can basically be found in a much more intensive, true-to-life and real way in the Rosicrucian mystery.

In a book such as for example *Knowledge of the Higher Worlds. How is it Achieved?* we can only bring what we want to say about human development in such a way that it is in a sense applicable to each human individuality which embarks on the path into the higher worlds in a specific way, to any human individuality. This gives such a book something of an abstract character for all its concrete nature, we might say a half theoretical character. Because we have to understand one thing: development is not development as such. There is no development as such, no development in general. There is only the development of the one or the other or the third, of the fourth or the thousandth human being. And as many people as there are in the world, so many developmental processes there have to be. Hence the truest description of the occult path of knowledge must in general have a character which in a certain sense is not congruous with an individual development. If we truly want to represent development as it can be seen in the spiritual world, then this can only happen if we frame the development of an individual person, if we implement in the individuality what is true for all human beings. If the book *Knowledge of the Higher Worlds. How is it Achieved?* in a certain sense contains the beginning of the developmental secret of every person, then the Rosicrucian mystery contains the developmental secret of a single person, of Johannes Thomasius.

So it was a long path from all those things which are occult developmental laws down to the individual, truly real person. And in this developmental process, on this path something had to be almost completely reversed which is contained in *Knowledge of the Higher Worlds* and which might become theoretical there. If it should not become theory, specifically if it should become art, it has to be reversed completely, because the laws of art are very special ones. And just as there are laws of nature, so there are laws of art which should not be handled with normal human consciousness because then the only thing to result is something like brittle allegory. The laws of art must be handled like nature itself handles its laws when it creates a human being, an animal or a plant. If what we can know about the world, looked at from one angle, is that we look into the world and it reveals its laws and secrets to us, then that which must appear in art and in each art is something which has to be laid into the artwork concerned from the other side through the opposing sense. That is why the worst possible interpretation of a work of art would be one which attempted to introduce concepts and ideas, laws which we know from some place else into a poetic work. And a person who would introduce abstract or symbolic concepts into a given work of art would not shape something artistic.

That is why it would be one of the worst methods with regard to works of art from the past, in which real occult forces were at work, such as in *Faust* for example, if we were to seek concepts and ideas which are familiar to us again in the works of art. Such bad habits were rife for a time in the theosophical movement in the most awful way. Indeed, I can recall something which happened last year when we performed Schuré's drama *The Children of Lucifer*, how the author of this drama, who is an artist in the best sense of the word, was horrified when someone approached him with the question: does this character mean 'Atma', does this figure mean 'Buddhi', this figure 'Manas', this one 'Kama Manas' and so on? This type of allegory would be impossible in an artistic process. That is why it has to be impossible in any explanation, in any interpretation. That is why we can also say that we should not reflect on: what in anthroposophical terms is Johannes Thomasius? There is only one answer to this question: as the main character of this poetic work he is nothing other than Johannes Thomasius. He is nothing other at all than this living figure of Johannes Thomasius which contains nothing but the developmental secret of an individual person, namely of Johannes Thomasius.

As soon as we talk about the individual characters in general there is one thing missing. The missing thing is what is indicated in the words of the drama in the lines: 'Within our circle there is formed a knot of threads that karma spins world-fashioning.' No development takes place at any point of human existence without the surrounding threads being knotted in this development which karma spins in cosmic existence. And we cannot draw any individual development without showing how everything plays in the occult environment, that is in the physical environment but as it is seen with the forces which are behind the physical environment. That is why Johannes Thomasius has to be placed into the human environment out of which his development grows into the real physical human world.

And that is why the drama had to have a dual introduction. The first introduction shows what the world looks like with regard to the external world in which the threads are knotted for Johannes Thomasius which spin karma in cosmic existence. We could ask: did what this world looks like from outside have to be shown, did it have to be shown particularly in the prelude? It had to be shown. And not everything would have been done if it had not been shown. It had to be shown because the world in which karma spins its knots is different at the time of the fifth millennium before the Christian era, different again three hundred years before the Christian era, and different again a thousand years after the start of the Christian period and different again in our present time. The exoteric external world is also a different one and it is connected with its karma with what becomes the environment for the person who is developing. Thus the circle is drawn from outside inwards. And inside there is then the small circle in which Johannes Thomasius himself stands. That is the second thing. In the outside world these are minor waves; in the smaller circle waves surged up high. But they can only show themselves as they foam up in the soul of Johannes Thomasius himself. That is why we are first taken to the physical plane. The physical plane is shown to us in such a way that the threads are indicated which are spun by karma everywhere within the physical plane.

Anyone who looks into any physical circle with occult eyes will find that everywhere the threads go from person to person and that they intertwine in a remarkable way. There are people who appear in life to have little to do with one another. But between soul and soul are spun the most important, the most significant threads. All these things are knotted. And all these things have gradually to be shown in such a way that there is a clear pointer, as it were, to any given knot. Another time they can only be shown in a subtle, indicative way because they are in the process of developing. These things have to be referred to where the matter takes place on the physical plane, where we are in a purely physical environment, where people come together from a great variety of backgrounds. Externally they talk about this and that. But in talking externally, they are manifestations of karma. All the people whom we meet at first on the physical plane are karmically linked with one another and that is the key thing: that they are karmically linked. There is not a single invented case; there is an occult foundation for everything. All of it threads which can live, and these threads are very remarkable.

You can get an idea of the remarkable nature of these threads when you put together figures such as Felix Balde and Frau Balde on the one hand and Capesius and Strader on the other hand. The content of what they say in their words is not the most important thing; the most important thing is that it is these persons who say it. And these persons are living persons, not persons who have been thought up. They are, for example, very well known to me. With known I do not mean thought up but standing and alive. They are real and particularly also the figure of Professor Capesius, of whom I have become very fond, is a figure taken from life. And it is our world. That is why there had to occur the remarkable event which is presented by the seer Theodora, who can sometimes look into the future and predicts the remarkable event which will still arrive before the end of the twentieth century as the next Christ event. That is something which can be karmically interpreted. It would be wrong if there was an equally clear pointer to other events. Then the karmic relationship which exists between Frau Balde and Professor Capesius is indicated in the peculiar connection which the fairy tales told by Frau Balde have on Capesius.

Karmic threads are indicated which arise in Strader's heart to the seer Theodora since he is particularly moved by her. All of these are threads which lie in an occult way behind what takes place externally on the physical plane. These threads are spun by karma as if aiming for a point. This one point is Johannes Thomasius. That is where they meet. And within the story on the physical plane a light is illuminated in the soul of Johannes Thomasius, a light which creates terrible waves in his soul but which at the same time sparks his esoteric development as a very specific individual one, as the crossing of his own karma with the cosmic karma. That is why we see the impression which is made on him by what exists around him on the physical plane, and how the greatness in his soul, the unconscious, presses up to the higher worlds.

Now this journey into the higher worlds must not start rudderless. It must be steered and guided. There then enters into all these relationships the person whom you see described as the actual leader of this circle, but at the same time as the one who knows about the cosmic relationships, as the one who sees through the knot which karma spins in cosmic development—Benedictus comes in. And he becomes the leader. The karma at work in Johannes Thomasius, which would work perhaps through millennia, or millennia of millennia, is ignited at a very specific moment through a karmic relationship between Benedictus and Johannes Thomasius which is subtly indicated in the scene in the meditation room. Here we stand at a point at which a human being destined for development through karma strives up into the higher worlds. And so that he does not strive upwards like a blind person he is guided in the right way by Benedictus. What is meant by that will be revealed when now a number of the passages concerned are performed.

The recitation of the whole of Scene 3 follows: Benedictus, Johannes, Maria, Child.

Maria: I bring to thee this child who needs some word
             From out thy mouth.

Benedictus: My child, henceforth each eve
             Thou shalt come unto me to hear the word
             That shall fill full thy soul ere thou dost tread
             The realm of souls in sleep. Wilt thou do this?

Child: Most gladly will I come.

Benedictus: This very eve
             Fill thy soul full ere sleep embraceth thee,
             With strength from these few words: 'The powers of light
             Bear me aloft unto the spirit's home.'

             (Maria, having taken the child away.)

Maria: And now, that this child's destiny doth flow
             Harmoniously through future days beneath
             The shadow of thy gracious fatherhood,
             I too may claim my leader's kind advice,
             Who am its mother, not by bond of blood
             But through the mighty power of destiny.
             For thou hast shown to me the way wherein
             I had to guide its footsteps from that day,
             When I discovered it before my door

Left by its unknown mother desolate.
And wonder-working proved themselves those rules
Whereby thou madest me train my foster-child.
All powers, that deep in body and in soul
Lay hidden, issued forth to light and life:
Clear proof it was that all thy counselling
Sprang from the realm which sheltered this child's soul
Before it built its body's covering.
We saw its early promise blossom forth
And radiate more brightly each new day;
Thou dost know well how hard it was for me
To gain the child's affection, at the first.
It grew up 'neath my care, and yet nought else
Save habit chained its soul at first to mine.
It only realized and felt that I
Gave it the nurture and the food that served
The needs of body and the growth of soul.
Then came the time when in the childlike heart
There dawned the love for her who fostered it.
An outer incident brought forth this change—
The visit of the seeress to our group.
Gladly the child did go about with her
And soon did learn full many a beauteous word
Steeped in the mystic charm that graced her speech.
Then came the moment when her ecstasy
Descended on our friend with magic power.
The child could see her eyes, strange smouldering light,
And, terrified unto the vital core,
The young soul found itself.

In her dismay she fled unto mine arms;
And from that hour did grow her love for me.
Since that same time she doth accept from me
The gifts of life with her full consciousness
Not with blind instinct: aye, and since that day
When this young heart first quivered into warmth,

Whene'er her gaze met mine with loving glance,
Thy wisdom's treasures of their fruitage failed,
And much already ripe hath withered up.
I saw appear in her those tokens strange
That proved so terrible unto my friend.

A dark enigma am I to myself,
And grow still darker. Thou wilt not deny
To solve for me life's fearful questionings
Why do I mar the life of friend and child,
When I in love attempt to work on them
According to the dictates of my heart
By spirit-lore instructed and inspired?
Oft hast thou taught me this exalted truth—
Illusion's veil o'erspreads life's surfaces—
Yet must I see with greater clarity
Why I must bear this heavy destiny,
That seems so cruel and that works such harm.

Benedictus: Within our circle there is formed a knot
Of threads that Karma spins world-fashioning.
Thy sufferings, my friend, are links in chains,
Forged by the hand of destiny, whereby
The deeds of Gods unite with human lives.—

When in life's pilgrimage I had attained
That rank which granted me the dignity
To serve with counsel in the spirit-spheres,
A godlike Being did draw nigh to me,
Who would descend into the realms of earth,
And dwell there, veiled in form of flesh, as man.
For just at this one turning point of time
The Karma of mankind made this demand.
For each great step in world-development
Is only possible when Gods do stoop
To link themselves with human destiny.
And this new spirit-sight that needs must grow

And germinate henceforth in souls of men
Can only be unfolded when a God
Doth plant the seed within some human heart.
My task it was to find that human soul
Which worthy seemed to take within itself
The powerful Seed of God. I had to join
The deed of heaven to some human lot.
My spirit's eye then sought, and fell on thee.
Thy course of life had fitted thee to be
The mediator in salvation's work.
Through many former lives thou hadst acquired
Receptiveness for all the greatest things
That human hearts can e'er experience.
Within thy tender soul thou didst bring forth,
As spirit heritage, the noble gift
Of beauty, joined to virtue's loftiest claim:
And that which thine eternal Self had formed
And brought to being through thy birth on earth
Did reach ripe fruitage when thy years were few.—
Thou didst not scale steep spirit-heights too soon,
Nor grew thy yearning for the spirit-land
Before thou hadst the full enjoyment known
Of harmless pleasures in the world of sense.
Anger and love thy soul did learn to know
When thy thoughts dwelt yet far from spirit-life.
Nature in all her beauty to enjoy,
And pluck the fruits of art—these didst thou strive
To make thy life's sole content and its wealth.
Merry thy laughter, as a child can laugh
Who hath not known as yet life's shadowed fears.
Thus thou didst learn to understand life's joy,
And mourn in sadness, each in its own time,
Before thy dawning conscience grew to seek
Of sorrow and of happiness the cause.
A ripened fruit of many lives that soul,
That enters earth's domains, and shows such moods.

Its childlike nature is the blossoming
And not the ground-root of its character.
And such a soul alone was I to choose
As mediator for the God,[83] who sought
The power to work within our human world.
And now thou learnest that thy nature must
Transform itself into its opposite,
When it flows forth to other human souls.
The spirit in thee ripens whatsoe'er
In human nature can attain the realm
Of vast eternity; and much it slays
That is but part of transitory realms.
And yet the sacrifices of such deaths
Are but the seeds of immortality;
All that which blossoms forth from death below
Must grow unto the higher life above.

Maria: E'en so it is with me. Thou giv'st me light:
               But light that doth deprive me of my sight,
               And sunder me from mine own self in twain.
               Then do I seem some spirit's instrument—
               No longer master of myself. No more
               Do I endure that erstwhile form of mine
               Which only is a mask and not the truth.

Johannes: O friend, what ails thee? Vanished is the light
               That filled thine eye: as marble is thy frame.
               I grasp thine hand and find it cold as death.

Benedictus: My son, full many trials have come to thee;
               And now thou stand'st before life's hardest test.
               Thou seest the carnal covering of thy friend;
               But her true self doth float in spirit-spheres
               Before mine eyes.

Johannes: See! Her lips move; she speaks.

Maria: Thou gav'st me clearness yet this clearness throws

A veil of darkness round on every side.
I curse thy clearness; and I curse thee too,
Who didst make tool of me for weird wild arts
Whereby thou willedst to deceive mankind.
No doubt at any moment hitherto
Had crossed my mind of heights thy spirit reached;
But now one single moment doth suffice
To tear all faith in thee from out my heart.
Those spirit-beings thou art subject to, I now must
recognize as hellish fiends.
Others I had to mislead and deceive
Because at first I was deceived by thee.—
But I will flee unto dim distances,
Where not a sound of thee shall reach mine ears;
Yet near enough that thy soul may be reached
By bitter curses framed by these my lips.
For thou didst rob my blood of all its fire,
That thou mightst sacrifice to thy false god
That which was rightly mine and mine alone.
But now this same blood's fire shall thee consume.
Thou madest me trust in vain imaginings;
And that this might be so, thou first didst make
A pictured falsehood of my very self.
Often had I to mark how from my soul
Each deed and thought turned to its opposite;
So now doth turn what once was love for thee,
Into the fire of wild and bitter hate.
Through all worlds will I seek to find that fire
Which can consume thee—I curse—Ah, woe!

Johannes: Who speaketh here? I do not see my friend.
I hear instead some gruesome being speak.

Benedictus: Thy friend's soul hovers in the heights above.
Only her mortal image hath she left
Here with us: and where'er a human form
Is found bereft of soul, there is the room

Sought by the enemy, the foe of good,
To enter into realms perceptible,
And find some carnal form through which to speak.
Just such an adversary spake e'en now,
Who would destroy the work imposed on me
For thee, my son, and millions yet unborn.
Were I to deem these wild anathemas,
Which our friend's shell did utter here and now,
Aught else but some grim tempter's cunning skill,
Thou durst not follow more my leadership.
The enemy of Good stood by my side,
And thou hast seen into the darkness plunged
All that is temporal of that dear form,
For whom, my son, thy whole love burns and glows.
Since through her mouth spirits spake oft to thee,
The Karma of the world could not restrain
Hell's princes also speaking thus through her.
Now only mayst thou seek her very soul
And learn her nature's inmost verity;
For she shall form for thee the prototype
Of that new higher life of humankind
To which thou dost aspire to raise thyself.
Her soul hath soared aloft to spirit-heights,
Where every man may find his being's source
Which springs to life and fullness in himself.
Thou too shalt follow her to spirit-realms,
And see her in the Temple of the Sun.—
Within this circle there is formed a knot
Of threads which Karma spins, world fashioning.
My son, since thou hast now attained thus far,
Thou shalt still further pierce beyond the veil.
I see thy star in fullest splendour shine.
There is no place within the realm of sense
For strife, such as men wage when they do strive
And struggle after consecration's gift.
Whate'er the outer world of sense begets

Of riddles soluble by intellect,
Whate'er this world engenders in man's heart
Born tho' it be of love or bitter hate
And howsoever direful its results:
The spirit-seeker must attain the power
In all these things to stand unmoved, serene,
Casting his gaze all unperturbed and calm
Upon the scene where such contentions rage.
For him must other powers unfold themselves
Which are not found upon this field of strife.
So didst thou need to fight to prove thy soul
In combat such as comes to him alone,
Who finds himself accoutred for such powers
As do belong unto the spirit-worlds.
And had these powers found thee not ripe enough
To tread the path of knowledge, they needs must
Have maimed thy powers of feeling, ere thou daredst
To know all that which now is known to thee.
The Beings, who can gaze into world-depths,
Lead on those men, who would attain the heights,
First to that summit whence it may be shown
Whether there lies in them the power to reach
To conscious sight within the spirit-realms.
And those in whom such powers are found to lie
Are straightway from the world of sense set free.
The others all must wait their season due.
But thou, thou hast preserved thy Self, my son,
When Powers on high stirred to its depths thy soul,
And potent spirits shrouded thee with fear.
Right powerfully thy Self hath fought its way
E'en though thy very heart was torn by doubts,
That willed to thrust thee into darksome depths.
True pupil of my teaching hast thou been,
First since that hour, so fraught with fate for thee,
When thou didst learn to doubt thy very self,
And gavest up thyself as wholly lost,

But yet the strength within thee held thee fast.
Then might I give thee of my treasured store
Of wisdom, whence to draw the strength to stand
Assured, e'en when mistrusting thine own self.
Such was the wisdom which thou didst attain
More steadfast than the faith once given to thee.
Ripe wast thou found, and thou may'st be set free.
Thy friend hath gone before and waits for thee
In spirit-worlds, and thou shalt find her there.
I can but add this guidance for thee now:
Kindle the full power of thy soul with words
Which through my lips shall grant to thee the key
To spirit-heights, and they will lead thee on
When naught else leads, that eyes of sense can see.
Receive them in the fullness of thy heart:
'The weaving essence of the light streams forth
Through depths of space to fill the world with life;
Love's grace doth warm the centuries of time
To call forth revelation of all worlds.
And spirit-messengers come forth to wed
The weaving essence of creative light
With revelation of the souls of men:
And that man, who can wed to both of these
His very Self, he lives in spirit-heights.'
O spirits, who are visible to man,
Quicken with life the soul of this our son:
From inmost depths may there stream forth for him
That which can fill his soul with spirit-light.
From inmost depths may there resound for him
That which can wholly wake in him his Self
To the creative joy of spirit-life.

A Spirit-Voice
(behind the stage): To founts of worlds primeval
                    His surging thoughts do mount—
                    What as shadow he hath thought

What as fancy he hath lived
Soars up beyond the world of form and shape;
On whose fullness pondering
Mankind in shadow dreams,
O'er whose fullness gazing forth
Mankind in fancy lives.

(The music starts while the curtain slowly falls.)

Those were the tones with which our dear friend Arenson[84] expressed in music what arises in my work as the echo from the higher worlds in the soul of Johannes Thomasius after he has shown himself capable, following the great event presented in the meditation room, truly to be able to rise to higher worlds; he has emerged from this experience with maturity. We should see something in the words which concluded the recitation sounding from the spiritual world in a very real way into the soul which to a certain degree has passed the test, if we may put it like that. The gravity is occasionally quietly indicated in words which contain more than we might initially think.

To begin with, we have to be clear that a knot is tied out of the threads of cosmic karma which at a holy site places before Johannes Thomasius a fact of the most magnificent and mightiest kind in its action. What actually happens?

Johannes Thomasius has to experience that a soul with which he is karmically connected in a wonderful way, as is shown later on in the Devachan scene, ascends into the spiritual world directly before him. It is a world historical moment when such a soul ascends into the spiritual world. We cannot now of course refer to everything connected with such a moment. But it is most certainly a real fact which anyone who is familiar with occult life knows in its terribly mighty shape with its light and shadow side. And such a person also then knows what happens in that respect in the physical world when the tremor occurs that a soul directly disappears into the spiritual worlds not in the serene progress of its own karma but called upon by cosmic karma. These are moments which are important for the evolution of humanity.

But these are also the moments in which real existing powers of temptation, which look into our physical world from the spiritual world in the same way as the good powers do, have the power to acquire physical envelopes which have been abandoned and turn them into the scene of the deceit and power of their temptation. Those are points which can be attacked; that is where they are released, as it were. And then the circumstances occur in which Maya comes to expression in the most terrible way. A person who perhaps has not advanced far cannot resist the minor deceptions of karma: but with regard to the major deceptions of karma, when it presents something of which at a certain level of development we can no longer fully believe that it could be like that, the soul recoils which has not passed through certain abysses of life. We can imagine that some might say they would have withstood what happened in the meditation room. But let them actually be there. The reality is something quite different from what we imagine in our thoughts. In reality there are still other forces involved. Anyone who does not believe that should try to imagine whether they have ever had the real experience of a human body which has been abandoned by its soul. People only know human bodies which are ensouled. There are simply other forces at play. And in order to withstand these forces, Johannes Thomasius had to be led precisely to this point in cosmic karma.

Now there are two things here. Johannes Thomasius first had to undergo what we normally call Kamaloka. That is the world in which what we are ourselves appears to us like a mirror-image, we might say. That is again something which appears a lot easier than when it happens in reality. And when it occurs in reality then it is not a picture restricted in space which tells us what it is but it murmurs to us from all parts of the world. Then the whole world is *us*. That is why in the scene in which it is shown how Johannes Thomasius descends into the depths of his soul, where he is under rocks and springs, it is not any single reflection which he implores which speaks to him out of his soul but everything resounds towards him, rocks and springs, the whole surroundings. And it happens that in such a moment the words which seem so tame in cosmic theories, in philosophical and intellectual works, turn into terrible forces. They resound from out of the whole world as if reflected from everywhere out of infinite space and are captured in the individual events of nature. 'Know thou thyself, O man!' That is how they resound when they are heard after they have lived in the soul for years and years. Then the soul faces itself in its loneliness, in its great abandonment. There is nothing other than the world. But this world is the soul itself. And this world contains everything that the soul itself is, including what is its karma, everything that it has done. In a work of poetry, only individual things can be highlighted. An old deed, the abandonment of a person, occurs. But it appears before Johannes Thomasius' soul in all its living nature. I can only cite individual words.

In this context Johannes Thomasius loses what he has to lose: the trust in himself, in his strength, even in being able to find healing in solitude for what causes him such torments on the physical plane when he hears it from out of the physical plane. Hence these words, which I would ask you to take in the way they should be taken as bursting the boundaries of the soul and filling it completely. When Johannes Thomasius hears out of all worlds the words 'Know thou thyself, O man!' his soul responds as if his I were not present:

> 'Tis thus I hear them, now these many years,
> These words of weighty import all around.
> I hear them in the wind and in the wave:
> Out from earth's depths do they resound to me:
> And as a tiny acorn's mystery,
> Confines the structure of a mighty oak,
> So in the kernel of these words there lies,
> All elemental nature; all I grasp
> Of soul, of spirit, time, eternity.
> It seems mine own peculiarities
> And all the world besides live in these words:
> 'Know thou thyself, O man. Know thou thyself.'

But which receives a mighty answer: 'Know thou thyself, O man!'. Then the whole interior turns around:

> And now—I feel
> Mine inmost being terrified to life:
> Without the gloom of night doth weave me round,
> And deep within my soul thick darkness yawns:

And sounding from this universal gloom
And up from out the darkness of my soul
These words ring forth: 'Know thou thyself, O man.'

(From the springs and rocks resounds: *Know thou thyself, O man!*)

You have to imagine the self going along with the world process. Normally we stand there, go with the hours and do not follow what is happening. We do not know what is happening and think that we are in our interior. But this happens knowingly. Knowingly he follows all elemental forces, goes with the course of the hours through the day and transforms into night.

The earth I follow on its cosmic course:
I seem to rumble in the thunder's peal,
And flash adown the lightning's fierce-forked tongue—

Everything gives him the impression: I am. That is the moment in which the I am becomes the demon of its own soul. In the face of that all self-assertion of the human being falls silent. And no sooner have we tried to speak it, the I am, then our own soul says:

Mine own existence snatched away from me.

Then our own being appears in a restricted way, in a limited shape:

I see what was my former carnal shape,
As some strange being, quite outside myself,
And infinitely far away from me.
But now another body hovers near;

Now he can speak not just with his own mouth but with the mouth of the other person. Here we have the person to whom he did an injustice:

'Ah, bitter sorrow hath he brought to me;
So utterly I trusted him of old.
He left me lonely with my sorrow's pain,
He robbed me of the very warmth of life,
And thrust me deep beneath the chill, cold ground.'

Now back again into his own body:

> Poor soul, 'tis she I left, and leaving her
> It was in truth mine own self that I left;
> And I must suffer all her pain and woe.
> For knowledge hath endowed me with the power
> Myself into another's self to fuse.

That is the beginning of a path which is then still characterized with the words which are meant to indicate at the end of the scene how the world and how solitude work. In the world everything that flows from the outside works in the most terrible way. From inside those things are at work which come from the inside so that solitude is the most populated thing there is. That is an examination which is employed for the purpose which is indicated in the words which were read to you:

> The Beings, who can gaze into world-depths,
> Lead on those men, who would attain the heights,
> First to that summit whence it may be shown
> Whether there lies in them the power to reach
> To conscious sight within the spirit-realms.
> And those in whom such powers are found to lie
> Are straightway from the world of sense set free.
> The others all must wait their season due.

At the moment we face here, consciousness would be lost and Johannes Thomasius would be thrown back into the sensory world if he had not been steadfast in the scene I indicated where he faces his own self. Two things were relevant here. Our own self, in so far as it has knowledge, has little strength—that deprives it of self-confidence. But it contains the eternal I of which it is not aware; that has great strength. That keeps him upright and allows him to surmount what he experiences in the meditation room as the desouling of Maria. Then all he needs is to be led upwards through Benedictus' words, through the power of those words.

And you have to see a secret of words in the words which were read to you. What is meant with them cannot simply be written in any old way, as so many other things can. These lines contain real cosmic forces right down into the sounds. And so the sounds cannot actually be changed. The opening of the gate to the spiritual world is truly given in these words. That is why they really have to be taken as they are said here. Something like this cannot be arbitrarily compiled—these lines for example:

> The weaving essence of the light streams forth
> Through depths of space to fill the world with life;
> Love's grace doth warm the centuries of time
> To call forth revelation of all worlds.
> And spirit-messengers come forth to wed
> The weaving essence of creative light
> With revelation of the souls of men:
> And that man, who can wed to both of these
> His very Self, he lives in spirit-heights.

Only then can sound into the soul from the other world what is intended to sound into it. But all of these things are just individual indications, as I said.

Now Johannes Thomasius is really removed to the spiritual world but he cannot directly ascend to the spiritual world to which everyone must ascend. He has to pass through the astral world. So then you have in the fourth scene a representation of the astral world in the way that Johannes Thomasius specifically has to experience it in accordance with his particular individual prerequisites. It is not a general description of the astral world but a description of this world in the way that Johannes Thomasius has to experience it in specific examples. This astral world is different from the physical one. Here it is possible to see a human being we encounter as they were several decades ago or we see a young person how they will be in the future. Those are all realities. In your soul you are still the same person today as you were when you were a 3-year-old child. What you see in the astral world is nothing like what the outer physical image of the human being shows. The physical image of the human being at every moment hides what was warranted beforehand and what will be warranted afterwards. So the gaze into the astral world has to achieve above all that we overcome the first Maya of the sensory world and see through time in its illusory power. That is why in the astral world Johannes Thomasius sees the person whom he has learnt to know on the physical plane as Capesius as he was when he was a young person. And he sees the person with whom he became acquainted in the physical world as Strader as he will be when he is an old man.

What does that mean? Johannes Thomasius knows Strader as he is now in the sensory world with the powers which are now in his soul on the physical plane. But that contains the prerequisites for what he will be decades later. We have to recognize that in this way if we want to learn about the human being. So time is torn apart. Time really is quite an elastic concept when we ascend into the higher worlds. From the physical world, Johannes Thomasius knows Capesius when he is old and Strader when he is young. Now they stand next to one another in the astral world: Capesius young and Strader old. Here time is not stretched forwards and backwards, but it is such that the one is shown in his youth and the other in old age. That is a perfectly real fact.

But something else is connected with that which actually reveals itself and which people today ridicule. And this is that there is more to our soul experiences than we normally think, that good and evil are not experienced in the soul unpunished (thus, for example, if we have a terrible or unjust thought this radiates into the depths of the world and then radiates back again), and that we are connected in our soul experiences with the elemental forces in nature. That is not an image. It is a reality in an occult sense when Capesius is taken before the spirit of the elements who guides every human being into their existence. Then it is actually also the case that Capesius stands before those things which are linked with the spirit of the elements, and what is linked with this is that when we experience anything in our soul it is connected with the elemental forces in nature. It is revealed to Johannes Thomasius that Capesius, and Strader too, can stir up the antagonistic forces in nature. That is why thunder and lightning follow in this world in response to what they experience themselves in their souls in pride or arrogance, in error or in truth or lies.

In the physical world, what people have in their soul as error or lies is something quite peculiar. Someone might stand before us, for example, in whose soul there live error and lies but he stands quite innocently before us. Yet at the moment in which we turn our astral gaze on him storms rage which we otherwise see only in the most terrible discharge of the elements on earth. Johannes Thomasius has to live through all that. And also all the things which can be revealed to him in the astral world of the peculiar connections which were not yet recognized by him when he encountered them on the physical plane.

The kind of designations which we find in this Rosicrucian mystery are not accidental. Designations such as, for example, the other Maria and so on all indicate certain relationships so that the one and the other Maria are not merely the two Marias but present themselves as the Marias with regard to all other people. And the other Maria, the mysterious figure of nature, reveals for Johannes Thomasius the soul which lives under the normal, conscious soul, remaining unheard and unperceivable for as long as human beings live only in the physical world. But you must not take these relationships and figures as symbols. In all these things the other Maria is in turn a real figure, just like the first Maria, a reality. And that is the only way they should be taken, that is what they are.

Everything that Johannes Thomasius experienced has passed before the eye of his soul. He has experienced the astral world. He can now bring this to consciousness when he says:

> So do I find within the soul's domain
> Those men who are already known to me:
> First he who told us of Felicia's tales,
> Though here I saw him in his youthful prime;
> And also he who in his younger days
> Had chosen for his life monastic rule,
> As some old man did he appear: with them
> There stood the Spirit of the Elements.

Johannes Thomasius has undergone all the things which destroy, as it were, time in front of his gaze. And what is it for which he has now become mature? He has become mature to turn his gaze into the astral world. Is the astral world free of delusion? No, it is not. But human beings can become certain of one thing in the astral world. And one thing becomes a certainty for human beings in the astral world if they enter it in purity, not with guilt, namely that there is a higher world which shines into the astral world like the astral world into the ordinary physical world. The only question is whether they can see it as it is in reality. The people who wander around in the world are themselves only a kind of mirage so that they themselves have something behind them which leads them into the higher world, so that they stand out against something quite different from what they might have been long or not so long ago, what they will become in the future. But certain delusions do not show us the astral world with which we are very much intertwined in the sensory world. Thus for example they do not show the relationship between the great forces of existence, the relationship between will, love and wisdom. That is something which is so difficult to recognize in its truth that it remains hidden in the astral world for a long, long time. It is not so easy to get behind that. And the relationships which are delusions in the sensory world continue into the astral world.

Such collaboration—this is something else which can only be indicated briefly—between will, wisdom and love occurs in the physical world through human beings. In the higher worlds it happens through those beings which send in their forces when on the physical plane the forces of the occult beings are submersed in human souls. That happens through the initiates in the temples in which the human representatives of the individual cosmic forces reside, in the temples in which human beings have already advanced so far that they no longer wish to represent the whole human being at once, where they have restricted themselves to representing one force. That is where these representatives reside. But when human beings look into the astral world they can see those sites where the representatives of the will, wisdom and love forces are in a picture filled with Maya. And here a terrible web between delusion of the sensory world and the astral world is spun.

And now I would have to speak for weeks on end if I wanted to explain what the situation is with regard to the form of higher power which presents itself as the initiate for the power of will as he is encountered by Johannes Thomasius on the physical plane and actually appears like a lightweight on the physical plane. Here the question can arise: are the archetypal forces of the will meant to exercise their influence through someone like that? And yet that is what they do. But we can understand that it is particularly through a perhaps less developed person that the force can enter which is meant to be a revelation of the forces of the will, just as the ray of wisdom can enter through a person such as Benedictus. For we have to understand the following. If we have here a wonderful flowering blossom, and lay a seed next to it then, it could be that the seed once it has grown will produce an even more beautiful flower. We will consider the flower as something very perfect now already but in truth the seed is something even more perfect in the reality of the world.

That is why there stand facing one another Benedictus, the great bearer of wisdom, and beside him the person who behaves in a curious way on the physical plane towards everything which is said about the spiritual worlds in that he rejects all of it in a curious way. Whenever he hears the group of people speaking about the spiritual world he says like a person who does not want to hear anything about the spiritual worlds: 'For my part I do seek in vain the bridge that truly leadeth from ideas to deeds.' It is a person who finds what leads to deeds in quite a different place and for whom all talk about the spirit is just empty words. You could tell this person as he now lives on the physical plane the most beautiful things about spiritual science; it would be empty words for him. The valuable thing for him is if the wheels of the machine work. And when he hears through the other Maria about the spiritual force which has united with her and has ignited in her the forces of feeling and love in order to do this or the other deed, he is once again the person who rejects everything and simply says: she does that because she has a good heart. He remains wholly on the physical plane and a lightweight of the physical plane. But he is an energetic, active, man of will. That is why he says:

> If this friend doth so many deeds of good,
> The impulse thereunto lies in herself
> And her warm-hearted nature, not in thought.
> Most certainly 'tis needful for man's soul,
> After the busy day of toil and work,
> With noble thought to edify the mind.
> But yet 'tis only schooling of man's will
> In harmony with all his skill and power
> To undertake some real work in life

Which will help forward all the human race.
When whirr of busy wheels sounds in mine ears,
Or when I see some creaking windlass drawn
By strong stout hands of men content to work,
Then do I sense indeed the powers of Life.

That is the person of will, the person of deeds. And you could talk to him about the spirit for days on end and his response would be: you could not turn a single crank with that, and how would people keep themselves fed? So you can keep turning the cranks during the day and when you have a bit of free time we can amuse ourselves by talking about the spirit. Those are the seed forces which have not yet emerged. But they are good forces. These are forces which are very important and which radiate into the world through the powers of will. We cannot proceed on a theoretical basis in this context when people hear about spiritual worlds and receive it in different ways, because it is very difficult to break through here. Anyone who fails to understand that something has to be seen in the seed which is a counter-image to the people we have just characterized experiences an illusion such as is represented in the subterranean temple. That is astral Maya. Whereas what Johannes Thomasius experiences in the scene with Capesius and Strader is reality, where he sees them at different ages describes Maya, a *Fata Morgana* of the spiritual world in the fifth scene which must initially discharge itself into the soul, which has to be passed through. That is why you have to take the fifth scene as something which is only justified in that reality is immediately injected into Maya.

This whole scene would contribute nothing to the development of Johannes Thomasius if it did not have the same relationship to astral experience as the concepts and ideas of the physical world have to our understanding of the world. What science is for the physical plane, that the Maya temple is for the astral world. As little as the concept is something we can eat, as little the Maya temple is a reality which is rooted in the spiritual world. But the concepts have to live in the world so that a real understanding of the world can occur. And this is the only way that something can be injected from another world which does in turn provide profound enlightenment for Johannes Thomasius; he can now recognize the way in which a certain knot is spun in cosmic karma in that Felix Balde has recognized that he should not bury the treasures of his soul by wandering through the world in solitude but that he must carry them to the temple.

Not until then is the opportunity given for Johannes Thomasius to see what we might call much more real circumstances in the spiritual world, including those circumstances which are of a more subtle and intimate kind—for example the way that the astral world reaches into the physical world, which happens when something occurs such as the inspiration of a human being like Capesius through someone who themselves does not actually know how much they have in their soul. Frau Balde does not know this in the mystery. In a person who has intellect and acts on the basis of that intellect everything passes through that intellect. That intellect contains nothing which could give us a knowledge about the forces in the world. All of that lies outside the intellect. In people who have a lot of intellect, a force which comes from the spiritual world can pass through that intellect and then continue. Then they will be able to talk in a beautifully theoretical way about the spiritual world. But the intellect has no influence on the inner occult degree, the content of the soul. Thus the things which arise from theories can enter the soul also without passing through the intellect; they can thus be available to a person who is receptive to their source and can call up there what Capesius for example describes on the physical plane. That is shown where he expresses what this woman actually means to him who lives out there in solitude with Felix Balde, when he says that he likes to listen to her speaking and that she then speaks the most profound ancient wisdom. It is important that we should fully understand what Capesius is saying. On the physical plane there is a woman whom he likes to listen to, who says things with her mouth which are full of occult sources. She cannot put it in special words. But when they reach the ears of Capesius he can say the following:

> If I would tell the tale, then must I touch
> A thing that verily doth seem to me
> More wonderful than much that here I've heard,

In that it speaks more nearly to my soul.
But were I in some other place, these words
Would hardly pass the barrier of my lips;
Yet here they seem to flow therefrom with ease.
In my soul-life there often comes a time
When it doth feel itself pumped out and dry.
It seems as though the very fountain-head
Of knowledge had run dry within my heart.
Then can I find no word of any kind
Worthy to speak or worthy to be heard.

This can happen. There are people who, however much they might
know, feel as if things have come to an end.

And when I feel such spirit barrenness
I flee to these good people, and seek rest
In their reviving, peaceful solitude;

Now his own soul opens because that is where the gate into the occult
world is for him.

Then Mistress Felicia tells me many a tale
Set forth in wondrous pictures, manifold,
Of beings, dwelling in the land of dreams,
Who lead a joyous life in fairy realms.
When thus she speaks, her tone and speech recall
Some oft-told legend of the ancient days.
I ask no question whence she finds these words
But this one thing alone I clearly know:
That new life flows therefrom into my soul,
And sweeps away its dull paralysis.

The reality of that is seen on the physical plane by Johannes Thomasius,
who is present but who first has to look into the astral world in order to
be able to explain it to himself. Frau Balde in particular therefore
appears to him in the astral image whom he now sees as she is in her
shape in the physical world. And she gives the spirit of the elements one
of her fairy-tale pictures of which she has told hundreds to Capesius. But

now the interaction comes with what occurs below the threshold of consciousness.

She tells the fairy tales to Capesius. And when she has told one which she herself does not understand then the forces arise in his soul which banish his soul paralysis; then he is able to tell things to his listeners again. That then sounds quite different from what Frau Felicia has told. Secret forces are also at play in Capesius. If we follow them to their origins we find that they are in the astral world. There we can then see how they provoke counter-currents. And they produce the kind of echo as the words of Frau Felicia produce in the soul of Capesius everywhere where there are elemental forces. Something similar also exists with regard to our brain. A little spirit lives in our brain who might think up the most wonderful things. When we search for what he is like out of the macrocosm, we find the earth brain. This thinks the thoughts at quite a different magnitude from how they appear in the small human brain. In their own brain human beings do not always see what they are actually stating. But it appears grotesque when it is reflected in this giant earth brain. And it must also be reflected. Hence the relationship between German, who appears on the physical plane, and then as the spirit of the earth brain. That, too, is something about which we could speak at length. But if we would see with the astral gaze what occurs in the solitary house when Frau Felicia tells fairy tales and we then looked at the spirit of the earth brain, then we would see many a secret—for example how this spirit of the earth brain is an ironist, sometimes also a mocker. And he has to be inclined towards mockery because there is a lot to laugh about with regard to what human beings do.

It is artistically justified that at the moment where he is displaced he also appears in the role he so often has to play and shows himself in his true shape. There we see, after the scene in which Frau Balde has told one of her fairy tales before the spirit of the elements, an enormous effect on the spirit of the earth brain who translates the fairy tale into quite different words. Frau Balde tells:

A being once did live
Who flew from East to West, as runs the sun.
He flew o'er lands and seas, and from this height

He looked upon the doings of mankind.
He saw how men did one another love,
And, how in hatred they did persecute.
Yet naught could stay this being in his flight,
For love and hatred none the less bring forth
Full many thousand times the same results.
Yet o'er one house—there must the being stay;
For therein dwelt a tired and weary man,
Who pondered on the love of humankind,
And pondered also over human hate.
His contemplations had already graved
Deep furrows on his brow; his hair was white.
And, grieving o'er this man, the being lost
His sun-guide's leadership, and stayed with him
Within his room e'en when the sun went down.
And when the sun arose again, once more
The being joined the spirit of the sun;
And once again he saw mankind pass through
The cycle of the earth in love and hate.
But when he came, still following the sun,
A second time above that selfsame house,
His gaze did fall upon a dying man.

And the spirit of the earth brain reflects that back, in quite an unjustified way of course:

A man once lived, who went from East to West:
Whose eager thirst for knowledge lured him on
O'er land and sea; with learned pedantry
He looked upon the doings of mankind.
He saw how men did one another love,
And, how in hatred they did persecute;
And every day anon he fondly hoped
His wisdom's goal was now at length in sight.
But, though the world is ruled by love and hate,
Yet could he not combine them into law.
A thousand single cases wrote he down,

Yet still he lacked the comprehending eye.
This dull, dry seeker after truth once met
Upon his path a being formed of light;
Who found existence fraught with heaviness
Since it must live in constant combat with
A darksome being formed of shadows black.
'Who art thou then?' the dry truth-seeker asked.
'Love,' said the one; the other answered, 'Hate.'
But these two beings' words fell on deaf ears;
The man heard not, but wandered blindly on
In his dry search for truth from East to West.

These things are indeed experiences of the astral world. Johannes Thomasius has to pass through them to ascend to the spiritual world.

And for today I will just say briefly that a real connection with the spiritual world is necessary for Johannes Thomasius which has already begun to be spun in the physical world in order to ascend to the spiritual world itself. And that is what you will hear afterwards, the connection with the karma, encompassing incarnations, which is only revealed in Devachanic vision. But there the Devachanic elements truly have to be at play. That is why I ask you to observe that everything lives in the weft and life of the Devachanic ocean. Here we cannot simply give a description, we can only ever come close to an indication of some things. But if we want to give a real description we have to go further. Do not believe that you know something when you speak of higher worlds and cite the words: sentient soul, intellectual soul and consciousness soul as referring to Philia, Astrid and Luna. These three figures are not in any way personifications of those three components of the soul or symbols of them. If you listen attentively to the vowels with which these three figures describe their own occupation, and if you listen out for what lives in the vowels, you can follow how in the sequence of the individual vowels, the individual words the thing is given which can clarify for us in quite a different way what is sentient soul, intellectual soul and consciousness soul. And if you remove something it is no longer the whole thing. That is why it is important to listen to the words in order to obtain an idea of the Devachanic element in the consciousness soul when, for example, Luna says:

> Soul substance will I warm,
> Life's ether harden too.
> That they may thus condense
> And may thus feel themselves
> As living in themselves
> And powerful to create,
> Dear sister, that thou may'st
> Prove wisdom's certainty
> To mankind's seeking soul.

The movement of the words contains in the description of Devachan something which otherwise cannot be expressed in any other way. We also have to pay attention to that. Because we are faced with the necessity when we speak of higher worlds to say it in many different ways. And what I could never say theoretically about the sentient soul, intellectual soul and consciousness soul, that you can hear, if you are willing to understand it, from what is contained in the characteristics of the three figures Philia, Astrid, Luna. But you will well understand that these three are not symbols or allegories for the sentient soul, intellectual soul and consciousness soul. If you ask yourselves, what are these three, the answer is: they are human beings who live there, Philia, Astrid and Luna human beings. That always has to be remembered.

How karma ultimately intertwines and how we can see as an image what Johannes Thomasius experiences as microcosm in the human soul, that we were able to show in the Munich performance in the whole of the final scene. The individual persons stood in their corresponding places in the way that karma works. Someone who was closer to a particular person was placed accordingly. If you imagine that as being reflected into the soul of Johannes Thomasius, then you will approximately have what is contained in this seventh scene, something it is very difficult to speak about.

There follows the recitation of the seventh scene by Marie von Sivers (Marie Steiner), introduced and concluded by the music of Adolf Arenson.

LECTURE 9

WHEN we look back on human development, initially as far back as history allows us, we encounter something very peculiar. We can test what we encounter there in a great variety of phenomena. Above all—and we will still see today how basically what I will say now applies to every human heart, to every human soul—we can test this human development against the various documents, traditions and writings that have been preserved. When we go back to the ideas that the individual peoples of antiquity had about the origin of the world, about the relationship of human beings to the world, about the sources of morality and goodness, we find that these ideas were laid down in sagas, in myths, in legends in a more or less beautiful, magnificent, mighty or maybe also less significant form among the various peoples on earth.

People today are very much inclined to treat these myths, sagas and legends as poetic writings and to say: peoples thought up these things in their childhood ages because they did not yet have the sources of today's sciences. They had all kinds of ideas how the world arose, the Greeks through their gods, the old Germanic tribes through their gods, and indeed as set out by the American peoples whose sagas have only become available to us in recent times and which coincide with what we find in those of other peoples. When we hear how Quetzalcoatl and Huitzilopochtli played a role among the central American peoples similarly, if more primitively, to other mighty, developed figures of other peoples, we can see that there are sagas and myths among all such peoples. And as I already mentioned, modern people are easily inclined to say: those are poetic writings, fantastical creations of the human spirit which wanted in this way to explain for itself how the various beings in the world, the various natural phenomena came about.

Among these various documents we now find a great one which a large number of you examined with me only a short while ago:[85] a great document, Genesis, the start of the Old Testament. And we saw in Munich the infinite depths which lie in Genesis. Some of you have also already heard the words out of spiritual knowledge about the different Gospels,[86] the last documents of this kind. We find such documents preserved which originated in various ages which we passed through in our previous incarnations, in which we participated in earlier lives on earth. Anyone making progress in spiritual knowledge must learn to understand that they were present in ages in which people spoke of, say, Zeus and Hera, Chronos and other gods, and spoke about natural phenomena in another way from today, in such a form as is contained in myths, sagas and fairy tales. All these things we have to consider. And we have to ask ourselves: how actually has that affected our souls which have taken in such things and which now—for most people, in a sense, without them knowing what filled them in those times—emerge again in our souls?

Now, let me describe to you quite simply how these documents affect anyone who begins by taking them as sagas, myths and poetic works but who then goes deeper into spiritual science and uses the latter as an instrument in order to understand these documents to an ever greater extent.

With the Old Testament for example, which most people today might read as a nice compendium of all kinds of images about the creation of the world, it will happen to them that they will gradually say to themselves: these things, which are reproduced there in such a remarkable way, contain an infinite wisdom. And they will increasingly realize that the individual words and phrases and sentences contain things to which, if we understand them properly, spiritual science quite naturally leads us today. There is perhaps no means more effective for letting our appreciation of such documents grow than to penetrate to a certain extent into spiritual science. For the most subtle discoveries which can be made in the field of spiritual science, the most powerful things which can be rediscovered with a great deal of effort through spiritual science, we discover afterwards in some biblical saying, let us say in Genesis.

But now a certain difference is revealed between the Old Testament and all other sagas and myths and documents. That is something we should remember. Take the sagas of the Greeks, the ancient Germanic tribes, even what is contained in the Vedas of the Indians, what is contained in the Persian documents, take everything of this kind. There is one huge difference in comparison to the Old Testament. This difference presents itself to the unbiased reviewer such that they find in all the other documents the riddles of natural phenomena, the riddles of everything which relates to natural phenomena—including human beings to the extent that they have a kind of natural existence, to the extent that the forces of nature push human beings in various directions—represented in a mythical way; but only in the Old Testament do they see the human being from the beginning as a moral soul being.

What science today has to say about these things rests on very shaky ground. It all collapses into nothingness if we look at these things in a way which is truly appropriate for the spirit. There is thus a fundamental difference so that we can say: everything else that we have by way of documents in the world reveals to us that human beings had mighty revelations from various sides, mighty revelations which were expressed in a mythical form and which were created on the basis of a profound wisdom, but which do not relate to the moral soul mysteries of the human being. That, then, is clear under all circumstances.

Now another difference presents itself if we compare the New Testament with all other documents of this kind. Here a completely different spirit rules from all other documents, including the Old Testament. How might we understand this difference if we approach the matter from an anthroposophical perspective? This difference will become clear to us if we first place another phenomenon before our soul.

Imagine a person who has never heard of spiritual science and who is a product of the scientific or any of the other sorts of so-called reasonable education of the present, who therefore does not have the opportunity to penetrate the old documents with spiritual science. We can imagine him to be a scholar, not a scholar at all—it doesn't really make a great difference—we imagine him as having no connection with spiritual science and assume that he then approaches these old documents, the Greek, Persian, Indian, Germanic documents and so on, he approaches these things with everything that modern thinking can give him. If he then really experiences not the slightest whiff of what is spiritual science, a peculiar phenomenon occurs. There will be a difference, depending on whether he is more poetically or soberly inclined, but on the whole we may say a phenomenon occurs. Such a person can in reality never understand the old documents any longer today; he cannot penetrate the way that wisdom is presented there. We can experience the most grotesque examples in this field. We need only refer to the most recent attempts to explain such ancient documents. Just at present there has been another booklet, which is actually of interest because it is so ridiculous, which makes a comprehensive attempt to explain all myths up to and including the Gospels starting with the first documents of the most primitive peoples. It is a booklet which is exceptionally interesting precisely because of the grotesque way, indeed its grotesquely stupid way, of grasping these things. The booklet is called *Orpheus*. It is by Salomon Reinach[87] who is famous in France as a researcher in this field.

Particularly among scholars he is an indicative example of a man who has not felt the slightest whiff of the way by which one can penetrate these things. A specific method is used for everything and it is all decreed away. All things are merely symbolic. No real beings stand behind Hermes, Orpheus and others. These figures are only symbols and allegories. It is not becoming to repeat among reasonable people what is given as an interpretation of these symbols; it is expressed in such a way that one does not really want to repeat it. In this way everything that is reality in the myths is proved out of existence and thus the reality of Demeter and Persephone is decreed away, is proved out of existence. All these names simply existed as symbols. This is done by a method by which one could easily prove to children after 80 years that a man called Salomon Reinach could not have lived in France at the start of the twentieth century, but that contemporary culture had encapsulated under the name Salomon Reinach what is presented in his book. That could be proved perfectly. Yet such things provoke a lot of attention nowadays. And by the same method evidence is now also put forward in Germany that Jesus never lived,[88] something which also caused a sensation recently.

We now ask ourselves: what is the real reason that we cannot penetrate these things today without spiritual science—and it is a fact that one cannot penetrate them without it—what is the reason? If we want to understand this reason, we have to look a little deeper into human development. We have to look some way back into human development. Then we see that we have to tell ourselves: the kind of sciences which people have today, the kind of sciences which are taught at the most basic level in schools about the sun and other things were not possessed by the ancients. The kind of sciences which are understood by the intellect, by reason. That is something towards which humanity had to progress. And our souls, when they were born in earlier incarnations, were quite certainly unable to take in such sciences because that did not exist, that was not incorporated into the culture.

But the further we go back in development, the more we find—no matter where we look for the reasons, which I have frequently set out for many of you—that human beings had a wisdom in quite a different form from today, a wisdom about spiritual things which people of today are not capable of expressing in their scientific form. But wisdom ruled the souls, lived in the souls. It was simply there. The initiated leaders of humanity above all had this wisdom, and it can be historically shown, if we have anthroposophical spirit, that an archetypal revelation, an archetypal wisdom was spread across humanity which came to expression in various ways depending on the stage of development here or there. If someone observes history in a truly anthroposophical spirit, they will find this archetypal revelation. Something else is, however, required. The ordinary current scientific human spirit must, if it wishes to penetrate to the true meaning of these documents, additionally undergo preparation—I am simply telling a fact now—a preparation which enables it to penetrate into the spirit of those old writings. This consists of studying the documents which can be directly studied today. These are the Gospels, these are the epistles of Paul. What is described there can directly bring us close to the archetypal revelation in the ancient documents so that we can understand it. That is a curious fact. But if a spiritual researcher in accordance with the prejudices of today had a certain dislike of approaching the Gospels—he might say it is only one religion among many—then it would show itself that he could not come to an understanding of the other documents either. There would always be a last final bit which would remain incomprehensible. But if he were to approach any phenomenon of the events in Palestine, and be it only in spirit, if he let himself be inspired by them, as it were, then a beam of enlightenment can in fact spread from the Gospels over the other documents. That is a fact and it can be experienced.

And then we will probably be willing to admit that these Gospels and these epistles of Paul are actually necessary for going back correctly into earlier periods. They cannot be ignored. If only we can truly read the spiritual documents, the Akasha Chronicle, it is not even necessary to go to the written Gospels—but we do have to go via the events in Palestine. Otherwise certain things with regard to what has gone before will always remain unclear. So I did not want to refer positively to the written word, but to the events and how they presented themselves to us in reality in human development. That is a very, very important fact.

I would like to throw a little light on this fact from another direction still. Let us remember what I said: we cannot jump over the Christ event if we want to understand what has been given as an archetypal revelation of humanity otherwise we will stumble and fall. If I want to describe how the matter actually presents itself, I have to say the following. Let us assume today's spiritual researcher investigates the past and he has no sense—the sense is the important thing—of the Christ event; he passes by the Christ event and approaches the other, earlier events in their development. He will find everywhere, truly everywhere that he becomes insecure. But let us assume we had such a spiritual researcher who was born and lived before the Christ event and who had progressed very far in respect of his clairvoyance and was very advanced also in other respects, who in a certain sense was prepared enough before the Christian period to have an overview of all of the past in such a way that at that time he could already have passed through the Christ event because he was ahead of his time. Let us assume that he lived five or six centuries before Christ and was prepared enough to go back via Christ to the earlier events like a spiritual researcher today, then we could literally ask ourselves: what would such a spiritual researcher have to be like in order not to fall prey to the luciferic or ahrimanic powers?

Let us assume such a person actually needed to go via the Christ event but this Christ event had not yet happened when he lived. Then it would turn out for such a person that he would either be content with a light heart with what arose, what he could see—then he would say all kinds of things which were not quite right—or alternatively he would reach the point where he said to himself: something is missing, I cannot find something when I turn my gaze backwards which I need for my path. And he would further admit to himself: here I become insecure. I must search for something that I need but it is not yet here on earth; it cannot be found in earth development.

I have painted for you, theoretically as it were, a personality of the fifth, sixth century before Christ which would have been prepared enough to find Jesus Christ in looking into the past. But because the latter was not yet on earth that person could not find him as an earthly fact. This theory became quite a reality for me a short time ago.[89] It was when I was able to visit our branch in Palermo this year. As I travelled on the ship towards Palermo it suddenly became clear to me: a riddle will resolve itself for you which can only easily be resolved through the direct impression here in this place. And it did indeed very soon resolve itself. The personality about which I spoke to you just now in theoretical terms immediately presented itself to me in the whole atmosphere of Sicily—I might say in the whole astral body of Sicily. It was very alive. A personality continued to live as it were in the whole atmosphere of Sicily who often appears as something of a riddle. It is the personality of Empedocles.[90] This ancient Greek philosopher lived in Sicily in the fifth century before Christ. He was, as external historians also know, a person who was deeply initiated in a great variety of things and performed magnificent things particularly in Sicily.

If we begin by looking at him spiritually, this personality presents itself in a curious way. In looking back at the development of Empedocles, following him in what he did as a statesman, architect and philosopher, how he travelled about, how he had his enthusiastic pupils, how he initiated them into the various secrets of the world, if we follow him spiritually in this way, then we discover that this was a personality who knew an incredible amount of what people today possess by way of scientific knowledge. This personality had a very modern spirit, a modern aura. Empedocles had indeed advanced so far that he asked about the origin of the world. And he would truly also have been so advanced that, after the way things turned out, he would have found Christ when he looked back. But Christ had not been there yet, he could not yet be found on earth, he was still missing on earth. These experiences caused Empedocles to waver[91] which in turn produced a particular kind of longing in him and this longing transformed itself in him—in quite a different way from the superficial people of today—into a passion to look at the world materialistically. Lucifer approached him. We just have to imagine in a living way how that happened. He was a modern spirit initiated into a great variety of mysteries, clair-voyant to a high degree. Through his modern thinking he was inclined to look at the world materialistically and there is also a kind of materialistic system from him in which he represents the world approximately in the way that today's materialistic chemists do through combining and separating the elements. Only he distinguishes just between the four elements. Depending on how they are mixed, he thought, the various beings are formed. This view produced in him a great passion to find out what was behind these material elements, what was in the air and in the water.

When we look back today through the Akasha Chronicle and look into air and water and fire and earth, we find Christ etherically in them. Empedocles was not able to find him. For him an immense urge arose to find something in air and water and fire and earth, to get behind what was in them. And we see this personality as he was gripped by this mighty urge to penetrate into what are the material elements. And that indeed leads him eventually to make a kind of sacrifice. Because it is not just a myth: he did throw himself into Etna to unite himself with the elements. The luciferic force, the urge to deal with the elements, drove him to combine himself with the elements in this way. This death of Empedocles continues to live in the spiritual atmosphere of Sicily. That is a great secret of this remarkable country.

And now consider this soul of Empedocles who shed his body in this way by burning it. It is reborn in a later period after Christ has already been there. Then it is a completely different situation for this soul. Previously it sacrificed itself to the elements, we might say, then it arises anew but in now looking back it sees Christ. And all elemental knowledge is created anew. What this soul knew is created in a completely new form. The personality of Empedocles was indeed reborn at a later time, only I cannot say at this time under which name.[92] But if we compare the later reincarnation of Empedocles which happened more in the north, if we compare this figure as it lived subsequently at the turn of the middle to the modern age with the Empedocles who threw himself in Etna, then we have a living picture of the giant impulse which arrived because the Christ event happened on earth in between.

But what happens in this way in one personality also happens for every soul. Also for your souls. Even if all these souls did not feel the mighty urge which Empedocles felt, they did look back into the past with a certain discomfort in the period which led up to the Christ event because it was not familiar to them, because the time was increasingly approaching in which the old knowledge disappeared. If we go back to earlier times, we will find that those who preserved the traditions of ancient knowledge stepped before the people; they told—let us put this before our souls—stories which if you like are contained in the Greek sagas, which were told to the ancient Greeks. But that was only a cause that the ancient Greeks when they, let us say, were in a special state— which at the time occurred to a greater degree than now—felt the truth of these sagas and that these sagas gave them a jolt to look into the spiritual world. But this inclination faded among people.

It came about that the inner force to look up into the spiritual world was lost to the degree that intellectual science approached. You can calculate, you can read in every little handbook the small extent to which our views, which today every child absorbs if not with the breast milk then with the school milk, go back. They go back to a few hundred years before the start of the Christian era. That is when there is a mighty caesura. If people want to go further back and understand the ancient documents they can no longer do so; they now appear to them as poetic works, as sagas and myths. That is something which we should indeed look at more closely. There will increasingly be people who without having inherited some aptitude to understand the ancient documents will fail to understand them. We will come to the view that behind everything that is considered to be science a wide field of mis-apprehension is spreading because most educated people are of the opinion that we now happily know how the earth moves and that what people in earlier times said about it was simply nonsense. It has already happened; we only go as far back as the view of Copernicus with regard to the movement of the earth. That is a somewhat late example. But even in geometry people only go back as far as Euclid. Before this time modern people see only black obscurity in this field. Thus modern people cannot find the wisdom, the archetypal revelation; they cannot find the way to penetrate it.

If we now really accept this as a fact, then something—and this can happen in even the most ordinary mind through a healthy sentience—then something can consolidate into a basic conviction which results from the highest anthroposophical studies. Human beings still have to reach the point at which they say: this is not the true form in which I see the world. If this were the true form, then they would not really need to undertake any research. Then no research would be necessary, then the world would have to appear as it is; but modern research does not accept it in *this* form either. There would be no Copernicanism if we accepted what the senses offer in its raw form. Here external science also questions sensory experience. If we go further, we can see that we cannot stop at what the senses provide, what the external experience of the physical world provides. That has to be corrected under all circumstances by human beings and also by external science. People might not normally admit that but it is nevertheless true. As soon as we understand ourselves—even just as ordinary thinkers with what we learn today—we have to say to ourselves: the purpose of everything is to look beyond sensory illusion otherwise there would be no science, there would be no thinking. But if this is the case, then there is actually something which allows us to understand quite easily in which direction the world is gradually developing. If we look at the matter a little in an anthroposophical light, then this will be affirmed. So if we tell ourselves that there was an archetypal wisdom, human beings were such that an archetypal wisdom was given to them which maybe they only saw in pictures but there was such an archetypal wisdom, but then with the development of humanity the understanding of that was increasingly lost, people understood this archetypal wisdom less and less—then in turn it is very clear: they understood it less to the extent that science, that the intellect and reason developed.

Now we can ask: what will have happened by a particular time? Let us imagine something, let us imagine a pre-Christian person who lived under certain conditions. He or she will have directed their gaze out into the world, will have seen many different things; but in addition the soul of this person contained the possibility of looking behind these things. This facility still existed. So for him or her was a fact that behind each flower there is an etheric body. That was fact for them. But this facility was gradually lost. It was lost because the intellect, reason as they are widespread today banished this facility. The two facilities cannot be combined; they are two opposing forces. It is simply the case—that is the common experience of all real spiritual researchers—that the reason, thinking in the normal sense, has a singeing, incinerating effect on what is an initiated view of things. So that the science of ancient spiritual vision, and thus an understanding of the ancient traditions, was lost in history to the extent that the intellect and reason in the ordinary sense made their appearance. Thus a number of centuries had to pass and the person whom I have just described had to be replaced by another one who might say to himself or herself: it would of course be a terrible preconception if one were to believe that truth was as it is represented through the senses in the world; it has to be supplemented in all cases by human reason. The belief in human reason was decisive. It has to start by dissecting things as they are; it has to tear into sensory appearances and understand them logically.

Such a person might perhaps have said: that is the advantage of human beings over other creatures of the earth, that they have reason, that they can understand cause and effect as they lie behind sensory things. They can explain these things, they can communicate from one person to another because they have language. Because that was soon recognized, that language is the daughter of reason. And such a person might say: the highest thing is, of course, reason. And if we want to obtain a proper picture of that person, we have to imagine someone who says: so, human being, trust only your reason, dissect everything with your reason, then you will come to the truth. Let us assume that such a person had come. I have described someone like that in theoretical terms but there was indeed such a person. One figure of this kind was Cicero[93] who lived a short time before Christ. You only need to look at him to see that he thinks precisely in this way, namely that reason can understand everything. It is not true that the world is such as it presents itself to the senses; but reason can understand everything. And specifically among the people who appeared shortly before Christ there is an invincible belief in reason. They call reason the God himself who resides in things. That is what Cicero does.

But let us assume for a moment that someone gets behind the secrets of this whole thing. Let us assume someone watches the whole thing in an unbiased way, the way that everything develops gradually. How would they describe this time? Let us assume that someone with a deep insight would watch this whole thing a century before Christ. How would the whole story present itself to them? Well, they would say: here we see two streams in humanity. The one of them is failing: the old clairvoyant power. In its place reason appears. It exterminates and eliminates the possibility in human beings to look into the spiritual world. A profound darkness will spread in respect of the spiritual world. Those who believe in the authority of reason might be of the opinion that they can look behind things with their reason. These people have completely forgotten what the reason is of which they speak. After all, such reason is merely tied to the brain; it cannot make use of any other instrument than the brain. It thus belongs to the physical world; it therefore has to share the characteristics of the physical world. Such a personality would therefore say: insist as much as you like on your reason and say that by means of it you can understand what lies behind things because these things are not true in themselves, but remember that this reason itself belongs to these things. You are physical beings like the others, your reason belongs to the physical world. And if you believe that this reason is the one thing through which you can get behind everything else, you are pulling the rug from under your own feet.

That is what such a personality would have said. And they would have continued: certainly, human beings are inclined to make more and more use of reason, to insist more and more on reason. But in doing so they are building a wall in front of the spiritual world because they are using an instrument which cannot be applied to the spiritual world, which is locked into the physical world. And yet humanity is developing precisely towards cultivating this instrument. And this personality might have added if they had been fully aware of the course of events: if human beings return to the spiritual world at all, then the possibility has to be given that they do not just want to make use of their reason, this tool which only works in the physical world, but that they receive a stimulus which enables them to ascend again—a stimulus which drives reason itself up into the spiritual worlds. But that cannot happen unless something dies in human beings which establishes in them the firm belief in the sole rule of reason. That has to die.

We therefore have to imagine human beings as descending further and further into the material world, developing the brain more and more. If people became so dependent on their reason, they could no longer escape from it. Because then their physical body would make them believe: let us do away with everything which our earth reason cannot grasp. But this is the physical body which, by developing itself in a subtle way, anaesthetizes human beings so that they cannot understand that as a result they stay in the physical world. If you envision that, you will understand that human beings are actually caught in a kind of trap in this respect. It is not possible for them to get out of themselves. Current human development has brought human beings to the point at which they cannot get out of themselves, at which they run the risk of being gradually completely overwhelmed by their physical corporeality. Is there anything that can help human beings in this situation? If the possibility arises in this period, in which reason has arrived at this point, that reason can be altered so that the part of it can die which blinds it, then it has to die. But there has to be an impulse through which those things which could overwhelm human beings in their sole belief in reason is overcome once and for all. Feel the power of this impulse, feel that this was the meaning of human development. Corporeality has developed in such a way that it would have overwhelmed human beings; and human beings would have reached the point at which they believed that they would have to remain within the physical world and yet could get behind Maya—not considering that they are Maya themselves with their reason—if something had not come which helped them to emerge as soon as they accepted it and which could counter falling prey to the physical, something which truly works down as far as the etheric body so that the latter has the possibility of killing what leads to such an error. Otherwise human beings would have remained in the trap of their overwhelming corporeality.

And now let us leave the person who might have spoken like that at the approach of Jesus Christ. Now let us see how a contemporary person might look at the matter, one of us. They can say: if I look in an impartial way at how human beings have developed, how reason has grown stronger and stronger, at this instrument which is part of Maya, I am definitely in error if I just abandon myself to the progression of world development. If I fail to take up the impulse that the part can die away which lures me into such a course, then that progression is of such a nature that I cannot escape from reason. What should have happened? I have to be able to look back to the time in which this impulse entered. I must find something that points to an event in the historical development of humanity which indicates that the continuous course of development in a materialist sense has been turned inside out. If I looked inside me today and if I found something like that, what else would I have to find there? I would see reason extend further and further to a point at the start of the Christian period, where it just begins to take effect. But further back? There things turn dark, there things turn black, there I need something completely different. But then it grows lighter because there I have to encounter Christ. Everyone, if they wish to believe in the possibility at all that they make progress, that in the following incarnations something can be in them that drives them upwards, which prevents them from being overwhelmed by Maya, everyone in looking back must encounter Christ. That can provide the ascent for them.

Let us assume the Gospels did not exist, then we can say: we do not need them as anthroposophists, we do not need any Gospels; we only need to look at the course of human development in an unbiased way and to ask ourselves what would become of each human being if they could not look back to an event in which the whole meaning of previous development is turned upside down. Then we have to encounter Christ if we go back in development. The anthroposophist has to be able to find him and the initiate will find him under all circumstances.

That is a secret of Christianity. The documents can be challenged, certainly, and they are not historical documents. All the clever people, Jensen[94] and others, who decree the Gospels away in a trivially scholarly way, look at them as mere myths, do have a certain point because they only refer to external reason. But at the moment in which we are anthroposophists we can say: we do not need any Gospels, we only need the facts which spiritual science gives us itself and in going back through human development we will find the living Christ as Paul found him through the event at Damascus. That anticipates what we also can have if we seek Christ in an anthroposophical sense. For, after all, Paul was in a similar situation to a modern anthroposophist who does not want to recognize the Gospels. The Gospels did not yet exist in his time but he was able to go to Jerusalem. What he heard there, what is later described in the Gospels, did not convince him otherwise he would not have left Jerusalem. So a modern person today does not need to be convinced either by what they say. He or she only needs to be in a position to experience something through anthroposophy similar to what Paul experienced. Then we have an event at Damascus, then that person has proof of Christ completely without any documents as was the case with Paul.

Now it is quite natural that we refer with these things to something profound in human development, to something extraordinarily profound in human development. In a certain sense what existed for the reincarnated Empedocles in the fifteenth, sixteenth century, who looked back into earlier ages and then saw what he was not able to see previously, is the case for everybody, even the simplest person. Previously Empedocles had become so insecure that he threw himself into Etna. In the fifteenth, sixteenth century he looked back and what the first time could not be explained through anything was now explained through the Christ principle. And that made him one of the most remarkable personalities of the subsequent time.

In this way the matter presents itself for every human being without documents simply through going back. Later on all people will look back to earlier incarnations and will be able to distinguish precisely: those are incarnations which lie before, and those are incarnations which lie after Christ. And what the simplest soul feels instinctively today when it reads the Gospels will then appear in the form of knowledge. That is the difference between the Gospels and other documents, that they are the closest documents which have to be understood. That is a great, beautiful, mighty gateway, the Gospels. If we pass through that gateway it becomes light, whereas otherwise darkness spreads.

It is indeed so. It can happen to modern people occasionally, because Christianity is only at the start of its development, that the research path peters out with regard to earlier things. But if they return to a phenomenon in the life of Christ then they are inspired and it becomes light. And what the spiritual researcher finds can also be found by the simplest people. They can experience a reflection in their mind of what I have just explained. They can be thoroughly depressed through human weaknesses and errors but they have of course to tell themselves: what I am today I have become through all the generations. Because if they were to deny that then they would be claiming to be their own father and mother. It is therefore something which leads back to the whole of humanity and human beings can feel thoroughly depressed by all kinds of errors, illnesses, weaknesses which they have. But there is always the possibility to elevate ourselves, even for the simplest mind. I do not say that in an orthodox sense. What exists for the spiritual researcher also exists for the simplest mind. If it feels thoroughly weak, picks up the Gospels and reads them, then strength will flow out of the Gospels because out of them flows the power of the word which goes into the etheric body. The Gospels are powerful words. They are something which addresses not only the reason but goes into deeper layers of the soul, which not only builds on the reason which is found in Maya but which goes into more profound forces and can comfort reason about itself as it were. That is a great strength of the Gospels which is there for everyone and that is the mighty thing in these documents. That is what distinguishes them from everything else. These things can also be denied, but then the possibility of making progress of human beings as a whole is denied.

This refers to a fact which is not easy to understand just like that.

Thus you can also understand what was necessary to prepare the person whom I began by placing hypothetically before your soul, who about a century before the Christian era predicted: one had to come who gives the impulse which will bring about the turnaround.

This had to be a significant personality who was also properly prepared. In the circles of those with the knowledge, the attempt was made for a long time to bring about the possibility that at least some would understand the approaching time, understand what was being prepared: what on the one hand guides people into the trap and what on the other hand guides people to ascend through the appearance of Christ. That was taught prophetically. And the person who a little over a century before the Christian era was chosen to teach this prophetically in circles which could understand it, was an initiate from the Essene community which was close to the circles which Christ joined, and he proclaimed: he would come who would lead humanity to ascend again. The person who taught this within the Essene community was a very significant individuality. External history actually knows little about him but tales are handed down about him at least by some writers so that he is not just a mythological figure or is only named in spiritual science. He lived a hundred years before Christ and also had records made by one of his five or six pupils. One of the pupils of this personality, who spoke about Christ and proclaimed his coming, knew what this was about. This personality had a pupil who was called Mathai[95] who recorded the secrets about Christ. But the personality was Jeshu ben Pandira. Because he taught those things, he also had to go through the corresponding martyrdom. He was stoned in his region and after stoning—when he was dead—was hanged.

This Jeshu ben Pandira[96]—he must not be confused with Jesus of Nazareth—who was the great proclaimer of Christ, had recorded what he knew and this document then came into the hands of the person who inserted it with its secrets into the Gospel which we call the Gospel of Matthew. This is an important, an exceptionally important fact which must be understood: firstly the necessity of the Christ impulse; then, in spiritually scientific historical terms, how Jeshu ben Pandira in a certain sense even pre-empted as an image—in that he was first stoned and then was quasi crucified immediately afterwards—what then takes place as the Christ mystery of Golgotha. After all, Christ was not stoned but crucified. And in this death a wonderful thing occurs. At the moment in which the blood flowed from the wounds the thing was transferred into the earth's atmosphere which for those who, looking back on it, take this event into their etheric body, who pass through this event, who look into Christ's tomb as it were, then means that they enter a past filled with light as they pass through this point. In contrast, without this event darkness will spread over everything that lay before.

Reflect on what has been said today. It was my task to indicate it to you. It is such a large subject that only indications could be given. But I have kept these indications such that, if you examine what you know and carry it in your heart, you will learn the extent to which, through life and through our own soul, it is proved to be true regarding what I was held to talk to you today.

Lecture 10

Leipzig, 21 November 1910

During their beautiful association in friendship, which was of such significance for modern intellectual life, Goethe and Schiller exchanged works on which they were working and when Schiller received from Goethe parts of *Wilhelm Meister* he wrote to Goethe,[97] overwhelmed by the impression of the chapter he had just received: 'Of this we can be sure, the poet is the only true human being and the best philosopher is merely a caricature in comparison.'

At the time that might have sounded peculiar but for us today that is no longer the case. We put ourselves in Schiller's soul and are enlightened about the truth of his words when we measure them against the significant letter[98] which Schiller wrote to Goethe shortly after their friendship had begun. Both had discussed nature and their view of the world in their wide-ranging discussions. Schiller now brings to expression in the letter I have just referred to[99] how Goethe does not obtain his views by speculative means but seeks the necessity in the totality of the phenomena of the world. Everything was contained in Goethe's intuition and he had little cause to borrow from philosophy which, however, had a lot to learn from him.

Schiller therefore sees something in Goethe's way of looking at the world, in his inner attitude out of which he created his works, which introduces human beings to the secrets of existence in a particularly profound way. If we examine what takes place between Goethe and Schiller by way of thoughts and opinions we can see how Schiller blossoms in Goethe's imagination, in the inner truth of Goethe's imagination. Schiller at the time wrote his series of letters *On the Aesthetic Education of Man* in which he set out how people through their development can become full human beings, something which exists in potential in each person as their higher human being. Schiller found something in Goethe's radiating imagination which turns people into full human beings, he saw in it a way of living one's way to the thing which can enable a person truly to affiliate with the archetypal foundation of things.

When we hear great intellects talk about imagination in this way it is a different matter from the way that imagination is talked about today. Now, when it is contrasted with objective observation, it is as if the imagination is something arbitrary which caused people to combine things in an arbitrary way. [Gap in shorthand note.]

If we remember that Goethe might be described as an expert in his research into nature, the following words[100] are doubly relevant. Human beings strive to discover the secrets of nature and long for its worthy interpreter, art. Art and beauty are manifestations of secret laws of nature which without them could never be fathomed. When the imagination mixes the way of thinking which only arises from feelings and impulses with other gains of the human soul, we have to admit that it sometimes leads away from truth. It is not appropriate for science and research. But as the precursor of a higher cognitive ability it points the way to hidden connections between things which one would not see without it. But for certain fields of life it is an absolute necessity that what is combined by the imagination is shown to be true through research in strict external proof.

Accordingly Goethe's words or Schiller's position appear to make it necessary that we determine in Goethe how he sees something in the imagination which offers truth in its content in contrast to an arbitrary, random play which we can describe as the fantastical play of the imagination. If we try to fathom the laws of nature scientifically our observations force us to make a judgement. That is not the case with the imagination. Certain ideas or thoughts must be connected by inner necessity if they are to be justified as truth. Something has to be there which guides them in a particular direction inwardly from one thought to the next.

If we hear great intellects speak about such truths, we may certainly be permitted to measure their findings against the methods which are used by spiritual research and which lead to the truths which have often been discussed. These methods are the so-called clairvoyant ones which enable information about the facts and beings of the spiritual world. In presenting them, we will also touch on the lower forms of clairvoyance,[101] but briefly at most, because they can never lead to real goals. In contrast we will make the methods and significance of higher clairvoyance obtained through appropriate training the subject of our reflections.

Some who only know low-level clairvoyance, which may occur as somnambulism, consider it to be an illness. There are states in which the person has filled their soul life with images from other worlds. It is a kind of sleep, perhaps of such a minor degree that the layperson considers it as being fully awake. When such a 'clairvoyant' perceives images in a sleeplike state they can sometimes offer astonishing and peculiar things. They can be of a prophetic nature. Such a person can say things about illnesses before they have occurred or, what appears even more astonishing to the layperson, they know precisely to indicate what will remedy them. In such states the person concerned has a different world before them. Anyone who denies this has not done the research. But what is obtained through such low-level clairvoyance is not the subject of our reflections today but what is obtained by way of trained clairvoyance.

Clairvoyants starting out take each step consciously with strict control of themselves. The only question is this: how should we think of the development of such clairvoyants? If we want to define this in its essence, we can quite justifiably compare it with the means of external research. In science the researcher investigates the secrets of nature with the help of instruments. Trained clairvoyants also work with an instrument—it is indeed a very complicated instrument—without which they could not research anything. Their instrument is simply themselves—not in their everyday state but only once they have transformed their cognitive ability into a different soul constellation through spiritual-scientific methods and have created new organs, that is, when they can say things out of their own experience. It cannot be the case that the external senses are the end of all knowledge. Each new organ opens up new content in the environment. Hidden worlds can be around us. For the trained clairvoyant the otherwise hidden world becomes just as real as the external one. Just as for the blind person after an operation, a whole world streams towards the clairvoyant which is his or her experience.

We must not think that this can be achieved by external means. I can of course only give an indication of how it happens. I hope at a later time to be able to tell you more[102] about the way that such research is undertaken. People will be able to observe most truthfully when they take in what the sensory world tells them without being influenced by subjective effects. It is a matter of people giving nature the opportunity to express itself. The less subjective combination is involved the better. Human beings cannot avoid thinking about the external world from which they obtain their observations but it is certainly not the case that all their concepts, ideas and thinking flow into them from the external world. The essential things they nevertheless obtain from their interior. That can be seen, for example in the way that modern thinking came to conceive of the structure of the star system. Copernicus[103] and Galileo[104] saw the same thing which the eye could see since time immemorial. But the laws were only established by them. Copernicus added new things to the old observational material and thus did the vital work. The same applies to orthodox Darwinism. Similar things were observed before Darwin and Haeckel but they approached these things in a new frame of mind. We have to be clear that concepts and ideas are not what streams into us from outside but we have to produce them themselves. If you sail out into the ocean where you cannot see any land the sky appears to rest on the surface of the sea in a circular form. You will only understand why this is so if you can construct in your thinking the circle around the point in the middle. In this way you can obtain an understanding of all laws and then reality has to fit with that. Kepler[105] would never have been able to discover the trajectory of the planets if previously elliptical trajectories had not appeared in his spirit.

In this way we carry our ideas to the external things which tell us: we will fulfil what you have thought. And in this way you obtain an insight that the same thing which lives in your soul underlies this external sensory world as its laws. Now think for a moment that a person tries to focus on a thought which has been constructed in their own soul. If that person manages to abstain from all external observation and direct all their internal attention to the thought, a soul process takes place which is described as concentration. The human soul first has to keep to something which lives in the soul and focus on that with all its strength. Now it is of course not sufficient to do that once; it has to be repeated frequently. It is not effective to focus on images in the thinking which come from outside.

Now there is experience in this field, advice is available as to which type of concentration is best for developing the soul forces. There are certain core propositions. We do not need to be convinced of their reality from the beginning. The greater the lack of preconceptions the better. One instruction says for example: fill your soul with a certain content, focus completely on this soul content. You do not need to believe in it but must allow it to work in you, concentrate on it and you will find that you achieve an effect in your soul through the content. It may be that external truth does not apply to the proposition. That is neither here nor there. The important thing is the force which acts in the soul. You will see that experiences will set in with constant repetition.

Symbolic images are particularly effective. I would like to recall one in particular: the profoundly significant symbol of the black cross with the roses.[106] Here the aim is to place the abstract meaning of the rose cross before our soul, Goethe's 'dying and becoming',[107] namely the requirement that in developing our soul we have to ascend above the things of the sensory world so that it disappears and dies off around us. Those whose soul remains empty is only a 'sombre guest on this dark earth'. If you are successful and you are quite sure that something higher is growing out of the hidden depths of your soul, then you have become new in higher worlds. Dying in the cross, resurrection in the roses—that is what lies in the symbol of the rose cross. A spiritual element lives everywhere in the mineral and in the plant world and we can sense that the underlying spiritual element is the origin of the physical. The external world is ultimately only the physiognomy of the spiritual world. The human soul is like steel or flint; it sparks divine spiritual content in the life of the human soul. It is a matter of finding the right symbol. Someone might well say: you can think up all kinds of things about what the rose cross is supposed to mean. That is neither here nor there for the researcher. When we determine a law of nature in physics that tells us something, science says. The rose cross tells us nothing. But that is not the point. Symbols are most effective when they are multi-layered in their meaning. We put ourselves in a pure, inner activity of soul and in using the support of the symbol, to have a starting point, we concentrate in our soul on the symbol.

Let us look at what the soul does consciously here, that is the important point. What is at work in human beings are forces which are appropriate for awakening what is slumbering, experiences which give us the guarantee that we are dealing with an inner reality when human beings obtain the feeling: actually the cross was only a kind of bridge. Now I have received something in my soul, something quite different which arises in my soul, and experience which I cannot obtain from external things. Initially the pupil does not know whether he or she is faced with *Fata Morgana* or reality. It is important to develop additional abilities because even what has just been described is still a detour for the clairvoyant—it is images. The feeling sets in on the further training path: the important thing is what comes to expression in the images. If you press on your eye or stimulate it with an electric current, light can appear as a result of the inner constellation of the eye. That is broadly what it is like when the images appear; they flash through the soul like spiritual lightning. You know that when you face an object it is not produced by your eye but communicates itself to your eye. The same thing happens in the spirit. The visionary knows now with equal assurance that he or she has not made the object but that the object communicates itself through his or her inner organs. Indeed, the way that the images are now experienced is an expression of objective facts. In the same way that we distinguish between external imagination and perception it is necessary for the visionary to maintain his or her healthy senses because in hardly any other area is confusion so easily possible than in inner experience. That is why other things have to occur in parallel.

If the visionary could practise only what has just been described, he or she might go insane believing that they could make reality be magicked from appearance through their personality. It is necessary for human beings to learn to renounce everything in experiencing the higher spiritual world that is connected with their wishes and inclinations. Human beings currently behave differently psychologically. They might correct the external sensory impressions but it is all too easy for feelings and subjective inclinations to be involved. An experience of spiritual reality must be preceded by renouncing any wish that something might be like this or like that. Objective spiritual things can only be experienced once any sympathy has been excluded.

There is another essential factor. For those who are guided on the path to clairvoyance expertly, not amateurishly, who learn to see in a way that accords with reality, it is of great value that they do not embark on that path without certain prerequisites. It is a difficult path. We therefore have to acquire truths beforehand, information from those who have already undertaken such research. We can also embark on the path with less knowledge but then the soul world remains impoverished, its content is compressed like fixed ideas. That is how the clairvoyants come about who then for example believe that they have become one with God, describe him and so on. When those kinds of clairvoyants describe the higher worlds, their descriptions appear superficial. But for those who approach the higher worlds with the tested experience of the spiritual researcher, a diverse content of those worlds will appear to them and everything external in contrast will turn out to be a small extract of the big world. People who make those experiences their own know that they are not deceived by what they experience there. They can perceive spiritually with the same assurance as in the external world of the senses. That is trained clairvoyance.

What now has to happen for these higher senses to be developed? For spiritual science human beings are not just their external physical body but they also have the otherwise invisible etheric body and the astral body, the bearer of pleasure and pain, for their higher vision. You know what sleep represents for spiritual research. The physical and the etheric body have remained in bed while the astral body and I act from outside on the physical body. On waking, the astral body returns into the physical and etheric body, the sensory world reappears anew. Thus sleep is when the astral body and I leave the physical body. How, then, can human beings hear and see the sensory world? With eyes and ears, otherwise the world would be without colour, light or sound. When the astral body leaves the physical body it is in the spiritual world but it does not possess any organs. If it had such organs, it could perceive the spiritual world in the same way that it perceives its environment in the physical. If therefore human beings are to observe the spiritual world, they have to develop spiritual senses. That is done through the methodical training of the soul life. When the astral body leaves such a person who is trained in accordance with spiritual methods, the latter is in quite a different position than under normal circumstances. It is as if what was previously a chaotic mass in the astral body structures itself and develops organs. What was previously a nebulous, smoky mass becomes beautifully formed. That takes a long time. This process has for a long time been called catharsis, cleansing or purification. The inner human being is then cleansed of drives, lusts and passions. That is the first stage.

This first stage is followed by a second. When human beings return in the morning to their physical and etheric envelope, the outer organs have the stronger forces which drown out the subtle new tones of the inner organs. They are always present, but weak for as long as they are drowned out by the forces of the etheric body in the sensory organs. Human beings subsequently learn to handle their inner organs so that they can see the spiritual perceptions alongside the sensory perceptions. This process is called illumination, photismus. These are thoroughly real processes which are experienced.

Step-by-step the person applies in every detail the method which has been indicated to train himself or herself to become an instrument of perception. The training is intended to give their inner human being organs. Just as nature has perfected the external human being, the developmental path is continued and the person builds on what nature has started. When human beings obtain insight into the spiritual in this way, this is due to the fact that their inner human being has learnt to govern the physical and etheric body. Human beings have become their own master. Initially they obtain mastery over their etheric body. In the trained clairvoyant this happens in such a way that the etheric body adapts its forces to the astral body, it becomes elastic. If clairvoyance on occasion occurs by itself in pathological states, that is caused by something else. Although it is subject to the same laws, it is uncontrollable. When human beings are under particular influences or when they are ill the etheric body can become partially or completely free of the physical body; it can be loosened. That is not normal. Then human beings have an etheric body which is not tied to the physical body as is normally the case and it is therefore easy to handle. In contrast, the spiritual pupil strengthens the astral body and thereby helps it to master the etheric body. When illness occurs, a part of the etheric body can become free which is then handled by the astral body. Then, because this state is based on the same principles, some people can sometimes have real insights into the spiritual world but they are not reliable. This is not the path by which the strict results of spiritual research are obtained.

The question is sometimes asked: how can a pathological process produce extrasensory perceptions? Health and knowledge do not need to follow the same path. That is not a contradiction but it is not a recommendation either. In any event we are given an insight into the facts of the higher world. Just as we enjoy the world which surrounds us, we find in the spiritual world that which explains the sensory world to us. The information from spiritual researchers is based on processes which they have experienced themselves. In telling about it, they communicate facts of a world which can also be understood by ordinary reason, whereas our soul world is otherwise determined by what happens at a physical level. That the image of the rose can have an effect on me, for example, is possible because the forces of the rose stream towards me. It is the same in the spiritual field. Trained clairvoyants experience the spiritual external world in their soul life. They say to themselves: the sensory world is determined in its laws through beings whose work is revealed to me. I see how a blossom appears to me as it is worked on out of the spirit, out of spiritual foundations. I have to make sacrifices in my soul life in order to let the world of the higher spiritual beings stream towards me. Imagine that this world exists and is at work and that human beings could enter it. And around them is this world which the clairvoyant can see. It acts on human beings as a determining force which they do not see but which flows towards them in an unconscious way. The clairvoyant is not satisfied with seeing human beings only as they are structured externally.

The imagination can also work as a soul force which is fertilized by the spiritual worlds. There we have the real foundation of the imagination and can understand Schiller's words characterizing what is created in this way. Thus we can understand it when Goethe says: there is an imagination which is determined inwardly. There is speculation which combines and there is imagination which is fertilized by the forces which the clairvoyant sees. Schiller's whole life at the time meant that he could have no idea of spiritual science but he did have an idea and could feel that it is justified when Goethe ascribed the ability to the imagination to fathom certain secrets.

No matter how many external facts reason gives us, real imagination can be much truer. Human beings are predisposed to ascend into the worlds of the spirit because the corresponding abilities are slumbering in each person. Each person will also achieve that, no matter how many lives it takes. Until then they can let themselves be stimulated by art in which it is not just the sensory world which comes to expression but the creative spirit itself which has passed through the medium of the imagination. The latter is the external image of the former. Thus we may say that imagination and clairvoyance are set for human beings to participate in spiritual life, as a great goal, as something which some have already achieved and which is superior to all other existence. Trained clairvoyance leads human beings into the higher worlds. Its representative in the sensory world is the imagination. That is why it is of exceptional importance among the human soul forces. The imagination is the representative of clairvoyance in the sensory world.

LECTURE 11

LET us today in this branch meeting take as our starting point a number of questions of life which directly touch on human life. Then we will ascend a little to higher spiritual perspectives. I would like to start from two human characteristics, two human flaws or negative virtues which are perceived as being something unsympathetic, as something which reduces the value of human beings. Let us speak about what we call jealousy and mendacity.

If you look around you in life you will easily find that there is a quite natural antipathy towards these two human characteristics. And also if we look up to human beings who stand in life as leaders of other people we can see that they place value particularly on not having these two negative virtues. For example Goethe,[108] who spent a lot of time practising self-knowledge, thinking about his flaws, mentions: I have this and that flaw, these or those merits, but what appears most important to me is that I cannot count jealousy as such among my negative virtues. And the great Benvenuto Cellini[109] said he was glad he was not guilty of any lies. So we can see that these two great personalities felt the importance of fighting against these two human characteristics. And the most simple, naive person agrees with these leaders of humanity in their valuation of, that is to say their antipathy towards these negative values.

If we ask ourselves why these two characteristics are quite instinctively condemned, we will notice that there is hardly anything which corresponds so little to one of the most important earthly characteristics as do jealousy and lies. They correspond little to what we call empathy with other people. Because if we are jealous of someone then we will be little inclined to give ourselves over to the virtue which corresponds to the most profound, the innermost existential core, to the divine in the other person. For empathy only obtains value if we not only have feelings of empathy but if we can value the core, the spiritual being of the other person. But valuing another person as the basis of empathy entails that we accept their merits and can take pleasure in the successes, the developmental stages of the other person. And all of those things exclude jealousy. Jealousy is a characteristic which is connected with the strongest egoism in human beings.

The same thing can be said about lies. If we tell an untruth we breach the law establishing the bond which embraces all human beings with regard to the truth. Truth is truth for all human beings and there is nothing with which we can practise developing a consciousness which encompasses all human beings more than with truth. If we tell an untruth, we commit a crime against the bond which should stretch from human breast to human breast. That is how things present themselves when we look at them as human beings. And when we look at them from the perspective of spiritual science, we know that our previous incarnations have an effect in this life and that we are subject to various influences. We keep having to go through two great influences: the two influences which we call the luciferic and the ahrimanic influence. We do not today want to discuss these two from a cosmological perspective. We want to remain with human life and imagine that we have passed through many incarnations; and when we passed through our first incarnation the luciferic power acted on our astral body.

Since that time the luciferic power has been the power which has tempted our astral body. There are forces which Lucifer exercises on our astral body. It is basically the endeavour of Lucifer to obtain influence over the astral body of the human being on our earth. We have to seek him in everything which pulls the latter down. We have to seek him in all those characteristics which live in the astral body as egoistical passions, desires, drives and wishes and be clear that jealousy is one of the worst influences of Lucifer. Everything that can live in our soul and has to be registered as being jealousy belongs to his field and every time we suffer a fit of jealousy Lucifer is taking hold of our drives in our astral body.

Ahriman, in contrast, has influence over our etheric body and everything connected with a failure in our judgement can be traced back to him—both the accidental, when we reach a wrong judgement, and the intended, when we tell a lie. If we fall prey to mendacity then Ahriman is at work in our etheric body.

The interesting thing is that we feel these influences so strongly, that we have such a strong antipathy towards them when they occur and that people do everything to fight against these two characteristics of lying and jealousy. It would not be easy to find someone who deliberately admitted, 'I want to be jealous.' Although the expression 'I'm so jealous of you' is quite commonplace it is not meant in that sort of way. People do not mean actual jealousy by that. As soon as we notice that we are jealous or that we are lying we do everything to fight against that. In this way we are taking up arms against Lucifer and Ahriman in this field.

But now something frequently occurs which we should take into account when we devote ourselves to spiritual science. We can fight against the individual manifestations of jealousy and lying but when these characteristics are seated in our soul, when we have acquired them in previous incarnations and are now fighting against them, then they come to appearance as different characteristics. When we attempt to fight against a tendency towards jealousy that arises from earlier incarnations, then such jealousy puts on a mask. Lucifer says: human beings are fighting against me, they have become aware of their feelings of jealousy. I will hand these people over to my brother Ahriman. And a different effect occurs which is a consequence of fighting against jealousy. Characteristics which are fought against appear in different masks. And the jealousy against which we are fighting then frequently appears in life in the form that we feel greatly tempted to seek out the faults in other people and criticize them severely. We can encounter people in life who always manage to find the faults and shadow sides of other people as if they had a certain clairvoyant power; and if we try to get to the bottom of this phenomenon the cause can be found in that jealousy has turned into censoriousness and this appears to be a rather good characteristic to the people concerned. It is good, they say, to draw attention to the existence of these bad characteristics. But behind such censoriousness is nothing other than transformed, masked jealousy. And we should learn to recognize whether such characteristics are original or whether they are the transformation of other ones. Then we have to consider whether someone was jealous in their youth. Perhaps we have driven such jealousy out of him and now he has become a censorious person.

And lies too are often transformed in life and come to expression in another mask. Mendacity can lead us to feel ashamed of it. But it is not easy to eradicate it at the root and it is often transformed into a certain superficiality towards the truth. It is important that we know these things because then we can take into account what we come across in other people in life. Such people are satisfied with responses about which we ask ourselves: how can they be satisfied with that? They easily say: yes, yes, that's how it is! That is frequently the product of the transformation of what is really mendacity. We have to examine the law of karma particularly with regard to such characteristics. Human beings do not pay attention to that because they are the most forgetful race in comparison to all the others which prevail on the physical plane.

We might be acquainted with someone for example. We remain close to him throughout life and observe that some things change in him. After 30 years we are still close to him and if we look back on life we would find curious connections in his life. But the person himself knows nothing about this; he has forgotten everything. But we should really observe such things in life. We can then see crucial connections. A person might be jealous in his youth for example. Such jealousy does not appear any more later on and its transformation is evident in later years in that the person concerned reveals himself with the characteristic of a lack of independence, of wanting to be dependent on other people or of not being able to cope with standing on his own two feet, always having to have other people to give help and advice. A certain moral weakness occurs as a consequence of transformed jealousy and we will always see when someone has such moral weakness that we have here the consequence of transformed jealousy.

And transformed mendacity produces shyness in later life. Someone who was mendacious in their youth does not dare in later life to look people in the eye. In the countryside people have an instinctive, elemental knowledge of this which is not however conceptualized. It is said that one should not trust a person who cannot look you in the eye. Shyness and reticence, not resulting from modesty but from fear of facing other people, is the karmic consequence of mendacity even in just one incarnation.

What thus appears as moral weakness in one incarnation has an organizing effect in the next one. The soul weakness which is the consequence of jealousy cannot particularly destroy the body in the present incarnation where it has already been built up. But when we pass through death and return for another incarnation these forces work in such a way that they become organic weaknesses of the physical anabolic processes and we can see that a weak body is built up by such people who have transformed jealousy from a previous incarnation. When we say that a person is weak—but without prejudgement, because people would have to know what is weak or strong—if a person is easily receptive to different influences, has no resistance, then we know that his or her body is weak and that this weak body is a consequence of previously transformed jealousy.

But now we have to say to ourselves: if a child is born into a certain environment as a weak child we not only have to think of this inner karma as being at work but also that there are reasons why we have been brought together with people in our environment—there is nothing arbitrary. This side of karma in particular, that we are adapted to our environment, is incredibly easy to understand. An edelweiss for example can only flourish in the environment to which it is adapted. Human beings, too, can only flourish in the environment which is adapted to them. The simplest logic would have to say that, because we can only understand life if we take this into account. Every being fits with its environment, nothing is random.

Thus we are born among those people of whom we have been jealous or whom we criticized. And thus we stand with a weak body among those people of whom we were jealous in the previous incarnation in what they had achieved or something similar. It is incredibly important to know these things because only if we take this into consideration can we understand life. If a child with a weak body is born into his or her environment we should ask ourselves: how should we behave in this situation? The correct behaviour has to be the one which is morally the most high-minded: to forgive. That will be the best way to reach the goal and it is also the best education for the person concerned. It has an incredibly educational effect if we can lovingly forgive a weak child which is born into our environment. The person through whom that happens in a truly powerful way will see that the child grows stronger and stronger as a result. Forgiving love has to work right into the thinking because in that way the child can collect the strength to reshape his or her previous karma and take it in the right direction. The child will also grow physically strong. Such a child might often display characteristics which are unpleasant. If we love him or her—in our deepest heart—then this acts like an intensive medicine and we will soon find how effective this medicine is.

The corresponding thing applies if we take the other characteristic, mendacity. In one incarnation the person becomes shy in their later years. That is a soul characteristic. But in the next incarnation this characteristic works as the architect of the body. There the child not only appears weak but in such a way that he or she cannot obtain any true relationship with his or her environment—he or she is weak-minded. There we have to consider that we are the people who were often lied to by such a person and we should repay the bad things which happened to us with the best. We must try to teach such a person a great deal of what are the truths of spiritual life, then we will see how they blossom. We should always have the thought, such a person lied to us a great deal in a previous incarnation and we have to do everything to create a true relationship between such a child and his or her environment.

Here we can see if we look at these things that we are always called upon as human beings to help other human beings to bear their karma in the right way. Anyone who thinks we have to leave people to their karma does not understand anything about karma. If we found a person who lied to us and we believed he or she had to bear their karma we would show that we have no proper understanding of karma. Because the right idea would be that we begin by offering help. When it is said that we should leave a person to their karma, then this might at most be said in the esoteric field[110] but never in life.

Imagine we endeavoured to help other people in accordance with their karma. Take a person who has a shy nature. We concern ourselves with him lovingly. We thereby create a connection between this person and ourselves. We will then see that in this person something in turn comes back to us in later years. But we have to leave that to karma, we cannot speculate about it. We have to see it as our duty to help another person. And here I come to a subtle law. Everything that we do for someone else to help them to bear and overcome their karma will always lead not just to the other person being helped but also to something being done for ourselves. But what we do for ourselves, for example so that we make rapid progress, will not as a rule help us a great deal. Only those things can become productive for human beings which they do for others. We cannot do something good for ourselves. When we help a person to overcome their karma, the best results arise because what we do for others is of benefit for humanity. We cannot do anything for ourselves, that in turn has to be done by others. That is why we have to recognize in the highest sense: empathy for other people. If we develop such empathy in the highest sense then we will also feel in relation to jealousy and lies such an obligation of empathy towards other people. In this way we develop a feeling of solidarity which extends to all human souls.

Humanity is generally predisposed so that every individual person feels a connection with the whole of humanity. And in the way that it variously comes to expression in life this feeling should also live in his or her fight against Lucifer and Ahriman. In seeking to help frail people who have a physical body which has become weak under the influence of jealousy which has been overcome, in being clear how we should behave towards such people, it can become apparent to us how the world is filled with these impulses from Lucifer and Ahriman and how they can be overcome in the course of earth development. And then every person who follows such connections in their feeling will of necessity obtain an ever deeper feeling for humanity as such. In a certain sense every person has the opportunity to feel something which can connect them with all people. This feeling has changed a great deal in the course of human development.

If we go back three to four centuries, the feeling of what human beings possess in terms of general humanity was clearly pronounced in all people. If we carry on further back, back through the post-Atlantean cultures to ancient Atlantis—we were always incarnated then—and if we go even further back we come to an incarnation in which we descended for the first time into a physical body. Previously we were in something spiritual, people still told themselves three or four millennia ago. Such wise feelings can be found in all human beings around this time. And the soul asked itself: what are you through being a human being? And it responded: before I descended into my body for the first time, I was previously in an ocean of divine-spiritual life and interweaving. I was in it and all other human souls were also in it. That was our common point of origin. Such a basic feeling in human souls provided the possibility to have fraternal, generally human feelings since the origin of all human souls was felt to be a common one. And if we recall how in all ancient mystery schools human beings were acted upon to make them good human beings, so it was everywhere that they were referred to their common origin, to the emergence of all human beings from the common divine source in order to make human beings into good human beings and make them receptive for the most profound, intimate, moving feelings. And it was easy to make this resound in the soul. But it became more and more difficult. If, for example, this had been made to resound in the number of people who are sitting here, that would have created an overwhelming impression at that time.

But the feelings of humanity towards this common origin grew ever colder. This had to happen as humanity had to pass through a certain point of development. If I want to characterize it, we have to look at the future of humanity, to the goal of earth development.

Just as the origin is a common one and all human souls have arisen from a common archetypal ground, all human souls will come together again in a common goal. And how can we human beings find this goal so that we continue to develop when the earth has reached its goal and will sink and scatter as a material sphere under us human beings? How can we reach an understanding amongst us that we jointly move towards one future? Such an awareness of this communality has to go down into the deepest fibres of the soul. That is only possible in that we as human beings learn to feel about the future as the ancient human beings felt towards the origin of humanity. This feeling has grown increasingly cold in humanity. But the life, the feeling, the certainty has increasingly to grow warm in souls that there can be something which is common to all human beings as the goal of humanity. Whether we have reached this or another stage of development, wherever we may stand in life in that we are human beings, something must be able to take place in our soul so that we can say to ourselves: we are all striving towards one goal. And looking towards this goal we have to be able to say to ourselves: that is something which concerns every human being. We have to be able to find something in our most profound inwardness in which we come together in one point.

In occultism this is given with the name Christ. Because just as we could feel and know millennia ago that our souls are all born out of the common divine ground and origin, so human beings will increasingly learn to say: just as we find our way together in something common when we think, just as we can be in agreement in common thinking as it can live in all human heads, so there is something which can live like a common element in all hearts. There is something which like a lifeblood can flow through all human hearts. If this is increasingly aglow in us in future incarnations, then these will take such a course that when the earth has reached its goal so that it transforms itself into the future planetary state of Jupiter, human souls will come together, be one, in what is common to them, Christ. The Mystery of Golgotha had to take place for this to be able to happen. To this end Christ became human in Jesus so that this common stream of warmth can flow from human heart to human heart. The feeling for the common goal of humanity emanates from the cross on Golgotha. Thus the past is connected with the future. This is the goal of the future development of humanity. It is not important whether human beings retain this common name of Christ, but what is important is that all human beings learn to understand that the same feeling which human beings originally had of their common origin is transformed into a feeling of a common earth future.

Earth development is divided into these two halves: the one goes as far as the cross on Golgotha and the other from the cross on Golgotha to the time when the earth will end. And human beings have much, much to do to understand Christ and his development. And when this will have been understood, then human beings will find each other in the common goal for Jupiter development. And all our individual findings have the purpose to discover this Christian principle.

If we have attempted today to understand how karma can work to form the body from one incarnation to the next, then we understand how human beings can become ever more perfect in passing through the incarnations. Without calling him Christ, we are still speaking of Christ. We ignore the personal. If we have a child before us that lies to us, we tell ourselves: this child has lied to us, how can we help him transform his karma? We do not ask whether he has harmed us. We look at the child in its core and thereby we advance karma. A deep feeling of human togetherness will in this way increasingly assert itself in the world.

So that which we call spiritual science—if we really take it to mean an understanding of the life processes in the sense of reincarnation and karma—is the preparation for a true grasp of the Christ impulse in the world. It is not important what words people use, but anyone who truly comprehends this developmental law cannot be anything other than Christian, be they Hindu or Muslim or a member of any other religious system. The important thing is to take the impulse into one's soul which is the impulse for the common goal of humanity, just as once in ancient human beings there lived the impulse to look towards the common origin of human beings.

That is why spiritual science always leads to the Christ impulse. It cannot do anything else. We could therefore simply also understand spiritual science as it appears today by saying: even if the person who learns about it may not want to have anything to do with Christianity, if he or she becomes an anthroposophist they will in truth be led to Christ. In reality they would be led there even if they were to fight against it in words.

Thus we have today brought before our souls something that is directly connected with life. We have seen how we should behave when a child lies or feels jealous. We have to be clear that the karmic thread runs through all incarnations of the human soul, that karma is spun for it in line with its destiny, and that when we look back to the origin in

God and then look towards the goal of humanity we once again look towards God.

We look back to the culture of the ancient Rishis. They spoke about the origin of human beings. They pointed to the world in which human beings existed before they descended to their incarnations. This teaching penetrated through the centuries and millennia. The great Buddha taught it when he said: through their urge to incarnate human beings lost everything which created the connection with the world of our origins. His call was to leave the world of incarnation again so that the soul can live once more in the spiritual worlds of its origins. And the prophets, in proclaiming the coming of Christ, pointed to a future in which human beings would once again find their proper goal on earth. And then Christ himself appears and fulfils the Mystery of Golgotha. Then human beings can be led towards the divine-spiritual future of the earth through the Mystery of Golgotha.

There is perhaps nothing quite as moving as two sayings which are similar in the Buddha and in Christ and which can place before our soul the contrast between the ancient and modern time. The Buddha is standing among his pupils, he points to the body and says: I look back from incarnation to incarnation, how I always entered such a human body as I am wearing now. And this temple of the body has been built for me by the gods each time anew. And each time the soul seeks to enter this temple of the body in new incarnations. But now I know that it is no longer necessary for me to return to a temple of the body. I know that the timbers have broken and the poles have disintegrated. Through my knowledge I have liberated my soul from this body. The wish and desire to return into such a body has been killed off. That was the great, the mighty result of the ancient times which looked back to the origins of humanity. The Buddha and his pupils and successors strove to become free of the body. What a mighty difference to when Christ stands before his closest pupils and says—no matter how we understand it; we take it as the words of Christ, as they are—Christ says: destroy this temple of my body and in three days I will raise it up again.[111] He, Christ, does not long to be liberated from the temple of his body. He wants to rebuild it.

Not as if Christ himself would be here again in such a physical body in following incarnations. But what he teaches his pupils and all human beings is this: to return to this earth temple from incarnation to incarnation in order in each one to make the Christ impulse greater and more intensive, so that we human beings can take in more and more of this earth existence in order finally to stand there so we can say that we have worked on these incarnations to become more similar to Christ. And we become more similar to him in that we take into this temple of the body what Christ let stream out from the cross on Golgotha as his own being. This we let stream from human soul to human soul because that is the only way we can understand one another now. This is what is common to all human souls in the future of the earth. And then the time will come in which the earth will pass away, in which it will break apart and disintegrate, and in which human beings in a spiritualized state will pass on to the next incarnation on another planet.

The words of the great Buddha, 'I feel how the posts of the temple of my body no longer support me, how the timbers are collapsing'—they can stand before our soul as the end point of our common human origin. And when we look at what Christ says to his disciples: 'I will raise up this temple of the body in three days'—that can be for us like the beginning of the period which points to the goal of the earth. And we can extend these words because we can say: let this temple be destroyed in death, but we know that we will use the best forces we have made our own in this incarnation for the next one. We have received these forces in giving our soul to the cognition of Christ. In this way we will advance from incarnation to incarnation. When human beings raise up this temple of the body for the last time, they will have obtained an understanding of the future, common goal of the earth.

It is the Mystery of Golgotha alone which can be the common impulse for all humanity for the development of humanity and the earth.

LECTURE 12

I would like to speak today about some anthroposophical questions about life and then ascend from these questions about life, from the everyday to the all-embracing, to matters of principle. This is the most productive benefit of our striving, that we increasingly learn to judge life and its truth, its reality through spiritual science: learn to judge how such judgement itself can lead us into life in the most capable, the most active way, and how it can locate us in the place we have to fill in accordance with our karma, which we have to fill in accordance with our greater or lesser mission during the time in which we are incarnated in a physical body.

And here I first want to start with some characteristics in life—which present themselves every day in ourselves or in our environment—with characteristics whose import and significance we can only understand if we can look at them in the light of spiritual science. I would like to start with two negative virtues of life and then speak about some virtues; I want to start from the virtues of good will and satisfaction and the negative virtues of mendacity and jealousy.

Let us first consider the two negative virtues which we often encounter in life. It cannot be denied that in the broadest circles, both among the simplest people and among those who already belong to the leaders in life, there is a deep, deep dislike of and antipathy towards what we can call jealousy and mendacity. To begin by quoting some of those who belonged to the leaders in life, I refer to the sculptor Benvenuto Cellini[112] and to those passages in his autobiography where he says that in thoroughly observing himself he had to admit to many negative virtues but could say that serious mendacity was not one of them. This artist thus finds a certain satisfaction in being able to exclude mendacity from his character traits when observing himself. And Goethe[113] once said as the result of his self-observation that he had to admit to many things but that jealousy, this ugly negative virtue, had not actually gnawed away at his heart.

Thus we can see at the peaks of life how mendacity and jealousy are seen with antipathy; how people everywhere, who are used to looking at life in a somewhat deeper way, including where great abilities in life appertain to the soul, say: you have to avoid these negative virtues in particular. And who would deny that this thorough antipathy towards mendacity and jealousy extends through all, all layers of our humankind. You only need to think how much it would gnaw at your hearts if at a certain moment you had to admit in truly honest and proper self-observation: I am a jealous personality. In making such an admission, you would most certainly feel, if you resolutely had to admit this, that you had to take up within yourself something like a battle against jealousy, a fight against jealousy. This is a deeply rooted feeling, that mendacity and jealousy are ugly human characteristics.

Why do we actually have such feelings? Well, you see, people are not always very clear why they have such a deep antipathy towards this or that. They are often not very clear what slumbers in the more or less unconscious part of their soul life and undoubtedly exists. With regard to jealousy and mendacity human beings feel that they are in breach of something which is connected with our most human values. We only need to say one word and we will feel it. After all, spiritual science is intended gradually to make us aware that apart from the individual personalities who are incarnated in the flesh there is something like a unified, general human element which lives as the divine-human element in the same way in all souls. And here it is spiritual science which presents us with this as a great ideal and which gradually works towards an understanding of that general human element. And in an emotional way there is something in all human hearts which in a certain sense always says: look for the bond which holds all human beings together, which always winds from soul to soul, and you will find it.

And the corresponding feeling can be expressed in the word 'empathy'. Empathy is such a general human characteristic that we have to say: the bond which goes from soul to soul declares itself as if darkly in such empathy. And in turn we feel in the unconscious how particularly with mendacity and jealousy we violate empathy, the recognition of that which is common to all human beings.

What do we actually do when we tell a lie to someone? We do nothing other than build a barrier between them and us. The thing which should unite us, the common knowledge of a truth which should live in our and their soul if things were correct, this is what we tear apart in telling an untruth. In the moment that we tell an untruth, we fail to accept that we should actually also live in the other with the best part of our self.

And if we are jealous of someone, be it their abilities, be it other things in life, then we sin against empathy in the sense that we fail to recognize the person as what he or she should actually be, as something which is part of us, and about whose merits and gifts and luck we should actually be happy if we felt properly connected with him or her.

So we sin against the most beautiful thing in human life, against empathy, if we are jealous and mendacious people. And why is this actually expressed in such a vehement way in the dissatisfaction about these two characteristics? Why? Well, both characteristics can truly show us how what is located in our soul can propagate, can advance to the envelopes of our being and has significance for these envelopes.

Jealousy is something which clearly expresses itself for occult observation—if it is present in a person—in a very specific state of the astral body. And jealous people, however much they are able to hide their jealousy from the external world, reveal the characteristic of jealousy in their astral body. Our astral body has a very specific basic characteristic. Although it is different in each person and shows a great variety of differences in different people, it nevertheless has a certain basic characteristic. And when we look at it with clairvoyant observation as an aura, it has very specific colour characteristics. These fade in a disturbing way in jealous people—they fade, they become weak and dull. And the astral body of a jealous person in a sense becomes deficient in the force which it should channel towards the whole human organism.

With mendacity it is in turn such that it and each individual lie are expressed in the etheric body. The etheric body loses vitality and energy for life if people are mendacious. We can even note that externally. Strange as it may sound for our age, it is nevertheless true that in people who lie a lot wounds, for example, are harder to heal under otherwise similar conditions than in truthful people. Of course we cannot take that in absolute terms; there can also be other reasons. But all things being equal, wounds are more difficult to heal in mendacious people than in truthful people. It is good to look at these things in life. And it can also easily be explained. The etheric body of the human being is the actual life principle, it is what must contain the life forces. But the latter are undermined through mendacity. So the etheric body cannot provide as much vitality as is necessary for healing if the etheric body has been deprived of vitality through mendacity, if it is not always imbued with those movements, those circumstances which derive from truthfulness. We should take good account of these things because we will understand life better in many respects when we do.

Now you know that we have to look at what approaches human beings in the light of two powers who influence human life as it develops from incarnation to incarnation. We have to look at human life under the influence of the luciferic and ahrimanic powers. The luciferic powers are those which act on our astral body, which radiate the action of their forces into our astral body and tempt us in that regard. The ahrimanic powers are those which tempt us with regard to the etheric body. Indeed, it is Lucifer who takes us by the scruff of the neck, as it were, when we are jealous of people. Jealousy is a real luciferic characteristic, a characteristic which comes from Lucifer, whereas mendacity is a characteristic which comes from Ahriman, because Ahriman sends out the forces and powers which radiate into our etheric body.

Now we can say: it may well have been absolutely necessary that Lucifer and Ahriman were delegated by the wise cosmic powers to act on us to make us independent. In causing us to misuse our independence, they are in a certain sense enemies of the higher development of humanity. But even if they are the enemy of human beings in a certain sense in their higher development, they are very great friends and make quite peculiar compromises between themselves. We can refer particularly to such compromises when we look at human characteristics like jealousy and mendacity.

Jealousy! Any person who is not completely corrupted will do anything to fight against this jealousy in the moment where they have to recognize 'I am jealous by nature', and we do not need to be particularly virtuous in order to feel compelled to do that. But things are sometimes much more deep-seated than the extent of the strength which comes from the consciousness. And human beings sometimes imagine it to be too easy in combating such things. So it can happen that they fight against such things because they consider them to be ugly, but they do not go away because they simply change their form and reappear somewhere else. They then appear in masked form. And because we hate jealousy so much, we fight against it, but if the soul is not yet strong enough to fight it thoroughly, it disappears as jealousy but reappears in another form.

You all know the characteristic in people which we find so frequently and which we could call fault-finding and censoriousness, finding the faults in our fellow human beings. When someone says 'I am a jealous person, I do not want my fellow human beings to have advantages', they feel bad. They feel that they have to fight against that. But if someone can say 'that person has done something terrible', they feel that their censoriousness is justified in a certain way, they feel properly in their element. Just think if that were not the case how many tea parties and pub discussions would no longer have a purpose where frequently little else is done than allow fault-finding and censoriousness a free rein. And then people feel that they are justified in what they have done because they can say they cannot close their eyes to someone else's errors. The only thing is, it depends for what reasons we see the errors of our fellow human beings, whether we see them with the intention of improving life or whether we are following an inclination of our soul which frequently is nothing other than masked jealousy.

People fight jealousy because they hate it but they cannot get rid of it completely because they are too weak. So it is dressed up as censoriousness and continues in the soul in this way. When that happens we have not fought jealousy, we have simply forced it to metamorphose. What has happened in truth is that the person has fought against

Lucifer because the latter is the ruler over jealousy and many other things. But Lucifer then says to Ahriman, if I can put it like this: 'See, dear Ahriman, that person hates my regime of jealousy because he does not want to be jealous. You take him with regard to this characteristic.' Then Ahriman says: 'Yes, I will compress it into the etheric body.' And it is compressed into the etheric body as censoriousness, as fault-finding, as misled judgement about what surrounds the person. Because power of judgement is always connected with the movements and forces of the etheric body. In this case the regime with regard to our soul is transferred from Lucifer to Ahriman.

And thus many characteristics which we would hate and fight against if they were to reveal themselves to us in their original form appear in a masked shape. Then they sometimes appear in such a form that we actually find them quite justified and even feel good about having risen to doing the right thing in life. Then we are properly caught in the tentacles of the other power, the ahrimanic power. Then we must not forget that a characteristic is much more dangerous when it appears behind a mask than in its original form. That is why it is always good to ask when we see something or other in life: is that not perhaps simply a transformed negative virtue? It is exceptionally necessary that we learn to look at life truthfully in this way. We can basically only do that if we use the guidelines given to us by anthroposophical wisdom in order to look at life properly.

Now we have to say: the things which appear in life as this or that negative virtue, be it in its true form or in a mask, we can often see working karmically in a single incarnation. We do not need to wait for the transition from one incarnation to the next. We can see in one incarnation already the karmic effects of a characteristic which comes to appearance in a particular phase of life. And those who really want to look at life and pay a little attention to the fact that we cannot get to know life if we forget by tomorrow what happened today, but if we look at longer phases in human life, they will also find karma at work in *one* incarnation, in *one* life. It is truly necessary that we pay very careful attention in a certain sense to how the sins of life really only reveal themselves decades later. Of all the races, starting with human beings and stretching up into all the higher worlds, human beings are truly the most forgetful species. Even if we have known someone for decades, we forget what came to light decades ago; we like to let that disappear from our memory.

I have probably already mentioned a small example here which can once again show us how we have to look at life in greater periods if we want to recognize its true shape—something superficial which I just want to mention in passing. It is from the period in which I had the opportunity to observe many children in various families. When we educate children we do not, after all, just observe those children which we have to educate ourselves but also the more or less little offspring of the uncles, aunts, nieces and nephews and so on. And then we can make note of many things with regard to life. Well, it is a long time ago, the fashions change. At that time, when I was educating children, it was the fashion that quite a few doses of red wine were given by the educators to small children at mealtimes to strengthen them. That is what happened, it was thought to be a good thing. If one noted at the time this and this child received red wine and the other one did not, we can discover some remarkable things when we have the opportunity to observe, as I try to do, what has become of these children. I can say: the 2, 3, 4-year-old children of that time—now people aged 27, 28, 29—who were given red wine as children are fidgety, nervous people and sometimes find it exceptionally difficult to find their way in life.

We should not of course make those observations for just five years. That has become very commonplace today, that we try this or something else and if there is success in the following months it is suddenly a widely used medicine. In this field people are forgetful as well. The number of medicines which went out of fashion again after five years is also something which people have forgotten about again. But, as I said, if one extends one's observation over decades, then one can begin to get a sense of how life works. There is really a great difference between the children who were given red wine at the time and those who were not. But one would have to make one's observations for three decades before seeing that. And that is how it is. I interjected this to show that it is necessary not to be forgetful if we want to see karma at work, and that our observations have to extend over longer periods of time. The same thing applies to those things which appear more in the soul sphere.

When we compare the second half of a person's life with the first half and that person was mendacious or jealous in a certain period of their life or had jealousy under the mask of censoriousness, it is quite possible to see how the effect already appears karmically in the second half of life. Mendacious people always already show in a single incarnation a very specific karmic effect of mendaciousness: a certain shyness, the impossibility, we might say, to look a person directly in the eye. That will assuredly happen. Just try observing the matter. You will find it confirmed. Popular sayings sometimes have a deep and wise core. It is not for nothing that people say in many regions that one should avoid a person who cannot look you in the eye. Because that is the karmic effect of mendaciousness.

In contrast, jealousy or jealousy masked as censoriousness and fault-finding can be found in a later part of life in the same incarnation in such a way that the people concerned have the characteristic of not being able to stand properly on their own two feet, that they have the urge to lean on other people, that they need advice about minor things, that they would like always to run to other people for advice. Independence in life is lost through jealousy, fault-finding, censoriousness. Such people become weak in their soul.

Now we encounter these characteristics with their karmic effects in the soul when we look at the one incarnation. We will shortly take into account a little how these karmic effects come to expression when we go from one incarnation to the next.

But in order not to be one-sided, we will also consider good characteristics: good will and satisfaction. Everyone knows what a person with good will is. A person with good will is someone who feels satisfied in a certain respect when someone else is successful, achieves something, when they notice good characteristics in one person or another. Good will is present when we experience what the other experiences as if it were our own. Such good will in turn has a very specific effect on our astral body which is pretty much the opposite of the effect of jealousy. We can see how the lights of the astral body are illuminated when good will is expressed. The astral body becomes brighter and more radiating when there are stirrings of good will in the soul of the person. The aura becomes brighter, more radiating and thus richer, it becomes more saturated in itself and then it is enabled to pour into the human being first something like soul warmth and then even something of a feeling of good health.

And when we see a satisfied person in front of us, a person who is not inclined to be upset about everything from the beginning, to be dissatisfied with everything, then the etheric body shows us very specific characteristics. It is important that we look at this in turn in a specific way. Because actually we should be clear about how much of our dissatisfaction fundamentally really depends on ourselves. The one person cannot do enough to dig up those things everywhere which make him dissatisfied. And we feel that it is not only happier natures, but also better natures who are capable of ensuring that even if the worst things constantly approach us, we nevertheless have reasons to be happy about one thing or another. There are such reasons. And anyone who does not want to admit that they exist can only blame themselves. Satisfaction, particularly when it is caused by a better characteristic of our soul, strengthens the etheric body in respect of its vitality. And once again it is the case—all things being equal—that wounds or other things in satisfied people who have reason to be easily satisfied, not to become too upset about what happens to them, heal more easily than in someone who is grumpy and dissatisfied, who gets upset about everything and is never satisfied by anything—all things being equal, as I said.

And now we can in turn see quite precisely in one life—and this is important, that we thoroughly take account of this in educating children—that someone who at a certain stage of their life was thoroughly imbued with satisfaction and sought to find those things which can give satisfaction, perhaps despite pain and suffering, that in such people there is a karmic effect in the same life still, even if it happens decades later. This can come to expression in that from such people who endeavoured to be satisfied a certain beneficial harmonious effect in life streams out to their surroundings at a certain stage in their life. You know that this happens. There are people in whose surroundings others easily become fidgety, and those who simply through the fact that they are there calm others down. People who have endeavoured at one stage of their life to be satisfied obtain as the karmic effect for the next stage of the same life this possibility to have a harmonious effect on their surroundings, in a certain sense to be benefactors for their surroundings purely through the fact that they are there.

People of good will—we can always observe that—who have endeavoured to be of good will obtain the karmic effect that in later phases of their life they are remarkably successful in achieving all those things connected with them which they intend to do. We sometimes find that we cannot explain how for some people everything works, that they feel up to everything they do and that others are unsuccessful, that nothing works for them. That takes us back to the karmic cause of good will or bad will. You can observe these things which I have outlined for you in life. If you exclude the sources of error which exist you will see that life confirms what I have said.

If we now move from one incarnation to the next one, we have to say: in one incarnation the karmic effects can actually only reveal themselves in the soul. Here the effects of jealousy are revealed in certain weaknesses and in a lack of independence, the effect of mendacity in shyness, the effect of good will and satisfaction as I have described. We simply do not have the thorough, deep-seated influences on our physical organization in a single incarnation so that we could advance beyond the soul with the karmic effects. These things only work as far as the body, into the construction and organization of the body, in the next incarnation. And while we turn ourselves into people with a lack of independence in one incarnation through jealousy and censoriousness, they act to weaken the body in its constitution, in its structure in the next incarnation. A weak body is built by someone who was previously plagued by jealousy or by masked jealousy, by fault-finding and censoriousness.

But now we also have to say if we have concerned ourselves a little with what spiritual science otherwise shows us that it is by no means a coincidence if we are brought together in a new incarnation with a particular person. We are guided into the family, the environment with which we have a connection. And so you will not find it strange when I say: someone who was a jealous person in one incarnation will be reborn with people—be it that they are his parents or other people—of whom he was jealous, whom he judged or gossiped about. He is brought together with them. And we are perhaps brought together in that we come into this environment with a weak organization. At this point the matter becomes very practical, the teaching of karma comes close to the way we live life. Here we can say that when a child is born with a weak organization this is the consequence of the jealous disposition of the previous incarnation and we are the ones who were the object of that jealousy; and this child has been karmically brought together with us because we are the ones whom the child pursued with jealousy and the need for gossip. It is fruitful when we tell ourselves: if karma has any meaning at all, it is justified to look at the matter in this way. So let us look at it in this way.

Of course the matter only bears fruit if we ask ourselves: what should we do with regard to such a weak child? We only need to ask ourselves: what would seem to us the best thing to do morally in ordinary life if someone pursued us with their jealousy and fault-finding? Perhaps it is not always possible to do the best thing in ordinary, everyday life. But what would appear as the best thing for us? Well, quite certainly, forgiveness would appear to be the best thing for us. We can say that our life is not perhaps such that we can always forgive but the best thing is undoubtedly forgiveness, and forgiveness is the most effective and also the most productive thing in life. If we can already say about ordinary life that this is best, even if we cannot always practise it, forgiveness, then we can see that under all circumstances the real application of the principle of forgiveness is the right thing to do when we have to recognize what I have explained as the karmic effect from an earlier incarnation. When a weak child is born into our environment or is brought together with us, we have to tell ourselves that since karma must not just remain a theoretical idea we have to consider that we were the object of jealousy and gossip. Now in our deepest heart we can practise the feeling of forgiveness under all circumstances.

We can, so to speak, envelop such a child in an atmosphere of constantly activated feelings of forgiveness. If we did this in life, if we felt brought together with people who are weak, and if we did not just grasp the idea of forgiveness theoretically but kept activating the feeling 'I have something to forgive you' in our soul, I want to forgive you, and kept renewing this feeling, then this would be a practical introduction of anthroposophical sentiments into life. We would undoubtedly see an effect. Just try carrying this out in practice and we will see that the people whom we forgive in this way, and for whom we keep renewing the feelings of forgiveness if they are born weak into our surroundings, then blossom, that our feelings have a health-giving effect which allows them to blossom. And in this way we become healers, health-givers for the people with whom karma has brought us together. In this way anthroposophy becomes productive if we do not just consider it as a sum of ideas. It is basically quite an egotistical thing if we begin to develop an enthusiasm for anthroposophy because we are passionate about the ideas of anthroposophy which appear true to us. Because what do we satisfy in that case? We satisfy what is our longing for a harmonious world-view. That is very nice. But the greater thing is if we imbue our whole life with what arises from these ideas, when these ideas enter into our hands, into every step and into all the things we experience and do. Only then does anthroposophy become a principle of life and unless it does that it has no value.

We can also say something similar with regard to other characteristics. If, for example, we were a mendacious person in one incarnation and are reborn, then we are brought together precisely with those to whom we told a bucketful of lies. We frequently find if we are true occult researchers that a child is born into an environment to which he or she cannot obtain a proper relationship, in which he or she is not understood and he or she does not understand it. It sometimes happens that we have a particular effect on our surroundings. I don't know whether you have ever observed this, but it basically extends much further than just to other human beings. There are certain people who can make every plant grow—they simply have green fingers. Just because it is them, the flowers thrive. Other people can try as hard as they like, the plants simply die. That happens. The relationship between the individual beings of existence are much more complex than we generally think. These complex relationships are of course mainly between one person and another. And when karma brings us together with a child who has valiantly lied to us in a previous incarnation, the situation arises that we find it difficult to establish a relationship with that child. We should take note of that. We must not only judge that by our temperament but we also have to judge it karmically. We should say: it may be because perhaps we were often lied to by this child. Now we can help this child and make it strong.

How can we best forgive something which can be expressed by saying that someone has told us a lie. We forgive that best if we teach them a truth. In rectifying the lie we do something good for the other person, but have not thereby yet caused them to advance. We do the latter if we try to teach them a useful truth. We have to pursue a kind of policy in dealing with the other person that allows him or her to advance. If we are held to look at the matter karmically, it is of particular benefit when we try to be quite truthful towards people with whom we have been karmically brought together, of whom we know that they cannot find a relationship with us because they are shy. Then we will see how these people in turn blossom in our openness and how such openness is of great benefit for them. Thus we can see how we can obtain principles of life if we look at the action of karma in a practical way.

What we characterized earlier as the action of good will already in a single life can be seen in such a way that it truly acts to produce something like the harmonization of life, but initially in the soul. In people in whom that works from one incarnation to the next, we find that they have actually been born with a more happy organization which we can call 'skilful'. Good will, satisfaction in an incarnation produce suppleness and dexterity in another incarnation. It is true that this is the case because it can always be proven in the field of occult research. And it is quite possible to observe ourselves and learn something of the way that the previous incarnation acts into the present one. We can be quite certain that this is the case in people whose fingers are quite unsuitable for sewing on a button which has come off or people who, when they are meant to take a glass to the cupboard, will quite happily drop it—I am now exaggerating a little. But in more subtle nuances there are many people who are organized in such a way that they cannot do anything other than not move their fingers in the right way, that they always blunder. This is of deep significance in life, whether or not we can use the instrument of the body well or whether it offers treacherous obstacles at every moment. This is exceptionally important. And when we see a clumsy child growing up then we have to assume in most cases that he or she was lacking in satisfaction and good will. If we see skilfulness appearing, so that the person can almost do it beforehand when he or she touches something, then the whole thing is certainly the karmic effect of good will and satisfaction.

When we look at it like this, we may say: actually we can work in a wonderful way from one incarnation to the next. The opportunity opens up to be able to work on our next incarnation. And we will change a great deal for our next incarnation if we take the serious decision to observe whether we might not still have a little bit of fault-finding and censoriousness within us. If we attempt to check whether we have a little bit of these things in us, we may even find that we have them in us to a considerable extent. It would be a good thing if we attempted to check whether we have a little bit of them within us. Then we can start working on ourselves. And we may be able to prevent ourselves from being born in the next incarnation as weak and pale, prevent ourselves in this life even from becoming children with a lack of independence as it were.

When we look at these things, we will say to ourselves: it is no fantasy to see the individual incarnations like links in a chain for human beings and to look at the earth as a kind of training through which we learn to use what is offered to us in the individual incarnations so that we ascend higher and higher and progress further and further. Because why do we basically incarnate? We can best obtain a concept of that if we ask ourselves about the two great differences which exist between our incarnations in ancient pre-Christian times and our present incarnations which have happened after the Christ impulse was here. Because there is a very considerable difference.

The difference between our incarnations in ancient pre-Christian times and our present incarnations can best be described by saying: if we look back to the incarnations of people in pre-Christian times, the souls in this pre-Christian period all to a certain degree had retained something still of what all souls had at the start of the incarnations on earth. All souls had a kind of natural clairvoyance, being able to look into the spiritual world. And the progression of the incarnations precisely consists of this inheritance from the spiritual world, from our spiritual origins, gradually being lost, that people increasingly stepped out onto the physical plane and the spiritual world increasingly disappeared for them. The Christ impulse means that if we find the possibility of incorporating Christ in us, of combining him with our I, we begin once again to ascend more and more to what we were at the beginning, except richer. That we will once again be back in the spirit at the end of our incarnations in the way that we were there at the start of our incarnations is achieved by incorporating the power of Christ, by using our next incarnations in such a way that we incorporate more and more of Christ.

These are the great differences between the pre-Christian and post-Christian incarnations. We are actually still in a transitional period. We are profoundly pushed out onto the physical plane with regard to pure physical perception and we have actually today reached a climax in physical perception. For the Christ impulse is only at the beginning, and it is in following incarnations that people will begin properly to incorporate Christ, will only then start to grow fond of these incarnations because they give them the opportunity to experience something which can only be experienced through earth existence: the incorporation of the Christ impulse into the soul. We can observe even in great personalities how there is the mighty difference between the incarnations before the Christ impulse on earth and afterwards. Allow me to tell you about one event.[114]

Some time ago I had cause to address our southernmost European branch—I mean in so far as we are talking about Rosicrucian theosophy—in Palermo. And when I came into Sicily by ship from Naples I had the very specific feeling that here there was something to learn about occult facts which is difficult to investigate in the north. Because a personality, an individuality, whom I cannot name right now appeared who had a certain importance at the turn of the Middle Ages to the modern age. He became a talking point in our and in neighbouring regions and the occultist likes to ask about him: what was the situation with regard to the previous incarnation of this personality? That was an important research question for me and strangely I was given the hope as I arrived in Sicily that I might perhaps learn something about this question through the occult research which was possible there. And that soon turned out to be the case. It is of course something intimate which I am telling here but within our branches we no longer need to hold back completely with regard to such intimate things. There is something in the whole spiritual atmosphere of Sicily—I do not say the outer but the spiritual atmosphere—something very, very strange. And in pursuing this strange thing I was finally led to its source, to a great wise man who was active in Sicily and who is dismissed in the history of philosophy in a few words, but who is actually very little known outwardly, exoterically. It is Empedocles.[115]

If we now as occultists want to characterize Empedocles—and I will do that shortly—we have to say: in a certain respect Empedocles was far ahead of his time, he was too mature for his time. But in another respect he could not get beyond his time. There was a deep split in his soul. Empedocles is truly a great, all-embracing personality. He was active in Sicily not just as a philosopher, not just as a leader of the mysteries, but as a statesman, architect, and as all kinds of other things—he was a kind of organizer, this wonderful Empedocles. Now Empedocles lived in Sicily about four, five centuries before the Christ impulse and he had moved ahead of his time to the extent that he had the urge to immerse himself in the material aspect of the world. In earlier times people never submersed themselves in matter in such a purely external way as today. When they spoke about water, like Thales for example, they referred to something spiritual. Empedocles was the person who in a certain sense pre-empted a materialistic principle in that he compiled all existence out of the four elements which, however, he conceived of materially. And he conceived of the constitution of the world through mixing and separating this matter. He lost the spiritual because—in looking back on his incarnations as an occult personality—he should have found the Christ impulse. He would have been the right person for that.

When we look back today in the Akasha Chronicle we find the Christ impulse in a very specific place. But anyone living before the Christ impulse could not do that. They could not incorporate it as an earthly impulse because it had not yet existed physically. That is what Empedocles missed, what could not flow into his soul. He did not have the counterweight to the materialism arising in him. But because he was a personality with strong impulses, the impulses of the occultist, this made him act out such disharmony. This is what the truth turned out to be. This brought him to the point of wanting to be one with the material aspect of the four elements, just as otherwise when we seek the truth we want to unite ourselves with this spiritual aspect in the spirit. And he threw himself into Etna. He threw himself in because he wanted to be one with the elements. He sought to identify himself with the divine which appeared to him in a material image. And I would say that this product of the immolation in the fires of Etna still exists today as something fertilizing in the atmosphere of Sicily, like the effect of a sacrifice. There is something great and mighty present but it is based on this what we might call wrong, dismissive materialism—please do not misunderstand the expression 'wrong'—which was wrong for its time. Empedocles, who could not find Christ in looking back although he needed to find him, throws his life away. That is how it came about that he returned to life in such a curious way at the start of the modern age and lived there quite differently. The time has not yet come to speak of the personality in which he was reincarnated.

A wonderful view opens up of what the Christ impulse actually is in the course of development. The Christ event is situated right in the middle between the earlier and later incarnation of Empedocles. And when we compare the two incarnations, we can see in the individuality of Empedocles what the effect is when we look back as a spirit with the new way of looking at things and find the Christ impulse or do not find it. That makes a huge difference. Just as souls in ancient times had to go back from incarnation to incarnation to see how they united themselves with the divine-spiritual being in earlier incarnations, so we have to have the possibility—when we go backwards from our own incarnation and follow the time from our birth to the previous death and then from the latter to the previous birth and so on—to find the Christ impulse on this path. It has to be found specifically by spiritual researchers. The Christ impulse sparks a light whereas otherwise they are plunged into darkness at this moment and everything that existed lies in darkness. We need the Christ impulse like a torch precisely in the field of spiritual research because otherwise darkness comes, otherwise we cannot look with clairvoyance into the true ground of the Akasha Chronicle of ancient times.

That can be observed in a wonderful way in an example such as that of Empedocles. Here we can obtain a feeling of how these incarnations follow one another in our earth existence, how as it were human beings moved in a descending direction as far as the Christ impulse, how they stepped further and further out onto the physical plane, and how we are once again in the process of gradually ascending to spiritual regions. The last great spirit of descent is the great Buddha, the first great impulse for ascent Jesus Christ; and there is perhaps nothing that can give such a feeling of the mighty difference between the Buddha principle and the principle of Jesus Christ than if we consider what the great Buddha once said to his closest pupils with regard to his enlightenment, which is symbolically referred to as the enlightenment under the Bodhi tree. There Buddha says: 'When I look back to earlier incarnations, I see how I originated in the divine-spiritual ground of the world, how I have gone from incarnation to incarnation, always living with my spiritual core in the outer temple of the body, descending into the physical world. But now, in this incarnation, I have found the possibility of not having to return to an incarnation. I have gone from one bodily temple to the next; in each incarnation the deity has erected the temple of my body for me. Now that I am incarnated in it for the last time, I feel how in this bodily temple the timber is collapsing and how I no longer need to return to such a temple.' Because that was his teaching, that true striving has to aim to leave behind our activity on earth, must no longer have a connection with the bodily temple but strive towards the final incarnation when we can leave it in order to continue to live purely in the spirit. That was the last reference to the descent of human beings, to a memory which human beings could have of the archetypal wisdom, of what stood at the start of the human race.

Oh, it is moving to see the Buddha standing there, saying: 'I have proceeded from one bodily temple to the next; now I feel that it is for the last time.' If we compare this—ignoring all the metaphysical background—with the intimate words which Christ spoke to his closest pupils, with his saying: 'Destroy this temple and in three days I will raise it up again'[116]—then we can see that there was the great longing in the Buddha for the timber of the bodily temple to collapse and for there no longer to be a necessity to return to it, but that in Christ there was the promise 'Destroy it, and in three days I will raise it up again'. Here we find expressed the love for the earth world, for the following incarnations of human beings in which they find the possibility to keep rebuilding the temple of their body so that they can keep learning and ascending, so that when the earth has reached its goal the earth itself becomes a corpse, falls away so to speak from the soul nature of humanity as a whole just as our body falls away from the soul when we pass through the portal of death. But then human beings will have ascended further and further. In being Christianized, human beings have become capable of transferring their lives to new stages of existence as humanity as a whole. Christ's words do not mean that he intends to return into a physical body himself but that he will return to the principle of building the body, that he will remain with earth existence until the end of the earth.

I tried to express that in what I have Theodora, the seer in the Mystery Drama, say,[117] where you can see how Christ will become more and more familiar in human life although he will not return to a physical body. But he will be experienced in the physical temple of the body of human beings. And his words 'Destroy this temple and in three days I will raise it up again' contain the promise: 'Yes, I will make it true that I can enter into human souls so that increasing numbers of people can come who can say as Paul did, "Not I, but Christ in me." '

So we can see how we can look at spiritual science on a small scale as a principle of life in that we obtain the possibility to see the karmic effect of certain characteristics of our character, our soul, between birth and death, and in seeing their effect continue into the bodily organization of the next incarnation. And so we can see how spiritual science on a large scale presents us with the noblest ideals and tells us what will become of us—Christianized human beings—when the earth will become a corpse and fall away from the soul element of human beings, when human beings will be called upon to progress to other planetary states. Thus spiritual science can give us the greatest ideals and flow into the most minor circumstances of life. That makes it practical for life and that is what it can and should increasingly become.

If we become anthroposophists in the sense that all our conduct— and be it in this or that place in life which might appear to be far removed from actual anthroposophical activity—is imbued in every detail by an anthroposophical attitude, by anthroposophical reflection and thinking in every detail, only then will have occurred what we can call the fulfilment of our being with anthroposophy. Anthroposophy must not be considered as a theory; it has to be seen at the same time as something to be practised in life but as a practice in life which needs to be learnt. And basically we have to be clear that we have to spur ourselves on through the true concrete content of anthroposophy if it is to become something we practise in life, and not to want to say: I understand this about anthroposophy and it is the correct thing—but that we first make ourselves deeply, deeply familiar with what spiritual science can tell us. Then it has to become a force in our life. And it cannot do that until we have imbued ourselves with it. But then it will become that on the smallest and on the largest scale, then we will obtain an outlook on the greater context of human progress and on the most minor facts of everyday life.

LECTURE 13

IF we go out into the streets of our large cities at this time, we find these streets filled with the things which our contemporaries want to buy for themselves to celebrate the festival which is coming up, to celebrate one of the major festivals which humanity can celebrate in the course of a year: the festival commemorating one of the mightiest impulses in the development of humanity. And yet, if we let pass through our hearts what will happen in the next few days in such a big city as this one, in which we find ourselves here, for example, to celebrate this festival of commemoration, if we ask ourselves if that corresponds to what should pass through the souls and hearts of human beings, if we do not surrender ourselves to any illusions but look truth straight in the eye, then perhaps we cannot avoid admitting to ourselves how little all the things which we see in preparation and perhaps also in the celebration of the Christmas festival fit on the one hand with what otherwise happens in modern culture around us, and how little they fit on the other hand with everything which basically should live deeply in the heart of human beings as a commemoration and thought of the greatest impulse which could have happened to humanity in the course of its development.

It is perhaps not to say too much if we express the opinion that not all the things have such a harmonious effect on our eye any longer which want to be imbued by the Christmas mood, which want to receive this Christmas mood from the things which we can see in our surroundings today. The effect is not so harmonious when our modes of transport go whizzing through the middle of the streets in which the Christmas trees or other preparations for the Christmas festival are set up. And if people today perhaps no longer experience this disharmony to its full extent then it is for the reason that they have already broken the habit of feeling the depth of inwardness which can be associated particularly with the forthcoming festival. Because what is left for the inhabitants of our cities of everything that gives depth to the Christmas festival is basically no more than a last echo which hardly any longer gives any idea of its greatness, a habit in which such greatness can no longer be perceived and which people have become used to in the course of the centuries.

It would be completely wrong if we were to look in a pessimistic mood at the fact that the times have changed and that it is impossible today in our major cities to develop the deep inwardness with regard to this festival which once existed. It would not be right to let such a pessimistic mood arise if at the same time we can have an inkling, as is the purpose of this group, of how humanity can once again approach this impulse in all its depth and greatness, something which should be felt particularly at this festival. Seeking souls have every reason to ask themselves in their soul: what should this Christ festival mean to us? And they may admit to themselves in their hearts: through spiritual science in particular something will be given to the whole of humanity once again which will bring in the fullest sense of the word that which can no longer be here now, and of which we must admit that it can no longer be here if we do not want to give ourselves over to illusion and fantasy and see something which has become a pure occasion for giving presents as being equivalent to what the Christ festival was for human beings for centuries: a festival whose celebration gave souls the joy of hope, the security of hope and the awareness of being part of a spiritual being which descended from spiritual heights, united itself with the world so that every willing soul can have a part of it.

A festival was celebrated throughout the centuries which awoke an awareness in souls that the individual human soul has a strong force in the spiritual power we have just characterized and that all human beings who are willing can come together in the service of this spiritual power, can come together in its service in such a way that they also find the right paths on earth to be as much as they can be as human beings for each other, to love each other as much as they can as human beings.

If, as seems appropriate, we wish on occasion to let the comparison act on our soul between what the Christmas festival has been through centuries and what it is to become again, then it can be a good thing to compare the mood which is prevalent in circles around us today through the cultural demands of the present with what the Christmas festival once was, and on the other hand with what this festival can become in souls once again precisely through spiritual science through a renewal which has become timeless as it were.

City people today are hardly capable any longer of completely appreciating to its full depth what is connected with our annual festivals. It is hardly possible to feel that magic which passed like a spiritual breath through the souls, through the minds of those who believed that they were carrying Christ in their heart during the great festive events at Christmas or Easter. To feel this magic which passed through humanity in these periods like a spiritual breath has become really quite difficult, particularly for city people today. Anyone who still had the opportunity to see even just a little of this magic wind which was able to pass through the souls and the minds in those times will undoubtedly have that as a wonderful, a magnificent memory. I myself only saw the last remnants as a child of what was able to pass of such a magic wind through the souls, through the minds in the villages in German regions—how in young and old, when Christmas time approached, something truly arose in the innermost depth of the soul which was different from the feelings which were otherwise present throughout the year. A few decades ago it was still possible to feel something like this in villages when Christmas approached, how souls decorated themselves inwardly in a natural way and really experienced something like: the physical sunlight has descended during autumn into the deepest darkness of night, physical outer darkness has increased. The nights have grown long, the days have grown short. We have to sit in our living rooms. Whereas otherwise at the opposite times of the year we go out into the fields and feel the golden sunlight stream to meet us in the morning, feel the warmth of the sun and can do things with our hands in the long days of summer, we now have to sit a lot in our living rooms, have to know that there is a lot of darkness around us, often have to look out of the window at how the earth is covered with its winter gown.

It is not possible to describe in detail all the beautiful, all the wonderful soul moods which arose in the simplest peasant huts during Sunday afternoons and evenings when Christmas time was approaching because we would have to describe intimate soul moods. We would have to describe how many a person who got into fights and engaged in mischief throughout the rest of the year felt tamed in their soul as something quite self-evident because they were filled with the thought that Christmas was nearing. They felt that the time itself was too holy for mischief to be allowed to be done during this time.

That is only a small look at something which existed extensively hundreds of years ago and which could still be seen decades ago as a last remnant in the villages. Once the family celebration of Christmas had withdrawn into the houses, it was possible to see how in the houses there would be an imitation of the little manger in the stable in Bethlehem and how the children were excited about everything associated with that when they saw Joseph and Mary, the shepherds in front, the angels above, sometimes imitated in quite a primitive way. Such an imitation of the manger could be found in almost every house in certain villages.

What withdrew into the houses was more or less the last echo of something else which we will still touch on. Then it was still possible to see some decades ago, once the main days of Christmas, 25 and 26 December, were over and the festival of Epiphany approached, how groups of performers went through the villages, last performers of the Christmas story. The actual Christmas plays had become quite rare by that time but it was still possible to see many instances of the Three Kings play as a last echo, perhaps even today still in remote villages. There were the Holy Three Kings dressed strangely in various ways with paper crowns and a star on their head who went through the village and in primitive voices, rarely without humour but holy and humorous at the same time, awoke everything that the soul was meant to feel following on from what the Bible said about the great Christ impulse in human development.

That is the key thing, that it was this mood which was poured into hearts specifically at Christmas time and in the days and weeks around it in which they were able to take in everything which was put before their soul in a simple and direct way and in which the whole village participated. Such grotesquely comedic depiction of holy scenes as they have become common in modern times in the imitation of the Oberammergau passion plays would not have been understood at the time when the memory of and thoughts about the great periods of humanity were still alive. Because people would not have wanted to experience the events of Holy Night and the Three Kings at any other time than in these days of the year, the Passion story at any other time than Easter. People felt a unity with what spoke out of the stars, out of the weeks, out of the seasons, what spoke out of snow and sunshine; and they wanted to hear the tale of what they wished to and should feel as told by the 'star singers' walking the rounds in a white smock and with a paper crown on their head, one of whom carried a star which was attached to scissors so that he was able to extend the star. They walked through the villages, stopped in front of the houses and presented their simple things. And the only thing that mattered was that people were able to take in at this particular time and with hearts attuned in this way what was intended to penetrate the souls of people in that time.

The things which I sometimes heard in the villages remain a beautiful memory for me, the way such simple rhymes were spoken by the 'star singers' as they wandered through the villages—such as the following for example:

The Oberschützen Star Singers[118]

In God's Name now our tale begins.
From Orient came the Holy Kings.
They ride with speed on distant ways,
Four hundred miles in thirteen days.
They ride by Herod's palace-walls
As Herod from his window calls:
Whither go ye, relax your speed!
To Bethlehem our journey does lead.
Ye Holy Three Kings be guests of mine,
I will draw plenty of beer and wine,
I will serve venison roast and fish;

To know of the newborn king is my wish.
In truth, we cannot tell just where;
We have to follow the star we bear:
Over the house the star will shine bright.
Over the mountains the holy men ride.
There found they Jesus Christ, our Lord,
Who is the Saviour of all the world.
Why is the hindmost oh so black?
He is the king from Ethiopia.

These things were organized in such a way that the whole village took part in them. At a particular line the star, for example, might be extended as far as possible. This Christmas or Three Kings star was the expression of the coherence between season, festival and human hearts. This was the greatness which spread through centuries over a wide region of our earth like a magic breath into the simplest minds. We have to place this to some extent before our soul, and as seekers of spiritual knowledge we are well placed to call it up before our soul because over the years in which we have been able to reflect on this great event we have been able to obtain a feeling once again as to the real power which has been given in that of which we are mindful in this festive period for all human beings and the whole of earth development.

Thus we may trust that we can obtain some understanding as to how in such earlier times the whole of the Christmas period—particularly among the peoples of the various German and eastern European regions[119]—was immersed in festive celebration, and how with the simplest means such festive celebration could be achieved. But perhaps today it is no longer anyone except the spiritual seekers who can understand what was the essence of the old Christmas plays.[120] What I have just presented to you as the star song is only a last ruin, a final remnant. If we went back through the centuries we would find how across wide regions the Christmas plays were performed when the time came, and whole villages were involved in what was presented. We may well say that in relation to these things, in relation to our knowledge of the Christmas plays we are no longer in a position to be anything but collectors of what is on the way to being lost. I myself, who still had the good fortune to have such a collector as an old friend, heard him tell many things about what he encountered as a scholarly collector of Christmas plays, particularly in the German-speaking areas of Hungary.

In those German language islands of Hungary in which the German mother tongue, the German vernacular had been preserved prior to the period of Magyarization in the 1850s and 1860s, quite a lot still happened in terms of Christmas plays and Christmas customs which had long sunk into oblivion in the main regions, in the German motherland. The individual colonists who had emigrated to the Slavic areas in the course of the preceding centuries retained their old Christmas plays and renewed them when they found the right people, who were always taken from among the villagers, to perform the Christmas plays. I can well remember—and you will perhaps grant me that I can judge this— the enthusiasm with which old Schröer[121] spoke about such Christmas plays, when he told how he had been present when the people had celebrated their Christmas plays during this festive period. We do not obtain any concept—this is no exaggeration—of the innermost being of the artistic until we have gone to these villagers and have seen how they gave birth to the simple art of the Christmas play from out of a most sacred mood.

The people who today think they can learn to declaim from this or that teacher, who go hither and thither to do these or those breathing exercises, whichever happen to be the right ones—there are many dozens of correct methods of breathing for singing or declamation— these people believe that the important thing is to turn the human body or larynx into the right sort of automaton to foster some art or other in a materialistic way. I only hope that this curious view will never really take root in our circles because these people have no idea how simple but real art was born out of the most sacred mood, out of a prayerful Christmas mood; how it was performed in a deeply Christian mood in the soul and breast of village lads who at other times of the year often played quite wanton and mischievous pranks. Because these simple people under their straw roofs knew infinitely more about the connections of the human soul, about the whole human being and about art than people today know in our modern theatres or the rest of the art scene, no matter how much people make a fuss about art being something which has to come from the whole human being and, if it is sacred art, from the sacred, pious mood of human beings.

You can see this, for example, from the four main rules as they still existed in the areas which Schröer was still able to visit.

When Christmas plays were performed in areas of upper Hungary, then as October or November approached the person to whom the Christmas plays had been handed down—never in written form because writing them down was considered to be a profanity—gathered together the people whom he considered suitable. And suitable in this Christmas period were really people of whom one would not otherwise have assumed it: wanton, naughty lads who had done their fair share of messing about during the year. But during this period the necessary mood entered these souls. There were strict rules for the participants in the Christmas plays during the weeks of rehearsal. Each one who wanted to take part had strictly to observe the following four rules.[122] We have of course to imagine ourselves in village life and consider what it meant in the life of the village not to be allowed to take part in such an event.

'Everyone who wants to be involved in the performance must 1) not visit floozies; 2) not sing any ribald songs throughout the whole period; 3) lead an honourable life; 4) obey me. All these things are subject to a fine, including any lapses of memory and suchlike.'

Is this not an echo of the consciousness which existed in holy places in the ancient mysteries where it was also thought that we cannot obtain wisdom through ordinary schooling? So here too there was a consciousness that a person as a whole in his or her mind and morals had to be purified if they were to approach art in a worthy way. Such things should be born out of the whole human being. And the Christmas mood made it possible that devoutness could exist in the roughest lads.

What I have just spoken about,[123] what Schröer and others were still able to collect in the way of Christmas plays, which were performed as if they were the remnant of something much older, is little more than a relic. We are looking back at much earlier periods, at periods of the sixteenth, fifteenth, fourteenth century and so on where the relationships between villages and towns were still quite different, where indeed the souls of the village inhabitants were immersed in quite a different mood at Christmas time through what was given to them through these plays, where with the simplest, and most primitive methods the holy legend was performed, the birth of Christ with everything in the Bible which belongs to it. And just as Christmas Day, 25 December, is preceded in the calendar by the feast day of Adam and Eve, so normally the play, which was thought of as the actual Christmas play, was preceded by the so-called Paradise play, the play about Adam and Eve in Paradise and how they fell victim to the devil, the serpent. It was possible to obtain a direct insight in the simplest regions into the connection which exists between the descent of human beings from spiritual realms into the sphere of the physical plane and the jolt which human beings received through the Christ impulse back up into spiritual worlds.

When human beings read the epistles of Paul they obtain a sense of the grandiose nature of the Pauline view about the human being who descended in Adam from the spiritual world into the sensory one, and about the 'new Adam', Christ, in whom the human being ascends again from the sensory world into the spiritual one; when human beings experience and feel this in Paul in a grandiose way—the simplest people down as far as the children could sense this in the depths of their heart, in the depths of their soul in an inward, loving and mindful way when at that time the Paradise play about Adam and Eve, about the Fall of human beings and the Christmas play about the revelation of Christ were performed for them one after the other. And the mighty caesura which came about in human development through the Christ event was felt at a very profound level. A reverse of the path of development, that was how the Christ event was experienced. The path from Adam to Christ was like the path from heaven to earth as it were. The path of Christ to the end of the earth period is a path from the earth to heaven. That was experienced in the most inward way when the two plays which have been characterized here a little were performed in a primitive way to thousands and thousands of people. Because the complete renewal through the Christ impulse of what is the human spirit was experienced.

We might perhaps also still feel something like an echo of what was experienced with regard to the reversal of the whole progress of humanity in the words which come from very ancient times, from the first Christian centuries, and which were very often spoken as late as the eighth, ninth, tenth centuries in regions in which Christianity had spread specifically within Europe. Something immense was felt in words such as the following:

> Ave maris stella
> Dei mater alma
> Atque semper virgo
> Felix coeli porta.
> Sumens illud Ave
> Gabrielis ore
> Funda nos in pace
> Mutans nomen Evae

When these words were spoken, people felt the path of human beings from heaven to earth through the Fall and the ascent of human beings from the earth to heaven through Christ, and this was felt in the two female figures, in 'Eva' and in the name which was attached to the Mother of Jesus, with which she was greeted as it were, 'Ave'. Ave is the reversal of the name Eva and when we read Ave backwards we get Eva. That was experienced in its full meaning, hence these words which also show what was experienced within the most elemental phenomena of nature and at the same time the human aspect which was experienced in the legend:

> Ave, star of the ocean,
> Divine young mother
> And eternal virgin,
> Happy portal of heaven that you are.
> Accepting the Ave
> As a gift from Gabriel
> You became our foundation of peace
> In that you reversed
> The name Eva.

The greatest mysteries, the greatest secrets of human development were experienced in such simple words. And in the reversal of the name Eva to Ave each person experienced in an inward way what can then be taken in a grandiose way from the epistles of Paul[124] when we read the passages about Adam, the 'old' Adam, and about Christ, the 'new' Adam. This mood was then present when in the days of the Christmas Festival the Paradise play, which presented the Fall, and the Christmas play, which represents the hope which can come to every human soul in the future if it incorporates the power which lies in the Christ impulse, were primitively performed one after the other. But such a feeling also requires an attitude of mind in which we have to be clear that it can no longer exist in that way today. Times have changed. The impossibility of looking into the spiritual worlds as it is given today for the most primitive and the most intelligent populations, such a fundamental materialistic element in the human mind did not exist at that time. An assumption of the existence of the spiritual world was self-evident. And a certain understanding of the spiritual world and its differences to the sensory world was equally self-evident. People today have little understanding of the way that the spirit could be felt up into the fifteenth, sixteenth century and how basically there was an awareness of spirituality everywhere.

If the repeat of one of the Christmas plays, a Christmas play from the upper Palatinate which is to be performed in our two art rooms,[125] is successful, then an understanding of the spiritual mood it contains may perhaps also be awoken once again outside our circles. For us some of the lines in such a Christmas play in particular should become an identifying mark of the spiritual sense that existed in the festive period in those who were intended to understand this Christmas play. When for example in one of the Christmas plays Mary, expecting the Jesus child, says, 'The time has come, I see the little child'—that means she sees the approaching child clairvoyantly in the days preceding the birth, as happens in so many Christmas plays—then let me ask you, where today could you find a similar tale for the same occasion? The times when there was a connection with the spiritual world, as it still existed consciously at that time, no longer exist. We should give ourselves over neither to an optimistic nor a pessimistic mood in that respect. We have to go to very remote primitive rural areas today if we want to find the vision of the child about to come in a few days. There are still such things.

This was the mood which was of course required for the immersion of what in these primitive memories and thoughts about the greatest event in human development was contributed to Christmas. Hence we have to find it quite comprehensible that this earlier poetry, this simple, primitive art, has been replaced by today's prose of the electrical railways and the automobiles which zoom along between the avenues of Christmas trees in such a grotesque way. It is impossible for an eye with any aesthetic sense to see the two things together: Christmas trees, Christmas markets, and automobiles and electric railways travelling between them. That impossibility is of course something which has become commonplace today, yet for the eye with any aesthetic sense it remains something impossible. But we nevertheless want to remain friends and not enemies of such a culture and understand that it has to be commonplace.

But we also want to understand how it is connected with the materialistic trait which runs through all minds, not just those in the cities, but also in the rural population. We can indeed eavesdrop on the materialistic mood as it sidles up to human minds. Go to the fourteenth, thirteenth century and you will find that people are fully aware that they mean something spiritual when they talk about the tree of knowledge in Paradise, for example. They know correctly what is being shown to them in the Paradise play, know to make the correct spiritual connection for what is represented as the tree of knowledge or the tree of life. Because superstition was by no means as widespread in those times than it subsequently became in the fifteenth, sixteenth, seventeenth century. In contrast we find in the fifteenth century for example near Bamberg—this can be verified historically—that people went out into the apple orchards at Christmas because they were expecting a particular chosen tree to physically and materially blossom at Christmas. The whole life of the mind of people had grown materialistic in the period which started in the thirteenth and fourteenth century, continued through the sixteenth, seventeenth century and existed not just in the towns but also in the souls of those who were simple villagers.

A lot of what was the old poetry still crept into the houses with their Christmas tree. But what wafted through the villages as the holiest mood like a mystery has turned to purely outward poetry, to the poetry of the Christmas tree which is still beautiful but nevertheless an echo of something great. Why is that so? Because humanity had to pass through a development in the course of time, because what was inward, great and important in one time cannot remain in the same form for all time. Because anyone who wanted to drag into another time what is great in one time would be an enemy of the development of humanity. Each time has its particular tasks and in each time we have to understand how to give life to what is meant to penetrate into the souls and hearts of human beings. Our time can quite certainly only immerse itself in that true Christmas mood, which we could intimate in our description, like a historical memory, like a piece of the past. But if we nevertheless include the symbol of the Christmas tree in our festive gatherings we do it precisely for the reason that we combine with anthroposophical spiritual science itself the thought of a new Christmas mood in humanity, a humanity which has advanced.

It is the task of spiritual science to lower the secrets of Christ in such a way into the hearts and souls of human beings as is appropriate for our time. Despite the fact that our modern modes of transport zoom past us when we step out of the door or maybe even fly away with us into the skies—soon these things will create the most mundane, most dreadful prose for humanity—human beings today must nevertheless have the opportunity to rediscover the divine-spiritual all the more strongly and significantly in a deepening of their soul, the divine-spiritual which appeared in such a simple way to the primitive minds of past centuries when they saw the holy child in the manger at Christmas time. We need other means today to awaken this mood in the soul. We may well wish to immerse ourselves in what previous ages possessed to find their way to the Christ event but we must also be independent of those times. The way that people in previous times felt their way into the secrets of nature was only possible in a primitive time. We need other tools today.

I want to give just one more idea of how people felt their way into nature when Christmas was approaching, felt their way into nature in a quite primitive way and yet spoke earthily in their mind out of an experience of the elements of nature. If I may tell you about another star song, you will perhaps feel properly only in a single place how the elements of nature spoke out of the soul. The rest is pretty primitive. But if you listen with greater care you will get a feeling of that natural mood from more of it.

For when the person whose task it was to gather together the actors for the Christmas play or the Three Kings play went with them, and when they made their appearance in various places, then they first of all greeted those who had come together because the abstract mood which exists today between actors and audience did not exist previously. People belonged together and everything was immersed in a common setting. Hence the actors made their appearance by welcoming those who were there and also those who were not there in a primitive way. That created a real Christmas mood.

The star singer speaks:[126]

> Beloved singers mine, let's gather as a clan
> Like fritters in a frying pan,
> Beloved singers mine, take up your place,
> We want to pass our while with singing in this space.
> Beloved singers mine, so strong and smart,
> With greetings do we want to start.
> Let us greet God-Father on His highest throne
> And let us greet also His only Son.
> Let us greet the Holy Spirit by name
> And then greet all three together again.

(Joseph and Mary enter the stage.)

> Let us greet Joseph and Mary mild,
> And we also greet the little child.
> Let us greet the ox and also the ass,
> Which stand near the crib with straw and grass.
> Let us greet them through sunlight and moonshine
> That shine on the sea and the river Rhine.
> Let us greet them through foliage and grassy blade,
> Through the holy rain that has wet us all made.
> Let us greet the emperor and his crown,
> And him who made it, a master of great renown.
> Let us greet the squire, Sir Palfi by name,
> Also his officers we greet the same.

Let us greet our fathers of the church, so stern,
Because this play they allowed us to learn.
Let us greet the judge and the jury elect
With worthy honour and respect.
The whole honoured community we greet
All who together here we meet.
Let us greet the honoured council of this place
By God ordained to serve in this space.
Let us greet them through the roots, large and small,
Which are in the earth, many and all.
Beloved singers mine, turn now to another thing.
To greet the star we shall now sing.
Let us greet the slats, so carefully matched,
To which our star is then attached.
Let us greet the scissors that can stretch out far
By which can wander around the star.
We greet all the little slats of wood
As many as make our star look so good.
Beloved singers mine, harken well to my words
We sang to the star and to all of its parts.
Now we greet our master singer with glee
And also his hat which here you see.
Let us greet our teacher, who indeed,
With God's help taught us what we need.
Beloved singers mine, note well this thing,
To all of these we did now sing.

Now I would ask you to take note of what it means to call on nature in this way, for everyone whom the players want to greet to be greeted with such a mood in their hearts, for such a mood to be felt in 'the roots, large and small, which are in the earth, many and all'. That is a feeling of the mood of nature itself. Thus we have to recognize how people at that time were united with everything that was holy, great and spiritual down as far as the roots of the grasses and trees. Anyone who can obtain a sense of this will feel in the line just quoted something grandiose with regard to the secrets of human development. The times in which this was natural, in which it was something self-evident are past and today we need other means. We need the means to take us to an even deeper source in human nature which in a certain sense is independent of external time. Because culture itself, the way it operates today makes it impossible for us to tie ourselves exactly to the seasons. Anyone who therefore truly understands the mood which could be felt as the Christ mood at holy Christmas in olden times will also understand what we are trying to achieve in that we want to deepen artistically again what we have been able to obtain from spiritual science, what we are trying to achieve in striving to give life to that source in human minds which can incorporate within itself the Christ impulse.

We can no longer directly awaken what is great at Christmas, much as we would like to awaken this impulse in our souls at this time in particular, but we will always seek it. And if we see a Christmas festival of human progress as such in what anthroposophical spiritual science is meant to be for humanity, and if we look at what ordinary people were able to feel when they were presented with the child in the manger in holy Christmas night, then we can say to ourselves: such moods, such feelings should awaken in us when we look at what can be born in our soul, when cognition of the spirit produces such a holy mood in our innermost source, purifies it to such an extent, that it can incorporate within itself the holy mystery of the Christ impulse.

From this perspective we also attempt to find the true art, the art which wells up out of the spirit and cannot be anything other than a child of devotion, a child of the holiest feelings. If we feel the eternal, the everlasting Christmas festival in this respect, and how the Christ impulse can be born in the human being, in the human soul, in the human mind, when we experience once again through spiritual science how this Christ impulse is something real which can truly be decanted into our souls as a living force, then the Christ impulse will not remain something abstract, something dogmatic through spiritual science. Then this Christ impulse, which arises from our spiritual movement, will become something for us which can give us consolation in the worst moments of our life, which can give us joy in the hope that when Christ is born in our soul, at the Christmas time of the soul, we can anticipate that at Easter the spirit will be resurrected within us.

Thus we must progress again from the materialism which has entered all spirits, all hearts, to something spiritual. Because the renewal which is necessary in the face of what is the prose of life today can only be born out of the spirit. If it is possible even when automobiles drive past outside, airships perhaps fly through the air, electrical railways zoom along—if it is possible in such rooms as these here to let something spread of the holy mood which can only be understood through what we obtain in the course of the whole of the year as spiritual knowledge, bringing Christ closer to us, and which in earlier times lived in a much more childlike mood, then there is hope that in a certain respect these meeting rooms will become 'mangers' which we can look at in a similar way to the way that the children and adults looked at the child, at the shepherds in front and at 'the ox and also the ass, which stand near the crib with straw and grass' when the manger was set up in the home or before that in the church. Here they felt that from this symbol there flowed into their hearts hope for all human love, for all human great- ness, for all earthly goals.

If on this day, which is meant to be dedicated and devoted to commemorating the Christ impulse, we can feel that throughout the year something is set alight in our hearts as the result of our serious spiritual-scientific striving, then our hearts will feel on this day: these are mangers, these our meeting places, and these lights are the symbols. These mangers through the holy mood that is within them, and these lights through the symbolism of their radiance—they contain some- thing that like Christmas, like Easter is intended to prepare a great period of humanity: the resurrection of the Holy Spirit, of the truly spiritual life.

Let us try to foster the feeling that our meeting rooms are mangers at Christmas time, places in which something great is in preparation away from the external world; let us learn to feel that, if we study busily throughout the year, our insights, the wisdom we have obtained can be concentrated on such a Christmas Eve into burning feelings—feelings which begin to glow like fire out of the combustible material which we have obtained throughout the year through the study of great teachings. And let us feel that in doing so we are cultivating the memory of the greatest impulse in human development. Let us feel how as a result the belief can live in these places that in the future what burns as holy fire and the light of secure hope will penetrate into humanity. Then it will be strong enough, powerful enough to penetrate, inspire, warm and illuminate also the hardest, the most mundane prose of life. Then we can experience the Christmas mood here as a mood of hope for the world's Easter mood which is an expression of the living spirit which is required for modern humanity.

We will celebrate Christmas the best way in our souls if we fill the next few days with this mood, fill them in such a way that we spiritually prepare the Easter of humanity, the resurrection of spiritual life, in our Christmas. Indeed, let our places of work become mangers at Christmas time. Let the child of light be born which is kindled throughout the year by contemplation of spiritual-scientific wisdom. Let Christ be born in the human soul in our places of work so that the spiritual life can be resurrected at the great Easter of humanity which in its essence must experience spirituality as a resurrection through the Christmas mood flowing out of our rooms into the general humanity of the present and the future.

LECTURE 14

STUTTGART, 27 DECEMBER 1910

The spirit whose incorporation enables the human soul to keep developing as the world progresses is an eternal one. But the way in which it lives and comes to expression in what human beings can feel, love and create on earth is new in each new age. And that is precisely the task of human beings in the progression of the world, to enable the spirit to assume these many consecutive forms through which it climbs up the ladder to the perfection of which we have an inkling—and of which we should actually have no more than an inkling, which we do not want to compress into clear concepts. If we think about the spirit and its development in the course of humanity in this way, then eternity and transience appear before our soul's eye. And in the specific cases as they keep appearing everywhere in life we can see how the eternal appears in the transient, how it comes to expression in the transient in order then to disappear again and reassert itself in ever new forms. We can also experience the symbols of Christmas as they surround us here as something which belongs to past forms of seeing the eternal in the external world in symbolic form.

For truly when we go out in the second half of December in our present time, particularly into the streets of our cities, and see out there the splendour of Christmas and everything that invites us into homes to celebrate Christmas, then it is painful for eyes which still have an aesthetic sense when they see these things spread out in the Christmas market and see zooming through them what cannot basically zoom through Christmas trees and Christmas symbols: automobiles, electrical trams and so on. In a certain sense these things no longer belong together in the way they can be experienced today. We feel the whole matter even more deeply when we visualize what this Christmas festival has become for many of the people who in the cities want to be the pillars of education in the present. A festival of presents, a festival which has retained little of the warmth, of the thorough depth of feeling which existed in connection with this festival in a not yet very distant past: it has become a festival of presents. The things which what we call our anthroposophical world-view, our anthroposophical understanding want to give us should once again include the very warm sentiments and feelings which passed through the soul on the high feast days of the old church year.

And we should learn to understand once again what a necessity it is for us, what a necessity it is for our souls at certain times to feel the full connection with the great world out of which human beings are born to renew our intellectual and feeling forces, but also our moral forces. For the Christmas festival was at one time a festival in which all morality, all humanness could be renewed, spreading a warmth in its symbols which is hardly possible to understand any longer in the mundaneness of today, the prosaic life of today. But for us, putting ourselves in these symbols could be something which can place before our soul a little of the sensations, the sentiments, the feelings which we ourselves can have towards this resurrection, which we sense as the anthroposophical resurrection of human beings, and which we can therefore also have towards the birth of the anthroposophical spirit in our soul. And there is a kind of connection between the older thoughts about the festival of Christ's birth and the newer anthroposophical thoughts about the birth of our anthroposophical ideas and sentiments, the whole of the anthroposophical spirit in the manger of our heart: there is such a relationship. And today it is perhaps the anthroposophist who is most likely to be able to immerse himself or herself in what was felt for long periods of time particularly at the Christian Christmas festival, which it will be possible to feel once again when something similar will be born out of the atmosphere which already surrounds us today, out of the atmosphere of materialism in the present time.

But in wanting to have such anthroposophical feelings about the

Christmas festival, we cannot restrict ourselves just to what was or is the Christian Christmas festival. Wherever we may look in the world and however far we look into distant periods of the past: something which can be compared, which can come close in thoughts and feelings to the feeling of Christmas, something of that nature has basically always existed everywhere. We will not go far today, we will only go to the feelings and sentiments which a person could have in our regions, in the regions of central Europe before the introduction of Christianity which corresponded to those as the Christmas festival approaches today. Let us take a brief look back at the times before the introduction of Christianity in Europe in which in a comparatively rough climate our ancestors in Europe had to provide for themselves in that they lived for the whole of the summer as a kind of herding or farming people in an intimate connection of their sentiments and feelings with the whole great natural world: in devout prayer to the rays of the sun, in fervent worship not in thought but in feeling and devotion, in fervent reverence towards the great world.

And when the old shepherd or cattle breeder in Europe was out in his rough fields, often in the burning hot sun, he then experienced not just something of outwardly physical nature but he felt an intimate connection of his whole being with what shone towards him in the physiognomy of nature. He lived with his whole heart in nature. Not just that the physical rays of the sun were reflected in his eyes, in his heart the sunlight spiritually kindled a rejoicing about summer which basically had its focus in the fires which then became St John's fires. The whole of nature wanted to rejoice in human hearts, the spirit of nature resound from human hearts.

That was how people felt throughout the year. And thus people also felt themselves in an intimate communality with the animal world which they cared for. Then autumn came, then came the times in which severe winter set in. I am thinking of the times in which severe winters spread across the land of the kind which people today can hardly imagine. Then all the livestock had to be slaughtered leaving only what was absolutely necessary to keep. Then all outer life became silent; it was truly as if something held entry into human hearts which we can call a kind of death, of darkness in comparison to all the moods which passed through human hearts in the summer. These were the times in which there really was still an echo of ancient clairvoyant forces particularly through the specific characteristics of the climate and nature which existed in central Europe. The people who rejoiced in the summer as if nature itself was rejoicing in their hearts, these same people became silent and quiet in themselves in winter, as winter approached; they let arise in the interior something of the mood which should descend on human beings when they enter their own inner world in total disregard of the outer world in order to sense and feel the divine inside them.

So it was nature itself which gave the ancient people of Europe the possibility to fully immerse themselves in their own interior from out of their life in the external world. Such a descent into death and darkness was experienced, as November approached, for weeks as a festive period; it was experienced as the approach of what is called Yuletide. And what arose as a result of this mood is something which can really show us for how long basically the memory of the ancient clairvoyant states remained, particularly of all people in central and northern Europe. What then followed in the period in which approximately our January and February approaches was that people felt a harbinger of nature beginning to rejoice anew inside them, the new resurrection of nature. This they experienced like a harbinger of what they were to experience in the outer world at a time when snow still covered the fields, when icicles still hung on the trees and nothing could yet be seen in nature to announce the joyous power which then, before the joyous power announced itself, was still a complete being-in-oneself, resting-in-oneself. That was transformed in the soul in such a way that people were released from themselves.

This intermediate stage, which was experienced by our ancestors in the approach of what we today call spring, was experienced in the way that the clairvoyant experiences his or her astral body when this astral body is not completely purified and cleansed. It was experienced as if the spiritual horizon was filled with all kinds of animal shapes. And that is what these people also sought to express. That formed a transition for them from the actual profound festive mood of approaching winter and the mood which was to come over the soul again in the summer. It imitated symbolically what the human astral body shows, imitated in boisterous games, in boisterous dances, in animal masks the transition from completely resting-within-oneself to the joyous emergence into the greatness of nature. That is how it was.

If we immerse ourselves in something like this, if we imagine that the sentiment of the people, the sense of the people across very wide circles was immersed in such a mood, then we will understand how on this ground there also existed a feeling of plunging down into external physical darkness, into the external physical death of nature, how it was also fully experienced that just in this plunging down into the physical death of nature, into physical darkness the highest light of the spirit can be given, and how the mood of plunging down into physical death is directly transformed into the boisterous mood which was given expression in animal masks, in boisterous dances and boisterous music. Yet there was not yet present a full feeling that if human beings are to find the supreme, the highest light they must seek it in the innermost depths. But the inward, devoted connection with all forces, with the whole interweaving and life of nature created the ground into which could be lowered what was to be announced to humanity for its evo-lution through the Christ impulse.

It was simply necessary to tell the sentiments and feelings of these people spread across the regions of Europe—not, however, in dry philistine words but in such a way that what one wanted to say spoke through symbols to the mind—it was simply necessary to make understood: in the place where you plunge down into darkness, into the death of external nature, there you can find an eternal, an everlasting light if you prepare your soul to feel in the right way. And this light was introduced into human development through what has come to appearance in human development in the Mystery of Golgotha, in the events in Palestine.

It is characteristic that in the following centuries the stage was reached that in Europe the Christ impulse was felt most inwardly, most warmly in the Christ child, in the birth of Christ. If we want to assign any task at all to humanity in evolution, how should this task be seen? In no other way than that human beings have divine-spiritual origins, that they descended ever deeper from these divine-spiritual origins, became more and more related to and interwoven with external physical matter, the external physical plane. But then we have to feel that human beings can again travel this path in reverse through the mighty impulse we call the Christ impulse. How they can reverse their course and, in overcoming what has led them into the physical world, travel the path from below upwards to spiritual heights.

If we have these feelings, we can tell ourselves: in the way that the human I is within the physical body, what this human I is like today, it has descended from divine-spiritual heights and feels interwoven with and caught up in the world of the external physical plane. But something else underlies this I, what we might call an innocent I below the sinful I. Where can we at least begin to encounter the I which is not yet interwoven with the physical world? It is—when we look back on our own life as it takes its course between birth and death—where we extend our memory back to the moment in which our ego consciousness appears at a certain point in our early years. The I is there, even if people do not remember it: it is there and lives and weaves within us also where there is not yet a concept of the I, where this I, as it looks around in the external world, interweaves with the physical plane; where there is not yet a concept of the I but where the I is there in the innocent state of the child; the I which can be there as an ideal which should be achieved once again but only once it has been imbued with everything which human beings can experience in the school of physical life on earth. And so the human heart can experience this ideal with inner warmth, even if sober reason may find it difficult to put it into words. Become like your I when it does not yet have a concept of itself. Become like you could become if you were to escape into your childhood I. The childhood I then illuminates everything that is acquired by your later I. And in experiencing this as an ideal it shines in Jesus of Nazareth into whom Christ was subsequently incarnated.

On the basis of such feelings we can understand how an intimate trait of human growth, of further human development was able to take hold in the minds of the simplest people across the whole of Europe when they saw the incarnation of the human being who could develop to incorporate Christ within himself. So we can see that it represented real progress, a mighty step forward when the feelings associated with ancient Yuletide were introduced into the feelings which were asso-

ciated with the festival celebrating the birth of Jesus. That was a mighty
step forward. We might describe this step forward by saying: the light
of Jesus Christ was lit in the darkness in which the soul was meant to
collect itself in preparation of the jubilation and rejoicing of the new
summer.

We can find an echo of what actually happened in the people of
Europe in what for the nineteenth century, or at least its second half,
had become little more than the subject of scholarly researchers and
collectors. We can find an echo still in the old Christmas plays. Such
Christmas plays were already performed in a special way in ancient
medieval times at around Christmas. They awoke all the feelings, all the
things which the soul could have by way of life at about the same time
in the same regions as could be experienced by people in still more
ancient times when Yuletide approached, as I characterized it just now.
And if we look from the old Yuletide festivals I spoke about to the
medieval Christmas plays we can obtain a real feeling of the warm
impulse which struck the people of Europe with Christianity. Yes
indeed, something very special here descended into hearts, into souls.

It is now no longer as it was before. In the nineteenth century it had
become nothing more than the subject matter for scholarly collectors.
There is nevertheless something touching if one knew the older type of
German philologist, German linguistic philologists, the philologists and
researchers looking into myths, who immersed themselves in what has
remained of Christmas plays from earlier centuries not with indifference
but with love, with deep love. I myself had such a collector as a friend
who for a longer period was a professor at a school in Bratislava in the
fifties and sixties of the last century. For a long time he undertook
research there into the German population which had ended up in the
eastern part of Hungary from the West and he was familiar with the
peculiar attraction of the customs and the language of the Zips Germans[127] still living in northern Hungary at the time, who have been
Magyarized since then. He learned on one occasion that there were still
Christmas plays alive in a lonely village near Bratislava. And he, I am
referring to my old friend Karl Julius Schröer,[128] went there and tried to
investigate what still lived there in the people from ancient times. He
later told me many things about the wonderful impressions which he

obtained of the last remnants which had remained of Christmas plays from much, much older periods.

In one village there was an old man. In his family there was the tradition as a custom that when Christmas time approached he gathered together those in the village who were suitable to perform a Christmas play, a Christmas play which was intended to present in a simple form what we possess in the Christmas story, what the Gospels tell us as the Christmas story, as the story of Herod and the Three Kings. But if we want to understand the very special nature of such Christmas plays, then we have to have a concept of what life was like in more ancient times among the simple people. That has now passed and should not be brought back either. If I want to describe what is important in this respect, then I could put it no differently than to say: do not the snowdrops have a certain season when they blossom, or the lily of the valley or violets, by placing themselves in the whole of the macrocosm? They can of course be grown in a greenhouse at different times but it is actually painful to experience the blossoming violet displaced into a different season from the one in which it is placed into the whole macrocosm. There is little understanding of these things in our present time but it is a similar situation with regard to the people in older times.

What people in certain periods through the Middle Ages were able to experience when autumn and the Christmas period approached—when the dark nights arrived—what people were able to experience then in such a way that the experience of their heart placed itself in the context of what lived outside in nature, that these experiences were in harmony with the snow outside and the snowflakes and the icicles on the trees, what was felt then could only be experienced in the Christmas period. It was a very special mood—it was something which gave the soul strength and healing power for the whole of the year. It really did refresh the soul; it was a real force. When decades ago it was still possible to observe the last remains of these feelings in some places, these feelings did come to appearance. And I myself can say as a thoroughly external experience on the physical plane that it was possible to find the most immoral, worthless lads who when the days grew shorter did not dare in their soul to be impious. Those who got involved in fights the most fought the least and those who were less involved in fights did not fight at all in the Christmas period. It was a real force which lived in the souls. And the period in the weeks around holy Christmas was immersed in this whole world of feeling.

What was it that people felt? What people experienced was indeed compressed in sentiments, in feelings: descent of human beings from divine-spiritual heights to the deepest point on the physical plane; reception of the Christ impulse, reversal of the path of human beings, ascent to divine-spiritual heights. That was felt in everything connected with the Christ event. That is why people liked to present not just the Christian events but, just as the feast day of Adam and Eve on 24 December was linked with the day of Jesus' birth on 25 December, the Paradise play was performed, with directly afterwards the Christmas play presenting the impulse of the ascent of human beings once again to divine-spiritual heights. It was a profound experience when in the Paradise play the name Eva was pronounced—the mother of human-kind from whom human beings originated, who then descended into the valley of physical life. That was listened to on one day and on the next day the reversal of that path of humanity. That is already indicated in the sound which was intended to express this reversal: Ave Maria! Ave was experienced as the reversal of Eva: Ave—Eva. It affected people profoundly when they heard something like the words, for example, which sounded innumerable times in ears and hearts from the fifth, sixth, seventh, eighth century onwards, and which were comprehended.

What we would say approximately is as follows:

> Ave maris stella
> Dei mater alma
> Atque semper virgo
> Felix coeli porta.
> Sumens illud Ave
> Gabrielis ore
> Funda nos in pace
> Mutans nomen Evae
>
> Ave, star of the ocean,
> Divine young mother
> And eternal virgin,

Happy portal of heaven that you are.
Accepting the Ave
As a gift from Gabriel
You became our foundation of peace
In that you reversed
The name Eva.

And in what was performed as the Paradise play people experienced something which had to be immersed in a Christmas, a holy mood. That was indeed deeply felt; and we may say this among anthroposophists: does this not remind us of the attitude towards truth in the mysteries—it was something greater there, of course—when we hear described the way in which the players in the Christmas plays rehearsed and prepared themselves, their behaviour before and during the Christmas plays? We know that the mysteries are thought of in such a way that the truth was not received in the mundane way which can be filled with any human mood. Anyone who feels something of the sacred nature of truth will find it a nonsense that truth could really be found in the prosaic, mundane lecture halls of the present. In the latter people have no idea that truth must be sought with a cleansed, purified, with a prepared soul, and that a soul will not find the truth if it has not first been sanctified in its innermost part, has not been prepared in its feelings. People today no longer have any idea of this in a time in which materialism sees truth as the most prosaic thing.

In the mysteries, truth was approached after the soul had passed through the trials testing it for its purity, its freedom, its fearlessness. And we might well say: does it not remind us of this when the old man with whom Karl Julius Schröer became acquainted demanded of the singers he gathered together that they adhere to the old rules? Anyone who has lived in a village knows what the first rule means. The first rule was that during all of the preparations none of the players were allowed to visit a floozy. That means something incredible in a village; it means being immersed in the devoutness of what one was intending to do. No one was allowed to sing a ribald song during the rehearsal period, that was another rule. No one was allowed to want anything other than to lead a good and honourable life; that was the third rule. And the fourth point was that the performers had to follow in all respects the person in whose hand the tradition of the Christmas play lay, which was only reluctantly disclosed.

These things were collected in the second half of the nineteenth century and the old feelings disappeared. Subsequently I had one more experience of the devoutness, the immense inwardness with which those who as scholars still had a connection with the people and remained, for example, in the scattered linguistic outposts of Hungary collected the old plays and songs. I came across a play about Herod when I was in Sibiu at Christmas time[129] where the teachers at the school in Sibiu had spent a lot of time collecting such plays. And so it was still possible in the second half of the nineteenth century to become acquainted with the collectors of what still lived on the ground of what I characterized with regard to Yuletide. Do not think of it in theoretical terms but imagine this warm magic touch of Christmas mood as it lives in these Christmas plays. It gives us at the same time a concept of the regeneration of the human being, of the belief of human beings through the Christ impulse in something divine-spiritual. Rehearsing such Christmas plays—it could indeed be something very instructive for us in our present time in which the idea of the way that art grows out of devoutness, out of religion, out of wisdom has long been lost.

Today, when people like to see art as something separated from everything else, when art has degenerated into formalism, for example, today we could learn a lot from the whole way that art was a blossom of humanity. As simple as it appeared in the Christmas plays, it was a blossom of the whole person's being. First the lads who performed the plays had to be devout, first they had to take into their whole being something like an extract of the whole Christmas mood. Then they had to learn to speak rhythmically in a strictly regulated way. Today, when the art of speaking in the old sense has been completely lost, when people no longer have any idea how rhyme plays a tremendous role and rhythm plays such a role, and how every movement of these people, who otherwise wielded the threshing flail, was rehearsed down to the very last detail, how they were completely immersed for weeks in rhythm, intonation and devotion to what they were meant to per-form—an awful lot could be learnt from this particularly for a real understanding of art today. Today, when artistic speaking, for example, has been lost to such an extent that barely more than the meaning is spoken whereas at that time the particularly attractive thing in these Christmas plays was that rhythm, tone, gesture, the whole human being spoke, it was truly something great even to see the last remnants.

When the days of Christmas were over, the Three Kings went about—at no other time than after Christmas. I myself can recall how I saw the Three Kings going about in the villages. They went from house to house. They had a star on scissors. It was flung far by extending the scissors. Flinging the star stood in harmony with the rhythm of these Three Kings, dressed in the most primitive way, who however prepared a proper festive mood through their whole manner and in the way they carried these things among the people at the right time, in the way they lived in it in self-abandonment. Our time can no longer understand this unless a mood can be reawoken which reflects that from out of what is to awaken in us as the life of the spirit we can be presented with something of a kind of timeless play, as has to be the case in our time, implemented in art through anthroposophy; this cannot, then, however be tied to festive periods but must be connected only with the eternal, with the eternal in the human soul which is not tied to the seasons.

Something which became a practical event for these souls could come to life in us: the Christ impulse in a particular time. Indeed, in a certain respect we are already deeply in a time in which materialism in the external world has taken such a great hold of all circles that quite different impulses are needed to renew the Christ impulse from the simple impulses which were at work in the Middle Ages. A renewal of the inward nature of human beings is needed, something which is the endeavour of anthroposophy, by raising the profoundest forces of the human soul, forces which are quite different still from those which we encountered in the symbols of Christmas, in the festive customs of Christmas. And as truthfully as we can learn specifically through anthroposophy to feel what went through hearts like a magic breath when the Paradise and Christmas plays were performed, all the things which went through hearts in these festive periods, as truthfully as we can experience this through anthroposophy, as honestly we should face the other fact that the eternal spirit must come to expression in ever new forms in human development. That is why the sight of the symbols of Christmas should be an incentive for us to assimilate in a Christmas mood what the world-historical mood in the anthroposophical way of understanding can be in our hearts.

After all, the person who experiences the secrets of Christmas Eve in the right way will look with hope to what follows as the second festival after the Christmas festival, will look at the Easter festival as the festival of resurrection where what is born at Christmas emerges victorious. And thus we are convinced of the necessity that all spiritual life, all cultural life as such must be imbued, saturated by what we call the anthroposophical way of understanding, anthroposophical feeling and thinking and intent. In the future, my dear friends, there will either be a spiritual science or there will be no science at all, only outer technical practice. In the future there will either be a religion imbued with anthroposophy or there will be no religion at all, only external churchdom. In the future there will be art imbued with anthroposophy or there will be no arts at all, because arts whose aim is to be separated from the life of the human soul will have a brief, ephemeral existence. So we look at something which shines towards us with the same certainty as the prophecy which is given us through Theodora in *The Portal of Initiation* about the renewal of the sight of Christ. With such certainty, we have in our souls the resurrection of anthroposophical spirit in science, religion, art and all human life. The great Easter festival of humanity stands before us as we sense it in our souls.

We can understand that there will once again be mangers, once again solitary, still quite solitary places in which will be born in childhood form what is to be resurrected among human beings. In the Middle Ages people were taken into the houses and shown the manger, an imitation of the stable with ox and ass, with the Jesus child, his parents and the shepherds. They were told: here lies the hope of the future of humankind. Let what we cultivate, what we intend within our anthroposophical places of work be modern mangers in our soul in which under the guidance of the one we call Jesus Christ the new spirit is resurrected, today still in childhood form, today still at the stage of being born in the individual anthroposophical branches of work, in the mangers, but bearing within itself the pledge that he will be victorious, that as human beings we will be able to celebrate through him the great Easter festival of humankind, the festival of resurrection of humankind in a new spirit, in the spirit we sense, we strive for as the anthroposophical spirit.

NOTES

Textual basis: The Copenhagen lectures were transcribed by Marie Steiner-von Sivers, the Nuremberg and Munich lecture by Georg Klenk (Munich). The sources of the other transcripts are unknown.

Responsibility for the second German edition on which this translation is based lies with Anna Maria Balastèr and Ulla Trapp.

The title of this volume was given by Rudolf Steiner for the Copenhagen lectures. All the other titles were chosen by the editors of earlier single editions.

Works by Rudolf Steiner within the *Gesamtausgabe* (GA—complete works) are shown in the notes with their bibliographical number.

1. Fragmente, Enzyklopädie V: *'Physiology.* Sleep is a mixed state of the body and the soul. The body and soul are chemically connected in sleep. The soul is evenly distributed throughout the body in sleep—the human being is *neutralized.* Waking is a separated—polarized state. In a waking state the soul is particularized—localized. Sleep is digestion of the soul; the body digests the soul (*withdrawal of stimulation through the soul*). Waking is the active state of stimulation through the soul—the body enjoys the soul. In sleep the *bonds of the system* are loose—when awake they are *tightened.'* Wasmuth 1900.
2. Enzyklopädie IX: *'Theory of the spirit.* The world of the spirit is indeed already open to us. It is always *revealed.* If we suddenly developed the necessary elasticity, we would see ourselves fully in it. Healing method for the current deficient state. Formerly through fasting and moral cleansing. Now perhaps through the strengthening method.' Wasmuth 2694.
3. Matthew 3:2.
4. Annals XV, 44.
5. Matthew 28:20.
6. 'These exalted beings have already travelled the path which the rest of humanity still has to go. They are now at work as the great "teachers of wisdom and the harmony of feelings of humanity",' Rudolf Steiner wrote to Anna Wagner on 2 January 1905. See also the relevant chapters in *From the History and Contents of the First Section of the Esoteric School. Letters, Documents and Lectures: 1904–1914,* GA 264.
7. 1770–1831.
8. 1775–1854.
9. 1770–1843.
10. See *Schelling. Gesammelte Werke*, Stuttgart and Augsburg, 1856–8, Volume 4, pp. 368 ff.

11. In October 1806 Jena was taken by Napoleonic troops (battle of Jena-Auerstedt).

12. 'Nature is the result of the idea in the form of otherness.' *Vorlesungen über die Naturphilosophie*, § 247.

13. Isaac Newton, 1643–1727.

14. 'For the rational, which is synonymous with the idea in that it simultaneously enters external existence in its reality, appears in an infinite wealth of forms, appearances and shapes...' *Hegels Werke*, Volume 8, Berlin 1833, pp. 17 f.

15. 'What is rational, that is real; and what is real, that is rational,' loc. cit. p. 17.

16. 1646–1716.

17. Cf. Rudolf Steiner, 'Zeichen und Entwicklungen der drei Logoi in der Menschheit', given to Edouard Schuré in May 1906, in *Beiträge zur Rudolf Steiner Gesamtausgabe*, Volume 14, Michaelmas 1965.

18. Theodor Schwann, 1810–82, *Mikroskopische Untersuchungen über die Übereinstimmung in der Struktur und dem Wachstum der Tiere und Pflanzen*, Berlin 1839.

19. Matthias Jakob Schleiden, 1804–81, 'Beiträge zur Phylogenesis' in *Archiv für Anatomie, Physiologie und wissenschaftliche Medizin*, Volume 5, 1838.

20. Ludwig Büchner, 1824–99. *Kraft und Stoff. Empirisch-naturwissenschaftliche Studien in der allgemein-verständlichen Darstellung*, Frankfurt a. M. 1855. Cf. Rudolf Steiner's essay in *Methodische Grundlagen der Anthroposophie*, Collected Essays 1884–1901, GA 30, pp. 383–90. Also 'Zur Herausgabe des "Magazins für Literatur" durch Rudolf Steiner. Mit einem Aufsatz von Ludwig Büchner' in *Beiträge zur Rudolf Steiner Gesamtausgabe*, Issue 7, Easter 1962.

21. Hermann von Helmholtz, 1821–94. Physiologist and physicist. Main works: *Über die Erhaltung der Kraft* (1847), *Handbuch der physiologischen Optik* (1856–66), *Die Lehre von den Tonempfindungen* (1862).

22. From the speech 'Über das Verhältnis der Naturwissenschaften zur Gesamtheit der Wissenschaft', given in Heidelberg on 22 November 1862, printed in *Vorträge und Reden*, Volume 1. Literally: 'Hegel's natural philosophy appeared to be absolutely meaningless, at least to scientists ... The philosophers accused the scientists of narrow-mindedness and the latter accused the former of meaninglessness.'

23. 1814–78. As a ship's doctor in the Dutch East Indies he observed in 1840 that venous blood was a lighter colour in the tropics than in a temperate climate. This observation was the starting point for his discovery of the law of the conservation of energy (energy principle) which he published in his paper 'Bemerkungen über die Kräfte in der unbelebten Natur' which appeared in Liebig's *Annalen*, Volume 42, 1842. This paper already contains the determination of the mechanical equivalent of heat from physical data which were known at the time and it has become a classic element of thermodynamics. Mayer did not receive the recognitions he was due until after a long dispute about priority with Joule, Helmholtz and others. His collected papers were published under the title *Die Mechanik der Wärme*, Stuttgart 1867.

24. Ernst Haeckel, 1834–1919.

25. Eduard von Hartmann, 1842–1906, writes in the foreword to the eighth

edition of his *Philosophie des Unbewussten*, Berlin 1878: 'Almost at the same time as this book (*Erläuterung zur Metaphysik des Unbewussten*, second edition, Berlin 1877), there appeared the second extended edition of the work *Das Unbewusste vom Standpunkt der Philosophie und Deszendenztheorie* with my name. The first, anonymous edition had been recognized as the best of all critiques of the philosophy of the unconscious and at the same time as the most brilliant justification of the scientific, mechanistic view of the world as opposed to philosophical idealism. The revelation that the work had been written by me and the detailed refutation of the critique added by me in the second edition should be sufficient proof of my command of the modern scientific standpoint in order henceforth to protect me from any accusation of shortcomings in this field. It was essentially to make an example of officially appointed and professionally spreading ineptitude if I went to the trouble of adding a detailed refutation of the critique of the scientific foundations of the *Phil. d. Unb.* [*Philosophie des Unbewussten*] by Prof. Oscar Schmidt (Leipzig 1877) in an annex.'

26. 1823–86.
27. 1809–82.
28. 1828–94. *Die Hauptprobleme der Philosophie in ihrer Entwicklung und teilweisen Lösung von Thales bis Robert Hamerling*. Vienna 1892. There is a review of the book by Rudolf Steiner in *Methodische Grundlagen der Anthroposophie 1884– 1901*, GA 30, pp. 329 f.
29. Johann Friedrich Herbart, 1776–1841, philosopher and educator.
30. 1858–1917. Cf. particularly Rudolf Steiner's *Riddles of the Soul*, GA 21, and *Menschenfragen und Weltenantworten*, GA 213, lectures 6–10.
31. Volume II of *Psychologie* by Franz Brentano, edited by Otto Kraus, Leipzig 1925, only contains the work *Klassifikation der psychischen Phänomene* which first appeared in 1911 as well as a few treatises from his estate.
32. 1838–1916. He saw as the highest law of all thought that it should solve its tasks with the least expenditure of thinking energy. *Die Analyse der Empfindungen*, Jena 1886, second edition 1922; *Erkenntnis und Irrtum*, fifth edition 1926. Cf. Rudolf Steiner *Vom Menschenrätsel*, GA 20, footnote p. 151.
33. 1824–1907. Second generation Hegelian. *Geschichte der neueren Philosophie*. 10 volumes, Mannheim and Heidelberg 1852–1877.
34. Karl Rosenkranz, 1805–1879. He writes in the introduction to his Hegel biography, Berlin 1844: 'Because does it not seem as if we people of today are only the grave diggers and memorializers of the philosophers who were the children of the second half of the previous century and who died in the first half of the present one?'
35. Immanuel Kant, 1724–1804.
36. 1840–1912. A leading figure in the renewal of Kant's critique. *Kant und die Epigonen*, Stuttgart 1865. Cf. Rudolf Steiner, *Methodische Grundlagen der Anthroposophie*, GA 30, pp. 169–70, 173 f., 529 f.
37. Eduard Zeller, 1814–1908. *Geschichte der deutschen Philosophie seit Leibniz*, Munich 1873.
38. Rudolf Clausius, 1822–88. His treatise 'Die bewegende Kraft der Wärme und die Gesetze, welche sich daraus für die Wärme ableiten lassen', Pog-

gendorff's *Annalen* 1850, contains the outline of the mechanistic theory of heat, i.e. thermodynamics in today's parlance.

39. 1848–1930. Cf. *Methodische Grundlagen der Anthroposophie*, GA 30, pp. 47, 246–52, 313–15.

40. Herbert Spencer, 1820–1903. Spencer wrote a multi-volume work *System of Synthetic Philosophy*.

41. 1842–1910. Cf. Rudolf Steiner, *The Riddles of Philosophy*, GA 18.

42. Vladimir Solovyov, 1853–1900. Cf. particularly Rudolf Steiner, *Der Goetheanumgedanke inmitten der Kulturkrise der Gegenwart, Gesammelte Aufsätze 1921–1925*, GA 36, pp. 62 ff.

43. Émile Boutroux, 1845–1921. See Rudolf Steiner's remarks in this regard in *Die Rätsel der Philosophie*, GA 18, pp. 558 ff.

44. On the previous day, 1 June 1910, the inauguration of the Rudolf Steiner branch in Copenhagen took place. Rudolf Steiner gave a powerful address on 'The symbol of the rose cross' of which only fragmentary notes have been preserved which are unsuitable for publication. We do however wish to record some passages, also for the sake of the historical moment and they follow below. After the introductory words, which highlight the foundation of an occult, western spiritual-scientific movement through H.P. Blavatsky and the president of the Theosophical Society, Olcott, 30 years previously, 1875 to be precise, it says:

'We will see in the coming three days that people in the last third of the last century required a new impulse. Many seeking souls would have withered if they had not been given H.P. Blavatsky's spiritual help and insight . . .

This new teaching can become a great blessing for humanity but also a great risk. Human beings need a new force if they want to advance but that contains a risk because human beings are weak and because the new thing can quickly turn into a sum of dogmas. These can then become a source of disunity rather than collaboration. That has already been the effect of many new teachings and they will continue to have that effect into the future . . .

Many people were able to find each other under the sign of H.P. Blavatsky and work together. It was too great to be grasped by one person alone but in the same way that refracted beams come together in the prism, so they gathered here under the sign of H.P. Blavatsky. The immense power of *Isis* and *Secret Doctrine*—even if they are one-sided—gives human beings a great opportunity and if we are dissatisfied we nevertheless have to understand that we have to decant into the movement what is required . . .

Western theosophy builds on the human being's own authority and freedom. It is the task of the western theosophical school to make a contribution so that this can be achieved in its true meaning through the symbol of the rose cross . . .

There is a characteristic of the symbol of the rose cross: it promises us that the spiritual life will flow in and that dogmas should not dominate the working material. Life, new life is the promise of the rose cross. Everything that forms from a book, an opinion or a conversation continues to new life which sprouts each time anew like a plant and keeps growing. Everything should grow like that and when a new revelation comes once again then it appears in new form. That is the promise of the Rosicrucian mystery: a spiritual life which forms from transformed soul life. It emerges as love, as creative activity in our life. It is transformed into striving strength. It is transformed like love and true fraternity arises. Human beings make war on one another because they have different intent. The inner is cause of the outer. If we are unable to love a brother because he is of a different opinion then we cannot work on the great issues. We have to understand, otherwise there is no love. True love has to be so great that it can encompass everything and understand all opinions . . .

That is what I wish to say today in response to the kind words addressed to me. On this point it has to be said that there can be dispute and hate if the name of a living person is used. These things will happen. We have to be clear that we must not pursue personal goals with such a name, otherwise it can easily be misunderstood. The name must not act back on other areas. The more thoroughly you forget this name the more it will benefit the matter, but never will I forget your work. That is the gift which you can give me. We have to learn that everything is impersonal and understand that the first duty consists of promising ourselves that we wish to contribute our work to great spiritual progress and make our hearts strong. Then we will also in truth find that which is powerful and which acts and blesses our work . . .'

45. This presumably refers to the Mazdaznan movement.
46. A device which reduces the acceleration which a body experiences through gravity, thus making it easier to observe the movement of falling bodies.
47. Johannes Tauler, *c.* 1300–61.
48. Meister Eckhart, *c.* 1260–1327.
49. Galatians 2:20.
50. *Circa* 582–493 BC.
51. In biology the theory that life is governed by different principles in contrast to the mechanistic view of the world.
52. Cf. Rudolf Steiner, *Der menschliche und der kosmische Gedanke*, GA 151.
53. See Lecture 2 of 26 May 1910 on pages 15–28.
54. Carl Unger, 1878–1929. Dr Ing., owner of a machine tool factory, a personal pupil of Rudolf Steiner's since 1905, member of the council of the German Anthroposophical Society, lecturer and writer. *Gesammelte Schriften* in three volumes, Stuttgart 1964 and 1966, Zurich 1956. He was shot and killed by a person with a mental illness before the start of a public lecture in Nuremberg on 4 January 1929.
55. Gideon Spicker (1840–1912) writes in his book *Am Wendepunkt der christlichen Weltperiode. Philosophisches Bekenntnis einer ehemaligen Kapuziners*, Stuttgart 1910: 'Thus we have metaphysics without transcendental conviction, epistemology without objective meaning, psychology without soul, logic without content, ethics without commitment and religion not founded in reason.'
56. The theory that light is a wave movement which propagates from a shining body in a similar way to sound from a sounding body.
57. See note 38.
58. Emil Du Bois-Reymond, 1818–96. *Über die Grenzen des Naturerkennens*, Leipzig 1827; *Die sieben Welträtsel*, Leipzig 1888.

59. About 300 BC.

60. Bernhard Riemann, 1826–66. *Über die Hypothesen, welche der Geometrie zu Grunde liegen*, Göttingen 1854. His geometrical studies were collectively described as Riemannian geometry. According to the latter, space and straight lines are finite but unbound and returning to themselves. There is no parallel line to a straight line and the sum of the angles of a triangle is greater than 180 degrees. Riemannian geometry in its most general form plays a role in Einstein's theory of relativity.

61. Nikolai Lobachevsky, 1763–1856. *On the foundations of geometry*, Kasan 1828. Lobachevsky developed a non-Euclidian geometry at the same time as but independently from the Hungarian mathematician and poet Farkas Bolyai. A characteristic element of this geometry lies in the theorems that two parallel lines are possible through a point lying outside a straight line and that the sum of the angles of a triangle are less than 180 degrees.

62. Henri Poincaré, 1854–1912. Mathematician, physicist and astronomer. He described mathematics as the free creation of the human spirit which used arbitrary signs to represent real relationships.

63. Ferdinand von Lindemann, 1852–1939. Professor in Freiburg, Königsberg and Munich. Translated Poincaré's *Science and Hypothesis* (Munich 1904) into German with his wife Lisbeth Lindemann.

64. Chapter 13, 'The value of life (pessimism and optimism)'.

65. See note 23.

66. Sadi Carnot, 1796–1832. *Réflexions sur la puissance motrice du feu et les machines propres à développer cette puissance*, Paris 1883, translated into German by Ostwald in 1892. According to this, the work undertaken in the steam engine is a proportion of the quantity of heat flowing from the boiler into the condenser; heat can only perform work in the *transition* from a warmer to a cooler body. Carnot's theorem, as it is called, as modified by Clausius (see note 38) forms the second law of thermodynamics.

67. See 'Über die Wechselwirkung der Naturkräfte und die darauf bezüglichen neuesten Ermittelungen der Physik', lecture given in Königsberg on 7 February 1854. Printed in *Vorträge und Reden*, Volume 1.

68. Literally: 'Should that make us afraid?... For many a long sequence of millennia, longer than our species has so far experienced, the current favourable state of inorganic nature appears secure so that we and many a long series of following generations have nothing to fear.'

69. In his lecture 'Über Helmholtzen's Beweis für den endlichen Stillstand des Weltalls, given in Königsberg on 28 May 1856. Printed in *Neue Studien*, Volume 1, Leipzig 1875.

70. One characteristic passage says: 'Now there is a difference in the nature of the movement because it can be produced in a finite or infinite way. In a finite way through an impulse or fall as the form of movement belonging to the individual bodies in the world which always has an external beginning and of necessity comes to rest again. But the movement of the individual cosmic bodies is produced in an infinite way in that they keep one another in balance through the interaction of their attraction and rotate around one another. Because the friction of the ether is equal to zero in this situation, as

we saw, this motion can keep generating itself without producing heat and without coming to a standstill. If there were no light in the universe, and if all the heat of the heavenly bodies had been exhausted radiating out into the endless wastes of the ether, the cold masses would nevertheless swing through the darkness with the same precision that they do now because the attraction of matter is a directly immanent function of the latter and gravitation in accordance with Newton's principles is inherent to all matter. The qualitative characteristics of matter, the processes it may contain, magnetic, electrical, chemical, thermal, are not relevant to the mechanism as such. Now since Helmholtz accepts Newton's principles, he must admit the possibility that the mechanical universe has to be able to exist in eternal movement and that expansion and contraction, i.e. temperature differences, is simply irrelevant in this regard. That is, he has to admit that the absolute stasis of the world is so little conceivable on the basis of the concepts of matter and gravity that, on the contrary, we have to assume the opposite . . . But is nature a machine? Is it ruled by the finite characteristics of circumstances as is necessary for a machine? Is it not the interaction of forces which does indeed rejuvenate the existence of nature in that their antagonism never lets it come to rest and through enabling transitions allows the return transformation of force into force, the restoration if imbalance? Space and time, ether and atom, mass and mass, darkness and light, coldness and heat, pole and pole, physical processes and the life of organic individuals produce the cosmos in indefatigable transformation so that with the sublime spectacle of its eurythmy we cannot help but exclaim as did the Archangel Raphael in Goethe's *Faust*: The sun resounds as it has always . . .'
From *Neue Studien*, Volume 1, by Karl Rosenkranz, see note 69.

71. The first edition said 'what philosophy has to say'. This was corrected analogously. It may not have been heard properly: 'philosophy' instead of 'theosophy'.

72. *Die Geheimnisse der biblischen Schöpfungsgeschichte*, 11 lectures given in Munich 16–26 August 1910 (GA 122).

73. Joseph Hyrtl, 1810–94. World-famous Austrian anatomist, professor in Prague, subsequently in Vienna. *Lehrbuch der Anatomie des Menschen, mit Rücksicht auf Physiologische Begründung und praktische Anwendung*, Prague 1846, twentieth edition, Vienna 1889.

74. See Rudolf Steiner, *An Occult Physiology*, 8 lectures in Prague, 20–28 March 1911, GA 128.

75. Play by Edouard Schuré. Authorized translation into German by Marie Steiner. See Rudolf Steiner/Edouard Schuré, *Lucifer—Die Kinder des Lucifer*, Dornach 1955.

76. By Marie von Sivers (Marie Steiner). She also recited the subsequent scenes. All translations of *The Portal of Initiation* in this volume by H. Collison, S.M.K. Gandell and R.T. Gladstone.

77. See Rudolf Steiner, *Geisteswissenschaftliche Erläuterungen zu Goethes Faust*, Volumes 1 and 2, GA 272 and 273.

78. Cf. Rudolf Steiner, *Occult Science. An Outline* (1910), GA 13.

79. Translator's note: In the section immediately following, the words of the

drama are quoted in the original German because Rudolf Steiner is commenting on the nature and effect of the sounds.

80. Bern, 12 September 1910, *According to Matthew*, GA 123, twelfth lecture: 'Take what I was able to describe in these days as *one* side of the great Christ event and be clear that thereby not everything has been said by any means . . . But the best thing which can accrue to us from this presentation of the facts is that we take them in not just with our reason and intellect but that we unite them with the innermost fibres of our soul life, with all our mind and the whole of our heart and allow them to continue to live there. The words of the Gospel are words which, if we inscribe them into our heart, turn into forces there which penetrate us and develop a peculiar vitality if we truly understand them. And we will see that we carry these life forces out into life.'

81. See *From the Course of My Life*, GA 28, chapter 12.

82. Cf. the preceding lecture, Basel, 17 September 1910, first paragraph.

83. In the first edition of 1910 there is the correction 'spirit' for 'god' in Rudolf Steiner's writing.

84. Adolf Arenson, 1855–1938. Rudolf Steiner asked him to compose the music for all four Mystery Dramas in Munich. At the request of Marie Steiner, the music was performed at the opening of the second Goetheanum, Michaelmas 1928, and also subsequently in Dornach.

85. See Rudolf Steiner, *Die Geheimnisse der biblischen Schöpfungsgeschichte*, GA 122.

86. The cycles on the Gospels given up to that point are contained in the following volumes of the complete works: *Menschheitsentwicklung und Christus-Erkenntnis*, GA 100; *Das Johannes-Evangelium*, GA 103, *The Gospel of St John*; *Das Johannes-Evangelium im Verhältnis zu den drei anderen Evangelien, besonders zu dem Lukas-Evangelium*, GA 112, *The Gospel of St John in Relation to the other Gospels*; *According to Luke*, GA 114; *Die tieferen Geheimnisse des Menschheitswerdens im Lichte der Evangelien*, GA 117; *According to Matthew*, GA 123; in addition, the first four lectures in *Exkurse in das Gebiet des Markus-Evangeliums*, GA 124, *Background to the Gospel of St Mark*, had been given.

87. *Orpheus. Allgemeine Geschichte der Religionen*, German edition by A. Mahler, Vienna 1910.

88. See Arthur Drews, *Die Christusmythe*, 2 parts, Jena 1909/11.

89. Of the two lectures held on 18 and 24 April 1910 in Palermo, the first one dealt with the 'The reappearance of Christ', reproduced based on the listener notes in *Das Ereignis der Christus-Erscheinung in der ätherischen Welt*, GA 118, *Reappearance of Christ in the Etheric*. There is no transcript of the second lecture in which Rudolf Steiner spoke about Empedocles.

90. See *The Christ Impulse and the Development of Ego-Consciousness*, GA 116, sixth lecture of 2 May 1910 in which the second lecture given in Palermo is also mentioned; *Das Markus-Evangelium*, GA 139, *The Gospel of St Mark*, first and seventh lecture.

91. Cf. Rudolf Steiner, *Die Rätsel der Philosophie*, GA 18, pp. 60 f.

92. One-and-a-half years later Rudolf Steiner names the historical Georg Faust as the reincarnation of Empedocles; see *Das Markus-Evangelium*, GA 139, first lecture.

93. Marcus Tullius Cicero, 106–43 BC. 'Cicero ... was part of the new academy and studied this philosophy with great zeal in that he was prepared to withdraw from the market and from all public business, were he to be excluded in Rome from all offices of state, and return to Athens in order to devote his life in peace and quietude solely to philosophy.' The new academy taught that 'all experiences of the senses are deceptive'. Plutarch's *Vergleichende Lebensbeschreibungen*, translated by Joh. Friedr. Sal. Kaltwasser, newly published by Otto Güthling, Leipzig n.d., Volume X, pp. 158 f.

94. P. Jensen, professor of Semitic philosophy in Marburg. *Moses, Jesus, Paulus. Drei Variationen des babylonischen Gottmenschen Gilgamesch. Eine Anklage und ein Appell*, third edition, Frankfurt a. M. 1910.

95. In the first edition this was erroneously given as 'Matthew'. See Rudolf Steiner's lecture of 6 September 1910 in *According to Matthew*, GA 123.

96. Cf. Rudolf Steiner, *Esoteric Christianity and the Mission of Christian Rosenkreutz*, GA 130, and the lectures in *According to Matthew*, GA 123.

97. 7 January 1795.

98. 23 August 1794.

99. 'Your observing gaze which rests so still and pure on things is never at risk of following the wrong path onto which both speculation and arbitrary imagination, following its own laws, stray so easily. Your intuition contains everything, and far more completely, which analysis laboriously seeks and only because it lies within you as a whole are your own riches hidden from you; because unfortunately we only know what we separate out. Intellects of your kind therefore rarely know how far they have advanced and how little cause they have to borrow from philosophy which can only learn from them. The latter can only dissect, but giving as such is not a matter for the analytical thinker but for the genius who consolidates under the dark but assured influence of pure reason following objective laws.'

100. 'Those to whom nature begins to reveal its open secret feel an irresistible longing for its worthy interpreter, art' (Sprüche in Prosa, 810)—'Beauty is the manifestation of secret laws of nature which would remain forever hidden to us without its appearance' (Sprüche in Prosa, 811). 'Maximen und Reflexionen. Aus Kunst und Altertum', Volume IV, 2: 'Error of the amateur: wanting to combine imagination and technology directly' in *Maximen und Reflexionen. Über Kunst und Kunstgeschichte*.

101. Cf. Rudolf Steiner, *Das Suchen nach übersinnlichen Erfahrungen. Spiritismus, Hypnotismus, Somnambulismus—ihr Wesen, ihre Geschichte und ihr Verhältnis zur Geisteswissenschaft*, four public lectures, Berlin 1904. Included within the complete works in *Spirituelle Seelenlehre und Weltbetrachtung*, GA 52.

102. In the Leipzig lecture of 4 November 1911, contained in *Esoteric Christianity and the Mission of Christian Rosenkreutz*, GA 130.

103. Nicolaus Copernicus, 1473–1543.

104. Galileo Galilei, 1564–1642.

105. Johannes Kepler, 1571–1630.

106. Cf. *Occult Science. An Outline*, GA 13, chapter: 'Knowledge of the Higher Worlds (Initiation)', also *Macrocosm and Microcosm*, GA 119, Lecture 8.

107. *West-östlicher Divan*, 'Selige Sehnsucht'.
108. Poems, proverbially:
     Egoist that I am!—If I didn't know better!
     It is jealousy that is the egoist;
     And whatever paths I may have trod,
     You've never met me on the path of jealousy.
109. 1500–71. Goldsmith and sculptor. Autobiography, Naples 1758. Translated from the Italian by Goethe, Tübingen 1803. Cellini frequently emphasizes his love of truth in it, thus in Book Three, chapter 8 and Book Four, chapter 7 where he refers to himself as a 'constant friend of truth and enemy of lies'.
110. In the parallel lecture held in Nuremberg on 12 November 1910, of which there is only a fragmentary record, it says in this connection: 'It is another matter if someone wants to undergo esoteric development. They can then be given advice how best to bear their destiny.'
111. John 2:19.
112. See note 109.
113. See note 108.
114. Cf. lecture of 13 November 1910, p. 141.
115. See note 90.
116. John 2:19.
117. In *The Portal of Initiation*, scene one, GA 14.
118. From *Deutsche Weihnachtsspiele aus Ungern*, described and communicated by Karl Julius Schröer. New edition, Vienna 1858 and 1862, p. 160. K.J. Schröer remarked about the last two lines: 'These lines have been taken out of context and do not belong at the end. Also, they were originally four lines so that they rhymed properly.'
119. In the first edition it said: 'German and *western* European regions'. This was corrected correspondingly.
120. Cf. Rudolf Steiner, 'Von den volkstümlichen Weihnachtsspielen. Eine Christfest-Erinnerung' and 'Zur Aufführung unserer volkstümlichen Weihnachtsspiele', both in *Der Goetheanumsgedanke inmitten der Kulturkrisis der Gegenwart*, collected essays 1921–5, GA 36; further the lectures Berlin, 19 December 1915, Dornach, 26, 27 and 28 December 1915, in *Unifying Humanity Spiritually Through the Christ Impulse*, GA 165.
121. Karl Julius Schröer, 1825–1900, Germanist, professor at Vienna Technical University, teacher and fatherly friend of Rudolf Steiner. See *Autobiography. Chapters in the Course of my Life*, GA 28; *Briefe*, Vol. 1, GA 38; *Vom Menschenrätsel*, GA 20; *Methodische Grundlagen der Anthroposophie*, GA 30.
122. See Schröer, *Deutsche Weihnachtsspiele aus Ungern*, p. 8.
123. See *Wehnachtsspiele aus altem Volkstum—Die Oberuferer Spiele*, Dornach 1990.
124. Romans 12–19, 1 Corinthians 15:45.
125. These art rooms, of which one had been installed in Berlin Charlottenburg and the other in the eastern part of Berlin (there were another two in Munich), deserve to be remembered. Because they certainly go back to the inspirational influence arising from Dr Steiner's social activities and respect for other people—even if the immediate initiative for this deed came from

the warm hearts of the two artists Fräulein Stinde and Countess Kalckreuth, who led the anthroposophical work in Munich, and was then also undertaken by Fräulein von Sivers and Fräulein M. Waller in Berlin. These art rooms were intended for the general public as hospitable places which not only offered warmth and comfort but also beauty, aesthetics and intellectual stimulation. The walls were covered in coloured hessian and everything down to the seating coordinated with the chosen tone. Each month there was a different exhibition of paintings: good reproductions of classic works of art and paintings by contemporary artists. There were evening performances with music and recitation, an introductory course to spiritual science and other areas of science, small drama performances, such as for example *Die Geschwister* by Goethe, and similar things. This is also where the 'Christmas plays from old tradition' were introduced in Berlin which could then be taken by the performers to other locations. It is worth mentioning that after the exertions of the day it was not always easy to undertake the long trek to the eastern part of Berlin by underground and tram on a foggy evening and to trudge the last bit through the snow in dark and remote streets. But the daily example of Dr Steiner's untiring work encouraged everyone else. And people learnt to know from their own experience the importance of the contrast when they entered the warm embrace of a bright room in muted red with the bleak stone surroundings of desolate working class quarters, and their eye fell on works of art which captured their gaze and refreshed the heart so that it could collect itself in subsequent words and music and liberate itself to some extent from the burdens of everyday life. In a modest and small way this offered food for the soul to those from the working population who sought the spirit. That had come to expression in many letters which Rudolf Steiner had received when he was still active in the workers' educational institute in Berlin. He was thanked for his belief that workers also needed spiritual and not just physical nourishment.

The world war brought changes here too. The large art room in Motzstrasse with its side rooms was transformed into a day nursery in which Fräulein Samweber, who had fled from Bolshevik Russia, worked devotedly to provide and care for the children, happily supported by the ladies from the Anthroposophical Society in this task which was reliant on donations. They had light, air and joy in the beautiful rooms at the front of the house. Dr Steiner made do with the much more modest rooms at the back. That is immaterial, but symptomatic of him. (Marie Steiner.)

126. See note 123.
127. Their migration to the Upper Zips region goes back to the twelfth to thirteenth century. The community of 24 Zips towns was autonomous with its own municipal laws until 1876. After 1945 only small groups remained in the Slovak towns.
128. See note 121.
129. In 1889. Cf. *Autobiography. Chapters in the Course of my Life* (GA 28), chapter 13, and *Beiträge zur Rudolf Steiner Gesamtausgabe*, No. 61/62.

RUDOLF STEINER'S COLLECTED WORKS

The German Edition of Rudolf Steiner's Collected Works (the *Gesamtausgabe* [GA] published by Rudolf Steiner Verlag, Dornach, Switzerland) presently runs to 354 titles, organized either by type of work (written or spoken), chronology, audience (public or other), or subject (education, art, etc.). For ease of comparison, the Collected Works in English [CW] follows the German organization exactly. A complete listing of the CWs follows with literal translations of the German titles. Other than in the case of the books published in his lifetime, titles were rarely given by Rudolf Steiner himself, and were often provided by the editors of the German editions. The titles in English are not necessarily the same as the German; and, indeed, over the past seventy-five years have frequently been different, with the same book sometimes appearing under different titles.

For ease of identification and to avoid confusion, we suggest that readers looking for a title should do so by CW number. Because the work of creating the Collected Works of Rudolf Steiner is an ongoing process, with new titles being published every year, we have not indicated in this listing which books are presently available. To find out what titles in the Collected Works are currently in print, please check our website at www.rudolfsteinerpress.com (or www.steinerbooks.org for US readers).

Written Work

CW 1	Goethe: Natural-Scientific Writings, Introduction, with Footnotes and Explanations in the text by Rudolf Steiner
CW 2	Outlines of an Epistemology of the Goethean World View, with Special Consideration of Schiller
CW 3	Truth and Science
CW 4	The Philosophy of Freedom
CW 4a	Documents to 'The Philosophy of Freedom'
CW 5	Friedrich Nietzsche, A Fighter against His Time
CW 6	Goethe's Worldview
CW 6a	Now in CW 30
CW 7	Mysticism at the Dawn of Modern Spiritual Life and Its Relationship with Modern Worldviews
CW 8	Christianity as Mystical Fact and the Mysteries of Antiquity
CW 9	Theosophy: An Introduction into Supersensible World Knowledge and Human Purpose
CW 10	How Does One Attain Knowledge of Higher Worlds?
CW 11	From the Akasha-Chronicle

Public Lectures

Lectures to the Members of the Anthroposophical Society

SIGNIFICANT EVENTS IN THE LIFE OF
RUDOLF STEINER

1829:   June 23: birth of Johann Steiner (1829–1910)—Rudolf Steiner's father—in Geras, Lower Austria.

1834:   May 8: birth of Franciska Blie (1834–1918)—Rudolf Steiner's mother—in Horn, Lower Austria. 'My father and mother were both children of the glorious Lower Austrian forest district north of the Danube.'

1860:   May 16: marriage of Johann Steiner and Franciska Blie.

1861:   February 25: birth of *Rudolf Joseph Lorenz Steiner* in Kraljevec, Croatia, near the border with Hungary, where Johann Steiner works as a telegrapher for the South Austria Railroad. Rudolf Steiner is baptized two days later, February 27, the date usually given as his birthday.

1862:   Summer: the family moves to Mödling, Lower Austria.

1863:   The family moves to Pottschach, Lower Austria, near the Styrian border, where Johann Steiner becomes stationmaster. 'The view stretched to the mountains ... majestic peaks in the distance and the sweet charm of nature in the immediate surroundings.'

1864:   November 15: birth of Rudolf Steiner's sister, Leopoldine (d. November 1, 1927). She will become a seamstress and live with her parents for the rest of her life.

1866:   July 28: birth of Rudolf Steiner's deaf-mute brother, Gustav (d. May 1, 1941).

1867:   Rudolf Steiner enters the village school. Following a disagreement between his father and the schoolmaster, whose wife falsely accused the boy of causing a commotion, Rudolf Steiner is taken out of school and taught at home.

1868:   A critical experience. Unknown to the family, an aunt dies in a distant town. Sitting in the station waiting room, Rudolf Steiner sees her 'form,' which speaks to him, asking for help. 'Beginning with this experience, a new soul life began in the boy, one in which not only the outer trees and mountains spoke to him, but also the worlds that lay behind them. From this moment on, the boy began to live with the spirits of nature ...'

1869:   The family moves to the peaceful, rural village of Neudörfl, near Wiener-Neustadt in present-day Austria. Rudolf Steiner attends the village school. Because of the 'unorthodoxy' of his writing and spelling, he has to do 'extra lessons.'

1870:   Through a book lent to him by his tutor, he discovers geometry: 'To grasp something purely in the spirit brought me inner happiness. I know that I first learned happiness through geometry.' The same tutor allows him to draw, while other students still struggle with their reading and writing. 'An artistic element' thus enters his education.

1871: Though his parents are not religious, Rudolf Steiner becomes a 'church child,' a favourite of the priest, who was 'an exceptional character.' 'Up to the age of ten or eleven, among those I came to know, he was far and away the most significant.' Among other things, he introduces Steiner to Copernican, heliocentric cosmology. As an altar boy, Rudolf Steiner serves at Masses, funerals, and Corpus Christi processions. At year's end, after an incident in which he escapes a thrashing, his father forbids him to go to church.

1872: Rudolf Steiner transfers to grammar school in Wiener-Neustadt, a five-mile walk from home, which must be done in all weathers.

1873–75: Through his teachers and on his own, Rudolf Steiner has many wonderful experiences with science and mathematics. Outside school, he teaches himself analytic geometry, trigonometry, differential equations, and calculus.

1876: Rudolf Steiner begins tutoring other students. He learns bookbinding from his father. He also teaches himself stenography.

1877: Rudolf Steiner discovers Kant's *Critique of Pure Reason*, which he reads and rereads. He also discovers and reads von Rotteck's *World History*.

1878: He studies extensively in contemporary psychology and philosophy.

1879: Rudolf Steiner graduates from high school with honours. His father is transferred to Inzersdorf, near Vienna. He uses his first visit to Vienna 'to purchase a great number of philosophy books'—Kant, Fichte, Schelling, and Hegel, as well as numerous histories of philosophy. His aim: to find a path from the 'I' to nature.

October 1879–1883: Rudolf Steiner attends the Technical College in Vienna—to study mathematics, chemistry, physics, mineralogy, botany, zoology, biology, geology, and mechanics—with a scholarship. He also attends lectures in history and literature, while avidly reading philosophy on his own. His two favourite professors are Karl Julius Schröer (German language and literature) and Edmund Reitlinger (physics). He also audits lectures by Robert Zimmermann on aesthetics and Franz Brentano on philosophy. During this year he begins his friendship with Moritz Zitter (1861–1921), who will help support him financially when he is in Berlin.

1880: Rudolf Steiner attends lectures on Schiller and Goethe by Karl Julius Schröer, who becomes his mentor. Also 'through a remarkable combination of circumstances,' he meets Felix Koguzki, a 'herb gatherer' and healer, who could 'see deeply into the secrets of nature.' Rudolf Steiner will meet and study with this 'emissary of the Master' throughout his time in Vienna.

1881: January: '... I didn't sleep a wink. I was busy with philosophical problems until about 12:30 a.m. Then, finally, I threw myself down on my couch. All my striving during the previous year had been to research whether the following statement by Schelling was true or not: *Within everyone dwells a secret, marvelous capacity to draw back from the stream of time—out of the self clothed in all that comes to us from outside—into our innermost being and there, in the immutable form of the Eternal, to look into ourselves.* I believe, and I am still quite certain of it, that I discovered this capacity in myself; I had long had an inkling of it. Now the whole of idealist philosophy stood before me in modified form. What's a sleepless night compared to that!'

Rudolf Steiner begins communicating with leading thinkers of the day, who send him books in return, which he reads eagerly.

July: 'I am not one of those who dives into the day like an animal in human form. I pursue a quite specific goal, an idealistic aim—knowledge of the truth! This cannot be done offhandedly. It requires the greatest striving in the world, free of all egotism, and equally of all resignation.'

August: Steiner puts down on paper for the first time thoughts for a 'Philosophy of Freedom.' 'The striving for the absolute: this human yearning is freedom.' He also seeks to outline a 'peasant philosophy,' describing what the worldview of a 'peasant'—one who lives close to the earth and the old ways—really is.

1881–1882: Felix Koguzki, the herb gatherer, reveals himself to be the envoy of another, higher initiatory personality, who instructs Rudolf Steiner to penetrate Fichte's philosophy and to master modern scientific thinking as a preparation for right entry into the spirit. This 'Master' also teaches him the double (evolutionary and involutionary) nature of time.

1882:   Through the offices of Karl Julius Schröer, Rudolf Steiner is asked by Joseph Kürschner to edit Goethe's scientific works for the *Deutschen National-Literatur* edition. He writes 'A Possible Critique of Atomistic Concepts' and sends it to Friedrich Theodor Vischer.

1883:   Rudolf Steiner completes his college studies and begins work on the Goethe project.

1884:   First volume of Goethe's *Scientific Writings* (CW 1) appears (March). He lectures on Goethe and Lessing, and Goethe's approach to science. In July, he enters the household of Ladislaus and Pauline Specht as tutor to the four Specht boys. He will live there until 1890. At this time, he meets Josef Breuer (1842–1925), the co-author with Sigmund Freud of *Studies in Hysteria*, who is the Specht family doctor.

1885:   While continuing to edit Goethe's writings, Rudolf Steiner reads deeply in contemporary philosophy (Eduard von Hartmann, Johannes Volkelt, and Richard Wahle, among others).

1886:   May: Rudolf Steiner sends Kürschner the manuscript of *Outlines of Goethe's Theory of Knowledge* (CW 2), which appears in October, and which he sends out widely. He also meets the poet Marie Eugenie Delle Grazie and writes 'Nature and Our Ideals' for her. He attends her salon, where he meets many priests, theologians, and philosophers, who will become his friends. Meanwhile, the director of the Goethe Archive in Weimar requests his collaboration with the *Sophien* edition of Goethe's works, particularly the writings on colour.

1887:   At the beginning of the year, Rudolf Steiner is very sick. As the year progresses and his health improves, he becomes increasingly 'a man of letters,' lecturing, writing essays, and taking part in Austrian cultural life. In August–September, the second volume of Goethe's *Scientific Writings* appears.

1888: January–July: Rudolf Steiner assumes editorship of the 'German Weekly' (*Deutsche Wochenschrift*). He begins lecturing more intensively, giving, for example, a lecture titled 'Goethe as Father of a New Aesthetics.' He meets and becomes soul friends with Friedrich Eckstein (1861–1939), a vegetarian, philosopher of symbolism, alchemist, and musician, who will introduce him to various spiritual currents (including Theosophy) and with whom he will meditate and interpret esoteric and alchemical texts.

1889: Rudolf Steiner first reads Nietzsche (*Beyond Good and Evil*). He encounters Theosophy again and learns of Madame Blavatsky in the Theosophical circle around Marie Lang (1858–1934). Here he also meets well-known figures of Austrian life, as well as esoteric figures like the occultist Franz Hartmann and Karl Leinigen-Billigen (translator of C.G. Harrison's *The Transcendental Universe*). During this period, Steiner first reads A.P. Sinnett's *Esoteric Buddhism* and Mabel Collins's *Light on the Path*. He also begins travelling, visiting Budapest, Weimar, and Berlin (where he meets philosopher Eduard von Hartmann).

1890: Rudolf Steiner finishes volume 3 of Goethe's scientific writings. He begins his doctoral dissertation, which will become *Truth and Science* (CW 3). He also meets the poet and feminist Rosa Mayreder (1858–1938), with whom he can exchange his most intimate thoughts. In September, Rudolf Steiner moves to Weimar to work in the Goethe-Schiller Archive.

1891: Volume 3 of the Kürschner edition of Goethe appears. Meanwhile, Rudolf Steiner edits Goethe's studies in mineralogy and scientific writings for the *Sophien* edition. He meets Ludwig Laistner of the Cotta Publishing Company, who asks for a book on the basic question of metaphysics. From this will result, ultimately, *The Philosophy of Freedom* (CW 4), which will be published not by Cotta but by Emil Felber. In October, Rudolf Steiner takes the oral exam for a doctorate in philosophy, mathematics, and mechanics at Rostock University, receiving his doctorate on the twenty-sixth. In November, he gives his first lecture on Goethe's 'Fairy Tale' in Vienna.

1892: Rudolf Steiner continues work at the Goethe-Schiller Archive and on his *Philosophy of Freedom*. *Truth and Science*, his doctoral dissertation, is published. Steiner undertakes to write introductions to books on Schopenhauer and Jean Paul for Cotta. At year's end, he finds lodging with Anna Eunike, née Schulz (1853–1911), a widow with four daughters and a son. He also develops a friendship with Otto Erich Hartleben (1864–1905) with whom he shares literary interests.

1893: Rudolf Steiner begins his habit of producing many reviews and articles. In March, he gives a lecture titled 'Hypnotism, with Reference to Spiritism.' In September, volume 4 of the Kürschner edition is completed. In November, *The Philosophy of Freedom* appears. This year, too, he meets John Henry Mackay (1864–1933), the anarchist, and Max Stirner, a scholar and biographer.

1894: Rudolf Steiner meets Elisabeth Förster Nietzsche, the philosopher's sister, and begins to read Nietzsche in earnest, beginning with the as yet unpublished *Antichrist*. He also meets Ernst Haeckel (1834–1919). In the fall, he begins to write *Nietzsche, A Fighter against His Time* (CW 5).

1895:   May, *Nietzsche, A Fighter against His Time* appears.

1896:   January 22: Rudolf Steiner sees Friedrich Nietzsche for the first and only time. Moves between the Nietzsche and the Goethe-Schiller Archives, where he completes his work before year's end. He falls out with Elisabeth Förster Nietzsche, thus ending his association with the Nietzsche Archive.

1897:   Rudolf Steiner finishes the manuscript of *Goethe's Worldview* (CW 6). He moves to Berlin with Anna Eunike and begins editorship of the *Magazin für Literatur*. From now on, Steiner will write countless reviews, literary and philosophical articles, and so on. He begins lecturing at the 'Free Literary Society.' In September, he attends the Zionist Congress in Basel. He sides with Dreyfus in the Dreyfus affair.

1898:   Rudolf Steiner is very active as an editor in the political, artistic, and theatrical life of Berlin. He becomes friendly with John Henry Mackay and poet Ludwig Jacobowski (1868–1900). He joins Jacobowski's circle of writers, artists, and scientists—'The Coming Ones' (*Die Kommenden*)—and contributes lectures to the group until 1903. He also lectures at the 'League for College Pedagogy.' He writes an article for Goethe's sesquicentennial, 'Goethe's Secret Revelation,' on the 'Fairy Tale of the Green Snake and the Beautiful Lily.'

1898–99:   'This was a trying time for my soul as I looked at Christianity. . . . I was able to progress only by contemplating, by means of spiritual perception, the evolution of Christianity. . . . Conscious knowledge of real Christianity began to dawn in me around the turn of the century. This seed continued to develop. My soul trial occurred shortly before the beginning of the twentieth century. It was decisive for my soul's development that I stood spiritually before the Mystery of Golgotha in a deep and solemn celebration of knowledge.'

1899:   Rudolf Steiner begins teaching and giving lectures and lecture cycles at the Workers' College, founded by Wilhelm Liebknecht (1826–1900). He will continue to do so until 1904. Writes: *Literature and Spiritual Life in the Nineteenth Century; Individualism in Philosophy*; *Haeckel and His Opponents; Poetry in the Present;* and begins what will become (fifteen years later) *The Riddles of Philosophy* (CW 18). He also meets many artists and writers, including Käthe Kollwitz, Stefan Zweig, and Rainer Maria Rilke. On October 31, he marries Anna Eunike.

1900:   'I thought that the turn of the century must bring humanity a new light. It seemed to me that the separation of human thinking and willing from the spirit had peaked. A turn or reversal of direction in human evolution seemed to me a necessity.' Rudolf Steiner finishes *World and Life Views in the Nineteenth Century* (the second part of what will become *The Riddles of Philosophy*) and dedicates it to Ernst Haeckel. It is published in March. He continues lecturing at *Die Kommenden*, whose leadership he assumes after the death of Jacobowski. Also, he gives the Gutenberg Jubilee lecture before 7,000 typesetters and printers. In September, Rudolf Steiner is invited by Count and Countess Brockdorff to lecture in the Theosophical Library. His first lecture is on Nietzsche. His second lecture is titled 'Goethe's Secret Revelation.' October 6, he begins a lecture cycle on the mystics that will become *Mystics after Modernism* (CW 7). November-December: 'Marie von Sivers appears in the audience. . . .' Also in November, Steiner gives his first lecture at the Giordano Bruno Bund (where he will continue to lecture until May, 1905). He speaks on Bruno and modern Rome, focusing on the importance of the philosophy of Thomas Aquinas as monism.

1901:   In continual financial straits, Rudolf Steiner's early friends Moritz Zitter and Rosa Mayreder help support him. In October, he begins the lecture cycle *Christianity as Mystical Fact* (CW 8) at the Theosophical Library. In November, he gives his first 'Theosophical lecture' on Goethe's 'Fairy Tale' in Hamburg at the invitation of Wilhelm Hubbe-Schleiden. He also attends a gathering to celebrate the founding of the Theosophical Society at Count and Countess Brockdorff's. He gives a lecture cycle, 'From Buddha to Christ,' for the circle of the *Kommenden*. November 17, Marie von Sivers asks Rudolf Steiner if Theosophy needs a Western-Christian spiritual movement (to complement Theosophy's Eastern emphasis). 'The question was posed. Now, following spiritual laws, I could begin to give an answer. . . .' In December, Rudolf Steiner writes his first article for a Theosophical publication. At year's end, the Brockdorffs and possibly Wilhelm Hubbe-Schleiden ask Rudolf Steiner to join the Theosophical Society and undertake the leadership of the German section. Rudolf Steiner agrees, on the condition that Marie von Sivers (then in Italy) work with him.

1902:   Beginning in January, Rudolf Steiner attends the opening of the Workers' School in Spandau with Rosa Luxemburg (1870–1919). January 17, Rudolf Steiner joins the Theosophical Society. In April, he is asked to become general secretary of the German Section of the Theosophical Society, and works on preparations for its founding. In July, he visits London for a Theosophical congress. He meets Bertram Keightly, G.R.S. Mead, A.P. Sinnett, and Annie Besant, among others. In September, *Christianity as Mystical Fact* appears. In October, Rudolf Steiner gives his first public lecture on Theosophy ('Monism and Theosophy') to about three hundred people at the Giordano Bruno Bund. On October 19–21, the German Section of the Theosophical Society has its first meeting; Rudolf Steiner is the general secretary, and Annie Besant attends. Steiner lectures on practical karma studies. On October 23, Annie Besant inducts Rudolf Steiner into the Esoteric School of the Theosophical Society. On October 25, Steiner begins a weekly series of lectures: 'The Field of Theosophy.' During this year, Rudolf Steiner also first meets Ita Wegman (1876–1943), who will become his close collaborator in his final years.

1903:   Rudolf Steiner holds about 300 lectures and seminars. In May, the first issue of the periodical *Luzifer* appears. In June, Rudolf Steiner visits

London for the first meeting of the Federation of the European Sections of the Theosophical Society, where he meets Colonel Olcott. He begins to write *Theosophy* (CW 9).

1904:   Rudolf Steiner continues lecturing at the Workers' College and elsewhere (about 90 lectures), while lecturing intensively all over Germany among Theosophists (about 140 lectures). In February, he meets Carl Unger (1878–1929), who will become a member of the board of the Anthroposophical Society (1913). In March, he meets Michael Bauer (1871–1929), a Christian mystic, who will also be on the board. In May, *Theosophy* appears, with the dedication: 'To the spirit of Giordano Bruno.' Rudolf Steiner and Marie von Sivers visit London for meetings with Annie Besant. June: Rudolf Steiner and Marie von Sivers attend the meeting of the Federation of European Sections of the Theosophical Society in Amsterdam. In July, Steiner begins the articles in *Luzifer-Gnosis* that will become *How to Know Higher Worlds* (CW 10) and *Cosmic Memory* (CW 11). In September, Annie Besant visits Germany. In December, Steiner lectures on Freemasonry. He mentions the High Grade Masonry derived from John Yarker and represented by Theodore Reuss and Karl Kellner as a blank slate 'into which a good image could be placed.'

1905:   This year, Steiner ends his non-Theosophical lecturing activity. Supported by Marie von Sivers, his Theosophical lecturing—both in public and in the Theosophical Society—increases significantly: 'The German Theosophical Movement is of exceptional importance.' Steiner recommends reading, among others, Fichte, Jacob Boehme, and Angelus Silesius. He begins to introduce Christian themes into Theosophy. He also begins to work with doctors (Felix Peipers and Ludwig Noll). In July, he is in London for the Federation of European Sections, where he attends a lecture by Annie Besant: 'I have seldom seen Mrs. Besant speak in so inward and heartfelt a manner....' 'Through Mrs. Besant I have found the way to H.P. Blavatsky.' September to October, he gives a course of thirty-one lectures for a small group of esoteric students. In October, the annual meeting of the German Section of the Theosophical Society, which still remains very small, takes place. Rudolf Steiner reports membership has risen from 121 to 377 members. In November, seeking to establish esoteric 'continuity,' Rudolf Steiner and Marie von Sivers participate in a 'Memphis-Misraim' Masonic ceremony. They pay forty-five marks for membership. 'Yesterday, you saw how little remains of former esoteric institutions.' 'We are dealing only with a "framework"... for the present, nothing lies behind it. The occult powers have completely withdrawn.'

1906:   Expansion of Theosophical work. Rudolf Steiner gives about 245 lectures, only 44 of which take place in Berlin. Cycles are given in Paris, Leipzig, Stuttgart, and Munich. Esoteric work also intensifies. Rudolf Steiner begins writing *An Outline of Esoteric Science* (CW 13). In January, Rudolf Steiner receives permission (a patent) from the Great Orient of the Scottish A & A Thirty-Three Degree Rite of the Order of the Ancient

Freemasons of the Memphis-Misraim Rite to direct a chapter under the name 'Mystica Aeterna.' This will become the 'Cognitive-Ritual Section' (also called 'Misraim Service') of the Esoteric School. (See: *Freemasonry and Ritual Work: The Misraim Service*, CW 265). During this time, Steiner also meets Albert Schweitzer. In May, he is in Paris, where he visits Edouard Schuré. Many Russians attend his lectures (including Konstantin Balmont, Dimitri Mereszkovski, Zinaida Hippius, and Maximilian Woloshin). He attends the General Meeting of the European Federation of the Theosophical Society, at which Col. Olcott is present for the last time. He spends the year's end in Venice and Rome, where he writes and works on his translation of H.P. Blavatsky's *Key to Theosophy*.

1907: Further expansion of the German Theosophical Movement according to the Rosicrucian directive to 'introduce spirit into the world'—in education, in social questions, in art, and in science. In February, Col. Olcott dies in Adyar. Before he dies, Olcott indicates that 'the Masters' wish Annie Besant to succeed him: much politicking ensues. Rudolf Steiner supports Besant's candidacy. April-May: preparations for the Congress of the Federation of European Sections of the Theosophical Society—the great, watershed Whitsun 'Munich Congress,' attended by Annie Besant and others. Steiner decides to separate Eastern and Western (Christian-Rosicrucian) esoteric schools. He takes his esoteric school out of the Theosophical Society (Besant and Rudolf Steiner are 'in harmony' on this). Steiner makes his first lecture tours to Austria and Hungary. That summer, he is in Italy. In September, he visits Edouard Schuré, who will write the introduction to the French edition of *Christianity as Mystical Fact* in Barr, Alsace. Rudolf Steiner writes the autobiographical statement known as the 'Barr Document.' In *Luzifer-Gnosis*, 'The Education of the Child' appears.

1908: The movement grows (membership: 1,150). Lecturing expands. Steiner makes his first extended lecture tour to Holland and Scandinavia, as well as visits to Naples and Sicily. Themes: St. John's Gospel, the Apocalypse, Egypt, science, philosophy, and logic. *Luzifer-Gnosis* ceases publication. In Berlin, Marie von Sivers (with Johanna Mücke (1864–1949) forms the *Philosophisch-Theosophisch* (after 1915 *Philosophisch-Anthroposophisch*) *Verlag* to publish Steiner's work. Steiner gives lecture cycles titled *The Gospel of St. John* (CW 103) and *The Apocalypse* (104).

1909: *An Outline of Esoteric Science* appears. Lecturing and travel continues. Rudolf Steiner's spiritual research expands to include the polarity of Lucifer and Ahriman; the work of great individualities in history; the Maitreya Buddha and the Bodhisattvas; spiritual economy (CW 109); the work of the spiritual hierarchies in heaven and on earth (CW 110). He also deepens and intensifies his research into the Gospels, giving lectures on the Gospel of St. Luke (CW 114) with the first mention of two Jesus children. Meets and becomes friends with Christian Morgenstern (1871–1914). In April, he lays the foundation stone for the Malsch model—the building that will lead to the first Goetheanum. In May, the International Congress of the Federation of European Sections of the

Theosophical Society takes place in Budapest. Rudolf Steiner receives the Subba Row medal for *How to Know Higher Worlds*. During this time, Charles W. Leadbeater discovers Jiddu Krishnamurti (1895–1986) and proclaims him the future 'world teacher,' the bearer of the Maitreya Buddha and the 'reappearing Christ.' In October, Steiner delivers seminal lectures on 'anthroposophy,' which he will try, unsuccessfully, to rework over the next years into the unfinished work, *Anthroposophy (A Fragment)* (CW 45).

1910:   New themes: *The Reappearance of Christ in the Etheric* (CW 118); *The Fifth Gospel; The Mission of Folk Souls* (CW 121); *Occult History* (CW 126); the evolving development of etheric cognitive capacities. Rudolf Steiner continues his Gospel research with *The Gospel of St. Matthew* (CW 123). In January, his father dies. In April, he takes a month-long trip to Italy, including Rome, Monte Cassino, and Sicily. He also visits Scandinavia again. July–August, he writes the first mystery drama, *The Portal of Initiation* (CW 14). In November, he gives 'psychosophy' lectures. In December, he submits 'On the Psychological Foundations and Epistemological Framework of Theosophy' to the International Philosophical Congress in Bologna.

1911:   The crisis in the Theosophical Society deepens. In January, 'The Order of the Rising Sun,' which will soon become 'The Order of the Star in the East,' is founded for the coming world teacher, Krishnamurti. At the same time, Marie von Sivers, Rudolf Steiner's co-worker, falls ill. Fewer lectures are given, but important new ground is broken. In Prague, in March, Steiner meets Franz Kafka (1883–1924) and Hugo Bergmann (1883-1975). In April, he delivers his paper to the Philosophical Congress. He writes the second mystery drama, *The Soul's Probation* (CW 14). Also, while Marie von Sivers is convalescing, Rudolf Steiner begins work on *Calendar 1912/1913*, which will contain the 'Calendar of the Soul' meditations. On March 19, Anna (Eunike) Steiner dies. In September, Rudolf Steiner visits Einsiedeln, birthplace of Paracelsus. In December, Friedrich Rittelmeyer, future founder of the Christian Community, meets Rudolf Steiner. The *Johannes-Bauverein*, the 'building committee,' which would lead to the first Goetheanum (first planned for Munich), is also founded, and a preliminary committee for the founding of an independent association is created that, in the following year, will become the Anthroposophical Society. Important lecture cycles include *Occult Physiology* (CW 128); *Wonders of the World* (CW 129); *From Jesus to Christ* (CW 131). Other themes: esoteric Christianity; Christian Rosenkreutz; the spiritual guidance of humanity; the sense world and the world of the spirit.

1912:   Despite the ongoing, now increasing crisis in the Theosophical Society, much is accomplished: *Calendar 1912/1913* is published; eurythmy is created; both the third mystery drama, *The Guardian of the Threshold* (CW 14) and *A Way of Self-Knowledge* (CW 16) are written. New (or renewed) themes included life between death and rebirth and karma and reincarnation. Other lecture cycles: *Spiritual Beings in the Heavenly Bodies and in the Kingdoms of Nature* (CW 136); *The Human Being in the Light of Occultism, Theosophy, and Philosophy* (CW 137); *The Gospel of St. Mark* (CW 139); and *The Bhagavad Gita and the Epistles of Paul* (CW 142). On May 8, Rudolf Steiner celebrates White Lotus Day, H.P. Blavatsky's death day, which he had faithfully observed for the past decade, for the last time. In August, Rudolf Steiner suggests the 'independent association' be called the 'Anthroposophical Society.' In September, the first eurythmy course takes place. In October, Rudolf Steiner declines recognition of a Theosophical Society lodge dedicated to the Star of the East and decides to expel all Theosophical Society members belonging to the order. Also, with Marie von Sivers, he first visits Dornach, near Basel, Switzerland, and they stand on the hill where the Goetheanum will be built. In November, a Theosophical Society lodge is opened by direct mandate from Adyar (Annie Besant). In December, a meeting of the German section occurs at which it is decided that belonging to the Order of the Star of the East is incompatible with membership in the Theosophical Society. December 28: informal founding of the Anthroposophical Society in Berlin.

1913:   Expulsion of the German section from the Theosophical Society. February 2–3: Foundation meeting of the Anthroposophical Society. Board members include: Marie von Sivers, Michael Bauer, and Carl Unger. September 20: Laying of the foundation stone for the *Johannes Bau* (Goetheanum) in Dornach. Building begins immediately. The third mystery drama, *The Soul's Awakening* (CW 14), is completed. Also: *The Threshold of the Spiritual World* (CW 147). Lecture cycles include: *The Bhagavad Gita and the Epistles of Paul* and *The Esoteric Meaning of the Bhagavad Gita* (CW 146), which the Russian philosopher Nikolai Berdyaev attends; *The Mysteries of the East and of Christianity* (CW 144); *The Effects of Esoteric Development* (CW 145); and *The Fifth Gospel* (CW 148). In May, Rudolf Steiner is in London and Paris, where anthroposophical work continues.

1914:   Building continues on the *Johannes Bau* (Goetheanum) in Dornach, with artists and co-workers from seventeen nations. The general assembly of the Anthroposophical Society takes place. In May, Rudolf Steiner visits Paris, as well as Chartres Cathedral. June 28: assassination in Sarajevo ('Now the catastrophe has happened!'). August 1: War is declared. Rudolf Steiner returns to Germany from Dornach—he will travel back and forth. He writes the last chapter of *The Riddles of Philosophy*. Lecture cycles include: *Human and Cosmic Thought* (CW 151); *Inner Being of Humanity between Death and a New Birth* (CW 153); *Occult Reading and Occult Hearing* (CW 156). December 24: marriage of Rudolf Steiner and Marie von Sivers.

1915:   Building continues. Life after death becomes a major theme, also art. Writes: *Thoughts during a Time of War* (CW 24). Lectures include: *The Secret of Death* (CW 159); *The Uniting of Humanity through the Christ Impulse* (CW 165).

1916:   Rudolf Steiner begins work with Edith Maryon (1872–1924) on the sculpture 'The Representative of Humanity' ('The Group'—Christ, Lucifer, and Ahriman). He also works with the alchemist Alexander von Bernus on the quarterly *Das Reich*. He writes *The Riddle of Humanity* (CW 20). Lectures include: *Necessity and Freedom in World History and Human Action* (CW 166); *Past and Present in the Human Spirit* (CW 167); *The Karma of Vocation* (CW 172); *The Karma of Untruthfulness* (CW 173).

1917:   Russian Revolution. The U.S. enters the war. Building continues. Rudolf Steiner delineates the idea of the 'threefold nature of the human being' (in a public lecture March 15) and the 'threefold nature of the social organism' (hammered out in May-June with the help of Otto von Lerchenfeld and Ludwig Polzer-Hoditz in the form of two documents titled *Memoranda*, which were distributed in high places). August–September: Rudolf Steiner writes *The Riddles of the Soul* (CW 20). Also: commentary on 'The Chymical Wedding of Christian Rosenkreutz' for Alexander Bernus (*Das Reich*). Lectures include: *The Karma of Materialism* (CW 176); *The Spiritual Background of the Outer World: The Fall of the Spirits of Darkness* (CW 177).

1918:   March 18: peace treaty of Brest-Litovsk—'Now everything will truly enter chaos! What is needed is cultural renewal.' June: Rudolf Steiner visits Karlstein (Grail) Castle outside Prague. Lecture cycle: *From Symptom to Reality in Modern History* (CW 185). In mid-November, Emil Molt, of the Waldorf-Astoria Cigarette Company, has the idea of founding a school for his workers' children.

1919:   Focus on the threefold social organism: tireless travel, countless lectures, meetings, and publications. At the same time, a new public stage of Anthroposophy emerges as cultural renewal begins. The coming years will see initiatives in pedagogy, medicine, pharmacology, and agriculture. January 27: threefold meeting: ' We must first of all, with the money we have, found free schools that can bring people what they need.' February: first public eurythmy performance in Zurich. Also: 'Appeal to the German People' (CW 24), circulated March 6 as a newspaper insert. In April, *Towards Social Renewal* (CW 23) appears— 'perhaps the most widely read of all books on politics appearing since the war.' Rudolf Steiner is asked to undertake the 'direction and leadership' of the school founded by the Waldorf-Astoria Company. Rudolf Steiner begins to talk about the 'renewal' of education. May 30: a building is selected and purchased for the future Waldorf School. August–September, Rudolf Steiner gives a lecture course for Waldorf teachers, *The Foundations of Human Experience (Study of Man)* (CW 293). September 7: Opening of the first Waldorf School. December (into January): first science course, the *Light Course* (CW 320).

1920:   The Waldorf School flourishes. New threefold initiatives. Founding of limited companies *Der Kommende Tag* and *Futurum A.G.* to infuse spiritual values into the economic realm. Rudolf Steiner also focuses on the sciences. Lectures: *Introducing Anthroposophical Medicine* (CW 312); *The Warmth Course* (CW 321); *The Boundaries of Natural Science* (CW 322); *The Redemption of Thinking* (CW 74). February: Johannes Werner

Klein—later a co-founder of the Christian Community—asks Rudolf Steiner about the possibility of a 'religious renewal,' a 'Johannine church.' In March, Rudolf Steiner gives the first course for doctors and medical students. In April, a divinity student asks Rudolf Steiner a second time about the possibility of religious renewal. September 27–October 16: anthroposophical 'university course.' December: lectures titled *The Search for the New Isis* (CW 202).

1921:   Rudolf Steiner continues his intensive work on cultural renewal, including the uphill battle for the threefold social order. 'University' arts, scientific, theological, and medical courses include: *The Astronomy Course* (CW 323); *Observation, Mathematics, and Scientific Experiment* (CW 324); the *Second Medical Course* (CW 313); *Colour*. In June and September-October, Rudolf Steiner also gives the first two 'priests' courses' (CW 342 and 343). The 'youth movement' gains momentum. Magazines are founded: *Die Drei* (January), and—under the editorship of Albert Steffen (1884–1963)—the weekly, *Das Goetheanum* (August). In February–March, Rudolf Steiner takes his first trip outside Germany since the war (Holland). On April 7, Steiner receives a letter regarding 'religious renewal,' and May 22–23, he agrees to address the question in a practical way. In June, the Klinical-Therapeutic Institute opens in Arlesheim under the direction of Dr. Ita Wegman. In August, the Chemical-Pharmaceutical Laboratory opens in Arlesheim (Oskar Schmiedel and Ita Wegman are directors). The Clinical Therapeutic Institute is inaugurated in Stuttgart (Dr. Ludwig Noll is director); also the Research Laboratory in Dornach (Ehrenfried Pfeiffer and Günther Wachsmuth are directors). In November–December, Rudolf Steiner visits Norway.

1922:   The first half of the year involves very active public lecturing (thousands attend); in the second half, Rudolf Steiner begins to withdraw and turn toward the Society—'The Society is asleep.' It is 'too weak' to do what is asked of it. The businesses—*Der Kommende Tag* and *Futurum A.G.*—fail. In January, with the help of an agent, Steiner undertakes a twelve-city German lecture tour, accompanied by eurythmy performances. In two weeks he speaks to more than 2,000 people. In April, he gives a 'university course' in The Hague. He also visits England. In June, he is in Vienna for the East–West Congress. In August–September, he is back in England for the Oxford Conference on Education. Returning to Dornach, he gives the lectures *Philosophy, Cosmology, and Religion* (CW 215), and gives the third priests' course (CW 344). On September 16, The Christian Community is founded. In October–November, Steiner is in Holland and England. He also speaks to the youth: *The Youth Course* (CW 217). In December, Steiner gives lectures titled *The Origins of Natural Science* (CW 326), and *Humanity and the World of Stars: The Spiritual Communion of Humanity* (CW 219). December 31: Fire at the Goetheanum, which is destroyed.

1923:   Despite the fire, Rudolf Steiner continues his work unabated. A very hard year. Internal dispersion, dissension, and apathy abound. There is conflict—between old and new visions—within the Society. A wake-up call is needed, and Rudolf Steiner responds with renewed lecturing vitality. His focus: the spiritual context of human life; initiation science; the course of the year; and community building. As a foundation for an artistic school, he creates a series of pastel sketches. Lecture cycles: *The Anthroposophical Movement; Initiation Science* (CW 227) (in England at the Penmaenmawr Summer School); *The Four Seasons and the Archangels* (CW 229); *Harmony of the Creative Word* (CW 230); *The Supersensible Human* (CW 231), given in Holland for the founding of the Dutch society. On November 10, in response to the failed Hitler-Ludendorff putsch in Munich, Steiner closes his Berlin residence and moves the *Philosophisch-Anthroposophisch Verlag* (Press) to Dornach. On December 9, Steiner begins the serialization of his *Autobiography: The Course of My Life* (CW 28) in *Das Goetheanum*. It will continue to appear weekly, without a break, until his death. Late December–early January: Rudolf Steiner re-founds the Anthroposophical Society (about 12,000 members internationally) and takes over its leadership. The new board members are: Marie Steiner, Ita Wegman, Albert Steffen, Elisabeth Vreede, and Günther Wachsmuth. (See *The Christmas Meeting for the Founding of the General Anthroposophical Society*, CW 260). Accompanying lectures: *Mystery Knowledge and Mystery Centres* (CW 232); *World History in the Light of Anthroposophy* (CW 233). December 25: the Foundation Stone is laid (in the hearts of members) in the form of the 'Foundation Stone Meditation.'

1924:   January 1: having founded the Anthroposophical Society and taken over its leadership, Rudolf Steiner has the task of 'reforming' it. The process begins with a weekly newssheet ('What's Happening in the Anthroposophical Society') in which Rudolf Steiner's 'Letters to Members' and 'Anthroposophical Leading Thoughts' appear (CW 26). The next step is the creation of a new esoteric class, the 'first class' of the 'University of Spiritual Science' (which was to have been followed, had Rudolf Steiner lived longer, by two more advanced classes). Then comes a new language for Anthroposophy—practical, phenomenological, and direct; and Rudolf Steiner creates the model for the second Goetheanum. He begins the series of extensive 'karma' lectures (CW 235–40); and finally, responding to needs, he creates two new initiatives: biodynamic agriculture and curative education. After the middle of the year, rumours begin to circulate regarding Steiner's health. Lectures: January–February, *Anthroposophy* (CW 234); February: *Tone Eurythmy* (CW 278); June: *The Agriculture Course* (CW 327); June–July: *Speech Eurythmy* (CW 279); *Curative Education* (CW 317); August: (England, 'Second International Summer School'), *Initiation Consciousness: True and False Paths in Spiritual Investigation* (CW 243); September: *Pastoral Medicine* (CW 318). On September 26, for the first time, Rudolf Steiner cancels a lecture. On September 28, he gives his last lecture. On September 29, he withdraws to his studio in the carpenter's shop; now he is definitively ill. Cared for by Ita Wegman, he continues working, however, and writing the weekly installments of his *Autobiography* and *Letters to the Members/Leading Thoughts* (CW 26).

1925: Rudolf Steiner, while continuing to work, continues to weaken. He finishes *Extending Practical Medicine* (CW 27) with Ita Wegman.

On March 30, around ten in the morning, Rudolf Steiner dies.

INDEX